Chronicles of Fort Clark, Texas

RESEARCHED AND PREPARED BY
Don Swanson

NORTEX PRESS Fort Worth, Texas

FIRST EDITION
Copyright © 2003
By Don Swanson
Manufactured in the U.S.A.
By Nortex Press
A Division of Wild Horse Media Group
Fort Worth, Texas
www.WildHorseMedia.com
ISBN 978-1-940130-38-5
ALL RIGHTS RESERVED.

Contents

Introduction.	vii
Scouts for the Army 1850-1872.	1
A. A. "Bigfoot" Wallace Mail Route, 1851.	3
Flag Officers	6
Infantry Regiments Garrisoned at Fort Clark, Texas. . . .	12
Major John B. Clark's Namesake Fort Clark	13
Howard's Well, 1854	14
Major General E. Kirby Smith, CSA, 1854	17
Dr. Albert J. Myers Diary, 1855.	22
Lower Road, 1855	28
Jeb Stuart, 1855	31
"I Married a Soldier or Old Days in the Old Army". . . .	38
Devil's River, 1857 (John B. Wood)	41
Captain Charles C. Gilbert, First Infantry Regiment, 1858	44
Harold A. Hamner, Captain, Second Texas Mounted Rifles, Commanding Officer, Fort Clark, 1861.	48
Trevanion T. Teel, 1861-57.	57
Company Headquarters, Fort Clark, Texas, March 19, 1861	63
Chaplain Elijah Guion, 1864.	66
Elm Creek, 1864	69

Fort Lancaster, 1864	71
Border Ruffian, 1864	74
Anacacho, 1865	77
West Prong of Nueces, 1865	79
Donald Jackson, Acting Assistant Surgeon, U.S. Army, 1866	82
Post War, 1866	91
Government Mail, 1867	93
June 1869	96
Seminole Negro-Indian Scouts Interred at Seminole Indian Scouts Cemetery, Brackettville, Texas	97
Seminole Negro-Indian Scouts, 1872	99
Headquarters Department of Texas, San Antonio, Texas	107
Headquarters 4th U.S. Cavalry, Fort Clark, Texas, May 23, 1873	110
Military Telegraph System, 1875	114
Chaplain D. Eglinton Barr, 1876	118
Kickapoo's War, 1876	122
Riot in Brackett, 1876	125
Sabinal Canyon, 1876	128
U.S. Army's Seminole Negro-Indian Scouts	131
November 29th, 1877	140
Mackenzie's Second Invasion of Mexico, 1876	142
Mexico's Reaction to Invasion, 1878	144
Doctor William C. Gorgas, Noted Army Doctor, Fort Clark, Texas, 1880	146
John Lapham Bullis, Whirlwind and Friend of the Frontier, 1881	149
Final Action of the Indian Wars, October 1881	163
Last Indian Raid, April 1881	165
Sgt. John B. Charlton, Fourth Cavalry Regiment Trooper, 1882	167

Brackettville–Fort Clark's Contribution in the
   Spanish-American War 179
Hazards of the Occupation 181
U.S. Army Turns to Bicycles for Mobility and
   Fort Clark's Bicycle Corp. 184
A Ghost Story from Fort Clark, 1894 189
Other Units That Served at Fort Clark, 1852-1945 192
First Cavalry Brigade Commanders 193
General Hugh S. Johnson......................... 194
General of the Army, George C. Marshall 200
Fort Clark's Chinese, 1919 206
I.G. Inspection, 1928............................ 209
Animal Sense Prevails, Trooper's Story, 1936 211
General Quinones, 1938 213
Recollections of an Airman Stationed on a Horse
   Soldier's Installation, 1939 216
Officer Quarters Assignment, Fort Clark, Texas 220
Maj. Gen. William C. Chase, 1942 222
Pecos River Viaduct............................. 225
Prisoner Chasing Duty 230
3rd Medical Battalion, Veterinary Troop, 1944 234
Officer's Quarters Assignment, Fort Clark, 1944 236
Last of the Cavalry Mounts, 1944 238
American Statesman, June 30, 1946 241
San Antonio Light, June 29, 1946 242
The Army's Training Is Lasting.................... 243
Fort Clark Guest Ranch, Old Guardhouse Museum
   1949-1964 244
About the Author............................... 246

Introduction

In 1975, when passing through Brackettville, Texas, I observed old Fort Clark, then a private recreational community development. As a history buff, I was intrigued by the fort and made a tour of the grounds. I then wanted to learn all about the history of this exciting Indian fort.

It was my fortune to meet many of the authors who had written on the history of Fort Clark. And it was my fortune to meet many of the troopers who had been stationed there. These meetings, combined with my love of history, gave me the opportunity to build this museum.

The collection of artifacts now in the museum also made me aware of the lack of any one document which recorded this information for future generations; thus was conceived the idea of the *Fort Clark Chronicles*.

These chronicles cover a wide range of subjects and dates and are collected from many publications, some of which are no longer in print.

Because it houses the history of this place, the museum at Fort Clark, like the *Chronicles*, has been a fulfillment of a dream. I hope future generations will come and enjoy.

—DON SWANSON

Scouts for the Army
1850-1872

Prior to 1872 when the Seminole Negro Indian Scouts came to Fort Clark and became proficient as scouts in the Military District of Nueces. Scouts or Guides were a civilian position hired by the Post Quartermaster and would be paid the whole sum of $50–$65 depending on knowledge of the area and his scouting abilities. There were four who received some historical recognition and perhaps there were more but records were scarce and wording on reports was direct and to point. Rokue "Roka" Maurice (1850s) was an old Mexican that the Comanches had stolen when he was a boy, and made him a slave for many years.

"Roka" had little use for the Indians, particularly the Comanches, so fighting and scalping was his long suit and several Indian encounters mention old "Roka."

Isaac Coxe is mentioned as the scout used by the Second Cavalry and early part of Civil War period. He evidently was well acquainted with the territory, conversant with the Indians, a natural sense of direction and uncanny memory.

Ike Coxe and Green Van led Mackenzie and the 4th Cavalry to Remolina for a raid on the Kickapoos and Lipans.

Much later (mid 1870s) there appears the Longorio brothers; Julian and Manual. Both were originally employed by the Quartermaster's Department and they also had been slaves of Indians as children. They evidently were spies for Cols. Shafter and Mackenzie. In 1879 and 1880 each enlisted in the Seminole Negro Indian Scouts Detachment. Julian served from 1879 to June 1889 while Manual served from May 1880 until January 1886.

About 1876, Lt. Col William "Pecos Bill" Shafter was needing information on the Indians of Mexico. He offered a reward of $500 for a live Indian he could interrogate. Julian Longorio was the man who could deliver but Julian had broken the neck of the captive by lassoing so he couldn't collect the reward. In March 1877, Julian was captured by the Mexican authorities as a spy for the "Gringo" army. Julian was one of two spies held in Piedras Negras jail by the

Mexican Government. Upon learning that Julian and Pedro Rodiquez were in the Piedras Negras Jail General Ord sent Lt. Col Shafter with troops to rescue them.

The troops surrounded Piedras Negras and closed in on the square but found the jail empty. The Mexicans had prior knowledge of the rescue effort and had removed the prisoners. Somehow Julian managed to get free without being shot because he appeared in the Seminole Scouts in 1879.

A. A. "Bigfoot" Wallace Mail Route, 1851

Richard Howard and A.A. "Bigfoot" Wallace made a bid for the San Antonio-El Paso Mail Route via Eagle Pass and Presidio del Norte in 1850 for $25000 per annum with service every two months but the postmaster disallowed the bid as too costly. The next bidder was Henry Skillman another of the party that had founded and built the Lower Road from San Antonio-El Paso. September 20, 1851, Henry Skillman was signed to establish mail route 6401 from Santa Fe–El Paso and the lower road to San Antonio.

Skillman operation first started with a wagon using six Spanish mules and spares herded along side by six or more former Texas Rangers well armed. "Bigfoot" Wallace became one of the most reliable and dependable drivers for the Skillman mail route.

Sometime in late 1852 or early 1853, Bigfoot Wallace was in charge of the mail coach, running from San Antonio to El Paso. "We had been traveling hard since 12 o'clock at night when we left Fort Clark in order to make the watering place on the Devil's River. It was here we would "noon it" (rest for couple hours, unhitch the team for watering and grazing.) After daylight on the road I noticed several Indian "smokes" rising up and disappearing but apparently they were a long ways off, and once we passed a considerable Indian's "Trail," where at least fifteen or twenty horses had crossed the road. Altogether, I didn't like the sign, and I told the boys (riding guard) to keep a bright look out, as I felt sure the Indians were hatching some devilment for our benefit. However, we reached the "water-hole" in safety about noon, watered all our animals, and hobbled them out to graze. I had eight men with me, most of them old Frontiersmen, who had seen much service and were good fighters as ever drew a bead upon an Indian."

Near the watering place there was about a quarter of an acre of very thick chaparral, and after we had taken a bite to eat, I told the boys to drag the coach up to the edge of the chaparral, and they could take a "snooze." I was determined to keep watch while the balance slept.

The appearance of the country around our encampment was enough to make one uneasy, for it had a real "Ingny look"—broken rocky hills, covered here and there with clumps of thorny shrubs and stunted cedars, and a little narrow valley or canyon between them, in which there was nothing but a few patches of withered grass.

Feeling pretty sure that danger was about now and as I came to this conclusion, I saw one of the horses raise up his head and look for a long time in a certain direction, and in a few minutes afterward a deer came running by as if it had been frightened by something behind it. I waited long enough to see that no wolves were after it, and then hurried to the camp and gave ole Ben a shake. "Help me bring in the horses" and between us we brought them all in and tied them securely in the chaparral, without waking any of the other boys.

Then Ben lay down again to finish his nap, but he sprang up as suddenly, "Cap, they are coming, I hear their horses feet." We then saw twenty-three Comanche warriors coming as fast as their horses could bring them right for our camp.

The Indians charged to a few feet of the chaparral were we were posted, and began to pour their "dogwood switches" (arrows) as thick as hail. But with our rifles and six-shooters we "emptied" four of their warriors from their saddles.

The Indians returned dismounted to give us another

"turn." They were yelling and screeching as if they thought we were a set of "green-horns." After "emptying" five more Indians they fell back but were reinforced by some forty more warriors.

After a conversation with their chief in Mexican, I told them we would camp at the California Springs (between the second crossing of Devils River and Beaver Lake) tonight in spite of the whole "Comanche Nation." They departed for the springs but we took the road back to Fort Clark. We rattled along at such a rate that we reached Fort Clark safely the next morning.

The commandant at Fort Clark (with Special Orders from Department of Texas to aid the mail) furnished us with an escort of twelve men and a sergeant, and we made the trip back to San Antonio without any further trouble from the Indians at that time.

=====

John C. Duval, *The Adventures of Big Foot Wallace*

Flag Officers

Rank of General: Brigadier, Major, Lieutenant, General of Army

OFFICERS THAT PERFORMED DUTY AT FORT CLARK
AS A FLAG OFFICER OR OBTAINED FLAG RANK LATER

NAME	RANK	UNIT	DATE SERVED
Anderson, Thomas M	Capt.	10th Inf.	1873
Anderson, Edward	Col.	13th Cav.	1919
Andrews, George	2nd Lt.	25th Inf	1877
Arnold, Abraham K.	Lt.	2nd Cav.	1856
Augur, Christopher C. B.	Gen.	Dept of Tx.	1874
Bacon, John M.	Capt.	9th Cav.	1869
Baldwin, F. D.	B. Gen	Div Comdr	1905
Baldwin, Theodore H.	Lt. Col.	10th Cav.	1899
Bankhead, Henry C.	Maj.	4th Cav.	1873
Barton, Seth (CSA)	2nd Lt.	1st Inf.	1853
Baylor, John R. (CSA)	Lt. Col.	2nd MTR(CSA)	1861
Bell, William H.	2nd Lt.	3rd Inf.	1860
Belknap, William G.	Lt. Col.	Engrs.	1855
Bernard, Rueben F.	Maj.	8th Cav.	1876
Biggs, Herman	2nd Lt.	1st Inf.	1858
Bliss, Tasker A B.	Gen.	Dept. of Tx.	1914
Bliss, Zenas R.	2nd Lt.	8th Inf.	1859
Blocksom, Augustus P	Maj.	1st Cav.	1903
Bomford, James V.	Lt.Col.	8th Inf.	1854
Bonneville, Benjamin L.E.	Col.	3rd Inf.	1860
Boudinot, T. E.	Capt.	5th Cav.	1930

NAME	RANK	UNIT	DATE SERVED
Brees, Howard J.	Maj.	1st Cav.	1907
Brett, Loyd M.	Maj.	1st Cav.	1905 (M.H.)
Brown, Robert A.	Maj.	14th Cav.	1912
Brown, Harvey	Col.	2nd Art.	1860
Brooks, William T. H.	Capt.	3rd Inf.	1861
Buell, John L.	Lt. Col.	11th Inf.	1874
Bullis, John L.	2nd Lt.	24th Inf.	1873-1881
Burke, Daniel W.	Maj.	23rd Inf.	1894
Byers, Joe	Capt.	5th Cav.	1940
Cabell, DeRosey C.	Capt.	1st Cav.	1903
Cameron, George H.	Maj.	14th Cav.	1912
Carroll, Henry	Capt.	9th Cav.	1872
Carlton, Caleb H.	Maj.	3rd Cav.	1887
Chase, William C. B.	Gen.	113 th Cav.	1941
Clitz, Henry R.	Col.	10th Inf.	1873
Coppinger, J. J.	Col.	23rd Inf.	1894
Corbin, Henry C.	Capt.	24th Inf.	1870
Cooney, Michael	Capt.	9th Cav.	1872
Craig, Malin	Capt.	1st Cav.	1904
Crandal, Fredrick M.	Maj.	24th Inf.	1878
Cress, George O.	Col.	306 Cav.	1918
Crane, Charles J.	2nd Lt.	24th Inf.	1878
Crittenden, George	(CSA)	Capt.	MTR. 1855
Curtis, James O.,Jr.	Capt.	5th Cav.	1941
Dawson, Samuel K.	Capt.	1st Art.	1859
Dickman, J. T.	1st Lt.	3rd Cav.	1897
Doubleday, Abner	Col.	24th Inf.	1871 (GCM)
Drake, Charles B.	Capt.	14th Cav.	1912
Duncan, J. W.	B. Gen.	Dept. of Tx.	1912
Dunlap John B	Lt. Col	112th Cav.	1941
Eastman, Seth	Capt.	1st Inf.	1853
Evans, Nathan G.	Capt.	2nd Cav.	1857
Edwards, C. R.	1st Lt.	23rd. Inf.	1895
Etringe, LeRoy	B. Gen.	1st Cav. Bde.	1928
Field, Charles W. (CSA)	1st Lt.	2nd Cav.	1857
Forsyth, George A	Maj.	9th Cav.	1868
Frazer, Joe W. Jr.	Capt.	2nd Cav. Div.	1943
Fremont, Johnthan C.	B. Gen.	1st. Cav. Bde	1903
French, Francis H.	2nd Lt.	19th Inf.	1882
French, William H.	Capt.	1st Art.	1859

NAME	RANK	UNIT	DATE SERVED
French, Samuel G. (CSA)	Capt.	Qtrmtr.	1852
Funston, Fredrick	B. Gen.	S. Dept.	1915
Gaston, Joseph A	Maj.	1st Cav.	1903
Gibbs, Alfred	1st Lt.	MTR	1854
Graham, William M.	B. Gen.	Dept. of Tx.	1897
Grant, Frederick D.	B. Gen.	Dept. of Tx.	1903
Greely, A. M.	1st Lt.	Sig. Corp.	1875
Green, Henry A.	B. Gen.	Cav. Bodr. P.	1916
Gilbert, Charles C.	Capt	1st Inf.	1859
Gillem, Alvan C.	1st Lt.	1st Art.	1859
Gorgas, William C.	Lt. Med.	Dept. FC	1880
Hare, Luther R.	Maj.	12th Cav.	1901
Hamilton, Schuyler	1st Lt.	1st Inf.	1853
Harjehausen, Arnold E	S/Sgt.	113 Cav.	1941
Hatch, Edward	Col.	9th Cav.	1874 (GCM)
Hatch, John B	Capt.	MTR	1856
Hawkins, Hamilton S.	B. Gen.	S. Div.	1931
Hayes, Edward M	Maj.	7th Cav.	1893
Hedkin, Charles A.	Capt.	3rd. Cav.	1908
Heintzelman, Samuel F.	Maj.	1st Inf.	1858
Hinks, Edward W.	Lt. Col.	25th Inf	1870
Holabird, Samuel B.	1st Lt.	1st Inf.	1854
Hood, John B. (CSA)	Lt.	2nd Cav.	1857
Hooker, Ambrose E.	Capt.	9th Cav.	1871
Hoyt, Ralph W.	B. Gen.	Dept. of Tx.	1911
Humphrey, Evan H.	B. Gen	1st Cav. Bg.	1935
Hunt, Lewis C.	Lt. Col.	20th Inf.	1878
Hunter, George K.	Lt.	3rd Cav.	1887
Johnson, Arthur	Lt. Col.	36th Inf.	1917
Johnson, Henry H.	B. Gen.	2nd Cav. Div.	1942
Johnson, Hugh S.(NRA)	2nd Lt.	1st Cav. Reg.	1904
Johnson, Richard W.	2nd Lt.	2nd Cav.	1857
Joyce, Kenton	B. Gen	1st. Cav. Bde.	1938
King, John H	Capt.	1st Inf.	1854
Lauback, Howard	2nd Lt.	23rd Inf.	1894
Lawton, Henry	Capt.	4th Cav.	1873
Lear, Ben	B. Gen.	1st Cav. Bde	1937
Lebo, Thomas C.	Capt.	9th Cav.	1872
Lee, Fitzhugh (CSA)	2nd Lt.	2nd Cav.	1857
Lee, J. M.	B. Gen.	Dept. of Tx.	1905

NAME	RANK	UNIT	DATE SERVED
Longstreet, James (CSA)	Capt.	8th Inf.	1854
Lowe, William W.	2nd Lt.	2nd Cav.	1857
Lynch, Edmund C.	Lt.	AAS11thOBs.S.	1927
Mackay, James O.	1st Lt.	3rd Cav.	1890
Mackenzie, Ranald S.	Col.	41st Inf.	1868
Magruder, John B. (CSA)	Lt. Col.	1st Art.	1856
Major, James F.	2nd Lt.	2nd Cav.	1856
Mansfield, J. K. F.	Col.	IPG	1854
Markley, Alfred C.	Lt.	24th Inf.	1877
Marshall, George C.	Lt.	1st Cav. Hdq.	1905 (TDY)
Maury, Dabney H. (CSA)	Capt.	MTR	1856
McCaskey, William S.	B. Gen.	Dept. of Tx.	1906
McClernand, E J	Lt. Col.	1st Cav.	1906
McClellan, George B	Capt.	Engrs.	1855 (TDY)
McKibbins, Chambers	B. Gen.	Dept. of Tx.	1899
McLaughlen, Napoleon B.	Maj.	10th Cav.	1878
Merriam, Henry C.	Maj.	24th Inf.	1877
Meyers, Albert J. A.	Surg.	Med. Dept. FC.	1855 (TDY)
Meyers, Albert L.	B. Gen.	Dept. of Tx.	1907
Merritt, Wesley	Lt. Col	9th Cav.	1872
Moore, Francis	Capt.	9th Cav.	1874
Morton, Charles	Capt.	3rd Cav.	1888
Mosely, George V. H.	2nd Lt.	9th Cav.	1900
Millikin, John	B. Gen.	1st Cav. Bde	1940
Mizner, John K	Maj.	4th Cav.	1873
Mower, Joseph A.	1st Lt	1st Inf.	1858
Nutter, William	Capt.	5th Cav.	1938
Oakes, James C.	Capt.	2nd Cav.	1857
O'Brien, Maxwell A.	Col.	113th Cav.	1941
Ord, E.O.C.	B. Gen.	Dept. of Tx.	1875
Ovenshine, Samuel	Col.	23rd Inf.	1895
Palmer, Innis	Capt.	2nd Cav.	1857
Parker, James	B. Gen	Bgde cmdr.	1914
Patton, George S. Jr.	Col.	5th Cav.	1938
Plummer, Joseph B.	Capt.	1st Inf.	1854
Prince, William E.	Capt.	1st Inf.	1852
Pugh, John Ramsey	Capt.	1st Cav. Bde	1940
Rose, Thomas R.	Maj.	18th Inf.	1880
Royal, William B.	1st Lt.	2nd Cav.	1856
Reynolds, J. J.	Col.	5th Mil. D.	1867

NAME	RANK	UNIT	DATE SERVED
Richardson, Robert C.	Col.	5th Cav.	1937
Rucker, Louis H.	Capt.	9th Cav.	1872
Ruckman, John W. M.	Gen.	S. Dept.	1918
Ruff, Charles F.	Capt.	MTR	1855
Ruffner, Clark	Capt.	5th Cav.	1936
Schafter, William R	Lt. Col.	24th Inf.	1871
Schofield, George W.	Maj.	10th Cav.	1877
Schofield, John M.	1st Lt.	1st Art.	1856
Shea, Leonard C.	lst Lt.	5th Cav.	1940
Shepherd, Oliver L.	Capt.	3rd Inf.	1861
Schriver, Edmund	Col.	IG	1873
Sheridan, Phillip H. M.	Gen.	Dept. of Mo.	1873
Sherman, William T	Lt.Gen	Gen. of Army	1882
Sibley, Caleb C.	Maj.	3rd Inf.	1860
Sibley, Henry H. (CSA)	Col.	Army N. Mex	1862
Simonson, John R.	Maj.	MTR	1855
Smith, Charles R.	Col.	19th Inf.	1883
Slaughter, James E. (CSA)	1st Lt.	1st Art.	1860
Smedberg, William B. Jr.	Capt.	14th Cav.	1912
Smith, Edmund K.	Lt.	Bdry. Comm.	1954
Smith, Persifor	B. Gen.	Dept. of Tx.	1852
Stanley, David S.	Col.	22nd Inf.	1882
Stearns, C. F.	Col.	5th Cav.	1939
Steever, Edgar Z.	B. Gen.	Dept. of Tx.	1913
Steinberg, G. M.	B. Gen.	Surg. Gen.	1895
Stoneman, George	Lt.	1st Drag.	1854
Stuart, J.E.B.	2nd Lt.	MTR	1854
Sumner, Samuel S.	Maj.	8th Cav.	1889
Sweitzer, Nelson B.	Lt. Col.	8th Cav.	1880
Sykes, George	Capt.	3rd Inf.	1860
Taylor, Holman H.	Stewart	3rd Texas	1898
Twiggs, David E.	B. Gen.	Dept. of Tx.	1859
Viele, Charles D.	Capt.	10th Cav.	1877
Vroom, Peter D.	Capt.	3rd Cav.	l889
Wade, James F.	Maj.	9th Cav.	1872
Wainwright, Jonathan	2nd lt.–B. Gen	1st Cav.	1906–1939
Ward, Federick K.	Lt. Col.	14th Cav.	1903
Wessel, Henry W.	Capt.	3rd Cav.	1888
Wheaton, Frank	B. Gen.	Dept. of Tx.	1894
Whipple, William D.	lst Lt.	3rd Inf.	1860

NAME	RANK	UNIT	DATE SERVED
Whistler, Joseph N. G.	1st Lt.	3rd Inf.	1860
Whitney, Clifford	Lt. Col	5th Cav.	1936
Williston, Edward B.	Capt.	2nd Art.	1878
Winans, Edwin B.	B. Gen	1st Cav. Bde.	1926
Wint, Theodore J.	Capt.	4th Cav.	1873
Young, Samuel B. M.	Capt.	8th Cav.	1878

(186–Updated 6-6-97)

Infantry Regiments Garrisoned at Fort Clark, Texas

1st Infantry;   1852–1855, 1858–1859
3rd Infantry;   1860–1861
4th Infantry: 1902–1902
5th Infantry;   1855–1856
8th Infantry;   1859–1859
10th Infantry; 1872–1879
18th Infantry; 1889–1894
19th Infantry; 1882–1889
20th Infantry; 1878–1880
22th Infantry; 1879–1882
23rd Infantry; 1894–1898
24th Infantry; 1869–1870, 1872–1872, 1876–1878,
25th Infantry; 1870–1872, 1873–1873, 1877–1878,
26th Infantry; 1906–1906
41st Infantry; 1868–1869 (combined with 38th to be 24th Inf.)
3rd Texas Infantry; 1898–1899 (duration of Spanish-American War)

Major John B. Clark's Namesake Fort Clark

John B. Clark joined the army from the state of Kentucky. He was Commissioned an Ensign May 20, 1813 in the Twenty-Eight (28th) Infantry Regiment of the U.S. Army. He served as an Ensign until April 9, 1814 when he was commissioned a Second Lieutenant. May 17, 1815 he was transferred to the Third Infantry Regiment as a Second Lieutenant. He was commissioned a First Lieutenant, May 7, 1817, in the Third Infantry Regiment. He was promoted to Captain in the same regiment, March 18, 1826. He was designed the Regimental Quartermaster on May 19,1826 and served in that capacity until September 1829.

He was commissioned a Major, November 26, 1845, by a transfer to the First Infantry Regiment. The First Infantry named Fort Clark, Texas in his honor instead of their current commanding officer, Colonel Riley, since Clark was deceased as of August 23, 1847 (approximately 56 years old). His cause of death is not listed but evidently not a battle casualty.

=====

Francis B. Heitman, *Historical Register and Dictionary of the United States Army*, Volume I, p. 304

Howard's Well
1854

In 1854 John Reinhart moved from Cibolo River to Seco Creek near D'Hanis. Shortly thereafter John Dunlap was in the area buying up a drove of cattle under a government contract, to be delivered at Fort Lancaster. Fort Lancaster was located at the mouth of Liveoak Creek where it empties into the Pecos River. John Dunlap lived at Fort Clark and was a civilian employee of the Quarter-master's Department acquisitioning cattle for posts in Military District of the Pecos.

John Dunlap employed John Reinhart and Capt. Joseph Richarz to help deliver the cattle to Fort Lancaster. Fort Lancaster was then far out on the extreme frontier with no settlement between. Once one had departed on the Lower Road (El Paso Road) from Fort Clark and Las Moras Village, there was nothing but open country and hostile Indians. These three men had demonstrated previously that they had pioneer's spirit for such a dangerous undertaking.

They proceeded along the Lower Road from D'Hanis to Fort Inge, up the Nueces Valley to Fort Clark, then on to San Felipe Springs crossed the Devil's River, through Dead Man's pass and on pass Beaver's Lake. The next water stop on the route was Howard's Well, 149 miles. This was sunken well to reach the water vein and in this period of the Indian Wars should have been named "Waterloo" because the Indians during the time made it a final stop for so many pioneers. It was named for Richard Howard, the surveyor, who was with party of Road Builders who founded the Lower Road in June-September 1849.

Dunlap's cattle drive up to Beaver's Lake was a normal cattle drive until they reached Howard's Well and as they started down Howard's Draw to the valley, they discovered a man on a mountain. This automatically overcame all the calm they had so far on this drive, they feared it might be an Indian lookout for a war party, and that they might lose their cattle and possibly their lives. The man, however, was a white man, watching the road back east for help. His party had camped the night before at the well and the next morning (this same day) had been attacked by a large war party of Indians. The man's party had consisted of nine men and five wagons.

At the time of the Indians' attack, the horses and mules were out grazing with one man watching them. The Indians made a dash from cover to capture the animals. The Indians played it a very smart trick by dividing their war party with a portion capturing the animals while the other portion waited to attack the white men. Concealed from view behind a hill the second party waited as the whites attempted to rescue their animals then they dashed from behind the hill to cut the men off from the protection of their wagons. The white men saw this maneuver in time to retreat back to their wagons realizing now their lives were more important than the horses and mules. Even the lone guard of the animals realized the tactic and being luckly mounted on a good horse, was able to make a wide sweep of the Indians and join his companions in the protection of the wagons.

The Indians gave up the attack on the white men secured the stock, and drove them off, passing within long rifle range of the chagrined owners, who gave the Indians one volley as a parting salute. One of these shots took effect on a horse ridden by one of the Indians, killing the animal in its tracks and throwing the Apache to the ground. He quickly mounted up behind another Indian and rode away. As the three cattlemen (Dunlap, Reinhart and Richarz) could do nothing for the nine white men, they went on and reported the matter at Fort

Lancaster. The commander of the post sent out teams belonging to the government and brought the wagons in.

After delivering the cattle to Fort Lancaster, Dunlap and his two men started back down the Lower Road. When they arrived at the crossing of the Devil's River they met a drove of 150 head of horses. Dunlap thought at the time that only three Indians were with them. It seemed an easy job to rout these Indian drovers, and capture the horses, although Dunlap's crew was only armed with pistols. They acted on the impulse and charged the Indians, but to their surprise seven more Indians appeared on the other side of the horses. They had been concealed, and now dismounted and remounted on fresh horses to give the trio of white men a battle and chase. The horses ridden by the cattlemen were jaded, and the situation began to look serious. The cattlemen immediately changed their charge into retreat. Luckily for them, the Indians did not follow up on the charge so the trio stopped the retreat. Dunlap said: "Boys, I believe the guns of those Indians were wet (it had been raining), and that was the reason they did not fire or charge us. We can go back and clean up on them." As they discussed this it became important for the three of them to take the ten Indians and 150 head of horses. So it was agreed, and they turned back to have a fight. The Indians saw them coming back, and left the horses and came yelling and charging at the white trio. Once more the trio had to beat a hasty retreat and sought protection in a big thicket where they could defend themselves. The Apaches decided the horse herd was more important and left the trio in their forest fort and returned to the herd. When the road appeared clear of Indians and horses, the trio did what they should of done in the first place, headed for Fort Clark.

=====

A. J. Sowell, *Texas Indian Fighters*, State House Press, Austin, 1986, pp. 195-197.

Major General E. Kirby Smith, CSA 1854

The Boundary Commission to which Captain Kirby Smith was now assigned (1854) as escort and botanist, was for the determination of the boundary, between the U.S. and Mexico, especially under the Gadsen Treaty of 1853. Three weeks after being assigned this duty at Fort Ringold he was writing to his mother from a Camp on Las Moras, near Fort Clark, Texas, while on his march to El Paso, the 31st of October 1854:

"I am now camped on a clear, limpid stream of crystal water which heads but a few yards above in a magnificent spring. A grove of venerable oaks over shadows my tent, furnishing a canopy of green and luxuriant foliage, while the waters rippling and murmuring over their pebbly bed, reflect in varied light, the rapid and graceful movements of the bass and trout sporting in their silvery home. You would laugh at my vagaries were I to tell you that this is the last jumping-off place of civilization. Yet indeed, so it is considered: and Fort Clark on Las Moras, looking west toward the bleak plains and trackless wastes of the Rio Grande is the last point on the great highway to El Paso where the face of the white man greets the emigrant on his tedious respite. Two companies of the First Infantry and one of the Rifles (Mounted Rifles) are here entrusted with the pleasant duty of keeping the Indians in check; through as in the case of most of our frontier posts, "THEY APPEAR TO HAVE BEEN STRUCK DOWN IN A DEFENSELESS POSITON FOR THE PURPOSE OF BEING KEPT IN CHECK BY THE INDIANS."

"The Lipans and Tonkaways have for some time been encamped in and around the post(awaiting completion of Texas Indian Reservations), and their grim visages and forbidding countenances, as they stalk about our camp, keep us bright, vigilant, and on the lookout.

"The government in its wisdom has seen fit to order the location of the Lipans on the Upper Brazos (Texas Comanche Reservation) with their inveterate enemies the Comanches. The Lipans have remonstrated in vain against being sacrificed to their powerful foe; and though for years friendly and our allies in expeditions against the prairie tribes, yesterday they stampeded and made for the Mexican frontier with all the stock they could drive off from the neighborhood of the post. (I remember the Tonkaways went on reservation but the Lipans would not, but left and went across the river into Mexico. They remained there and have been at war with us ever since." *Zenas R. Bliss Reminiscence* Vol. 1 page 91)

"We left San Antonio on the 23rd of October, with a train of forty wagons and an attendant suite of teamsters, attaches, frontiersmen and savant, traveling west through a beautiful region of country for ninety miles to Fort Inge, on the Leona. Here a notable change takes place in the character of the country. Rich luxurious vegetation, charming valleys and placid streams, are succeeded by a rocky, barren soil and rapid torrents. In the neighborhood of Fort Clark, thorny bushes, acacias, cacti, the plumed partridges, chaparral cock, horned frog and other peculiarities in the flora and fauna of New Mexico, become abundant. Game is plenty. Nature seems to delight throughout these vast wilds, in congregating her feathered tribes in immense conserves in proportion to the grand scale on which she has laid out the vast wilderness. Turkeys roost by tens of thousands along the streams. Acres upon acres of grass cover the prairies while different species of quail in countless covies, feed along the roadside. We are now about FOUR HUNDRED AND SIXTY MILES from El Paso, but have a wild, desolate region of mountain ranges and trackless wastes to pass over, which six years ago had never been trodden by the foot of white man. I believe our friends, Baldy Smith (Lt. W. F. Smith) and Henry Whiting (Captain W.H.C. Whiting) were the first to pass through this region when they made their adventurous trip in '49. We shall probably leave day after to-morrow. We are waiting two days to recruit our animals. We expect to arrive in El Paso before the end of November."

His later letter, the 15th of December, from a Camp below El Paso continues. "We remained three days at Fort Clark recruiting the animals and completing our outfit before launching upon the dreary wilderness which extends to El Paso. During this time it rained very hard and we found the road, which has been termed a natural turnpike, almost impassable. The soil was saturated; at time, on apparently a hard gravelly soil, the mules would sink to their flanks and have to be unharnessed and hauled out with ropes, and the wagons dragged through by hand. In many places detours of several miles had to be made over the mountain ridges. We were five days going about twenty-five miles; and between making roads, playing wagon-master, teamster, etc., you may conceive how considerably I have been enlarging my experiences."

"... the Vast plains surface have been cut into innumerably deep chasms by the retiring currents of water, and these chasms through a level country are termed canons (canyons). They are characteristic of the country from Fort Clark to the Rocky Mountains. From Devil's River to the Limpia Mountains (Sierra Diablos) is one vast network of canons (canyons), more or less intricately interwoven and varying from three hundred to twelve hundred feet in depth. The road winds through the canon of the Devil's River, crossing the bed of the stream seventeen times in course of twenty miles. In some places not much more than one hundred feet in width, cut through the strata of rock from six hundred to eight hundred feet deep, with the Devil's stream roaring and tumbling over rocks in its narrow channel and rushing through dark caverns of limestone cliffs."[1]

"In 1861 Captain E. Kirby Smith was commanding Company B, Second Cavalry in Texas. March 3, 1861, he resigned his commission in the United States Army and wrote his mother in Florida from San Antonio. "I've forwarded my resignation (commission in U.S. Army) and am enroute for Florida and the Southern Confederacy. Texas has demanded and received all the public property in the State and orders have been issued for the evacuation of the troops.

I do not know what has been done, I feel that I cannot, in the present coercive attitude of the North, remain any longer in service. I have been promoted to Majority (Major) and in a few weeks would have been a Lieutenant Colonel of Cavalry. Rank with me is no consideration, and I would rather shoulder a musket in the cause of the south than be Commander-in-chief under Mr. Lincoln.

After the surrender of all the public property in the State of Texas, by General Twiggs, then in command of the Texas Division of the Federal Army, to General Ben McCulloch in command of the Texas Militia, the latter sent a demand to Captain Kirby Smith, in command of Camp Colorado, for his surrender. The Captain refused to surrender the garrison. He had resigned his commission in the Federal Army, and was turning the garrison over to The United States Government, but so long as he was in command there he would fight for the protection of that garrison and all the property of The United States Government property committed to his care. And he strongly intimated that if General McCulloch chose to fight it would be all the worse for him. The demand for surrender was not pressed and there can be no charge of any dishonorable act in connection with Edmund Kirby Smith's withdrawal from the army of the United States Government to enter the service of the Confederate States."[2]

=====

1. For more information of that 1854 journey, see Chapter VI, *General Kirby Smith* by Arthur Howard Noll, Sewanee, University of the South Press, 1907.

2. Arthur Howard Noll, General Kirby Smith, Sewanee, Tenn. University of the South Press, 1907. The United States Boundary Survey along the Rio Grande was made from 1854 to 1857, when the survey crew was down the river from the Big Canyon they had to abandon their work because of Indians and return to Fort Clark to obtain an army of escort before the work could be continued. Clayton Williams, *Never Again*, Page 149

Dr. Albert J. Myers Diary 1855

(LATER, A GENERAL AND FATHER OF ARMY SIGNAL CORP)

Written January 7, 1855 while Dr. Myers was enroute to Fort Davis.

We arrived at Fort Clark about 2 P.M. About 5 P.M. an Express (U.S. Army Mail express between Fort Davis and Fort Clark) came in with the news that the troops who had gone over the road we were to follow had killed a party of seven Indians and captured a little squaw. (Troops were Company A and a Detachment of G Company, Mounted Rifles). They came upon them one morning unexpected and the Indians fled into the tall cane and grass which bordered the Pecos River. Fled not, however, before the whites had fired at random into a crowd of Mexicans (Comancheros) with whom the Comanches were trading. One Mexican was killed on the spot, others were badly wounded. We met them on their way down—as we left Fort Clark with our escort and I could not but pity one poor fellow who had ridden on horseback nearly 200 miles with his leg shattered fearfully by a musket ball.

As the command came up, the Texas Rangers (Capt. Travis & Co. C) and the Mounted Rifles spread themselves along the river and the grass was fired: as the flames drove each from his hiding place fifty balls were planted in his body, and so seven red-skins were massacred. Had the Comanches in proportionate numbers surrounded a few whites, the affair would have been styled a diabolical murder. As it is, we must try to look upon it as an execution. The war on this frontier is one of extermination. In the worst sense of the word, these tribes are savages. They are devils and the coldest blood must boil at the variations of the manner in which they have treated prisoners who have fallen into their hands. Not men, alone taken with arms in their hands, for they cannot but die, but innocent women and children. Orders are now issued to the troops to take no prisoners; to spare no one, to listen to no terms of peace until the race is cured by their punishment.

You can form an idea of the state of the country through which we were to pass. The Express Escort brought with them lances, bows, arrows, and other articles taken from the Indians. We examined them with the curiosity of those who might be forced to encounter them.

We stayed at Fort Clark until Monday A.M. when with an ambulance, a three wagons and an escort of ten men we started on our journey once more. This time to go 335 miles through a wilderness in which there is not a habitation. On the first evening we camped at a beautiful stream. I had seen no running water before in Texas, and to hear it rushing over the little rocks and tumbling into deep basins carried me back to my home, thought. Here too we saw beautiful fish; so they seemed at least, for I had seen none in fresh water since I watched them in "Eighteen Mile Creek" (Mud Creek).

Running water, an occasional tree and a hilly country characterized the road over which we passed on our next day's march-The hills among which we were riding were what is styled "truncated"—abrupt upon the sides, and perfectly flat upon the top, upon which you would often see a plain of a hundred acres. Toward evening the road began to wind over high hills, to plunge into ravines and to writhe and twist itself that our progress became difficult. Suddenly we labored down a precipitous slope, turned a corner and the whole beauty of "Devils River" broke upon our vision. I was in advance on "Pinkie" and was so elated that I swung my hat and gave a cheer, scaring by that rational proceeding a flock of ducks which would otherwise have contributed to our supper. I couldn't help it. I had seen no such rocks since Niagara and no such river for months. Castellated rock rose on either side to the height of one hundred feet from their foot, in places, a green as smooth as of cultivated extended to the waters edge. while among the hundred a changing forms of cliffs were scattered little groves of trees. Part of the river bed was dry, smooth and white as a marble floor for it was worn in solid rock. Over part, the water was flowing rapidly with a depth of about two feet. The pure bottom seen through purer water was singularly beautiful. We crossed the river and camped in a pine grove (cedar?) between high hills.

At daylight we were moving. Two men were seen in the distance, on close approach, found to be Texan Rangers (Capt. Travis' E Company) on the march to join their company which was with the expedition above. Now don't picture to yourself the Ranger*, as you read of him in newspapers, the personification of the brave and reckless-wild, perhaps but with a redeeming trait of lofty chivalry; but let me describe the animal and trust that you may have little to do with them. I have some under my control and can speak from experience.

Rangers are rowdies; rowdies in dress, manner and feeling. Take one of the lowest canal drivers, dress him in ragged clothes—those he ordinarily wears, as you see him, are altogether to clean—put a rifle in his hand, a revolver and big bowie knife at his belt—utterly eradicate any little trace of civilization or refinement that may have by chance been acquired—turn him loose, a lazy ruffianly scoundrel in country where little is known of, less cared for, the laws of God or man, and you have the material for a Texan Mounted Ranger, an animal—perhaps I should say brute—of which class some hundreds are at present mustered into service to fight Indians. There are exceptions. My invective is not meant for all.

I have gone, I see, far from my narrative. Revenons anousmoutons Rangers! They came up presently with a long yarn about seeing twelve Indians at Midnight. They described very graphically how "we hollered and they hollered"—as far as we could comprehend both sides were badly scared; both sides ran. It was nothing but two rangers scaring twelve. The twelve discharged with disgrace were going down the road and met the two coming up. The two brought letters from an officer at Fort Clark that they were to join our escort.

We had just started when we heard a great noise on the other side of the river, saw our escort scamper down the bank, then came a carriage-ambulance. More expresses sent after us. This was a Mexican guide (Roka Maurice) and as a little boy who had been five years a prisoner with the "comanches," now sent on as a guide to aid in tracking the Indians. This was the last we heard from Fort Clark. We were now sixty miles from that post and adding daily to the distance. We were in the Indian country where the white man goes now ready always to fight, for he knows that spying eyes are ever upon him and savage war-parties ready to strike at the first negligence. So we ride all day with arms in our hands, shooting now and then at deer or antelope that cross our path—sometimes marking down a bird or trying the range of a rifle at four hundred yards. Flocks of deer and antelopes raise their heads, look at us for an instant, and then rush crazy away into the distance, going as far as the eye can mark them at the same sweeping gait that carried them out of danger in the first twenty bounds. We cannot blame them, for though we flatter ourselves that our appearance is "killing" it may not be attractive to the deers(?) For my own part I should expect the most daring of my lady-acquaintances, meeting me, by chance, in my prairie costume to vanish, rending heaven with shrieks and "galloping"—ladies can't run in terror.

Danger comes openly on the prairies; there are no trees to hide a foe, and the savages of this country fight on horseback. They are the best horsemen in the world. In battle they gallop around you, throwing themselves out of the saddle and hanging over the horses' side keeping the body of their horse between their enemy and themselves, while only the foot is seen clinging to the saddle.

It required skill to do this alone, but in addition, these warriors manage to keep arrows flying from under their horses' necks with degree of certainty and rapidity that is disagreeable to contemplate.

=====

(Sorry I could not read the remainder of the copy. Refer to West Texas Historical Association Yearbook, Vol. XXIX, October 1953, General Albert J. Myers, The Father of the Signal Corp.)

*RANGERS–Referred to by Dr. Myers were a group of men the State of Texas recruited to augment the U.S. Army which was light in the number of troops available in Texas because many of the troops had been sent to the New Mexico Territory to stabilize the newly acquired territory. In the summer of 1854 Gen. Persifor F. Smith, Commanding the Dept. of Texas, made a requisition to Governor Pease of Texas for six companies of rangers to campaign against the Indian menace. These companies were to be mustered into the service of the United States on November 1 and their term of service was to be twelve months unless the President of U.S. discharged them sooner. Texas was divided into six districts which were to furnish the rangers. The Governor appointed the Captains from the districts to recruit their individual companies. The captains were: Giles S. Boggess, Tyler; William Fitzhugh, McKinney; John G. Walker, Nacogdoches; Charles E. Travis, Cameron; William Henry, Goliad.

The companies of Walker, Henry and Travis were assigned to Fort Clark. The companies reported in October 1854, three to Fort Clark and three to Fredericksburg. Evidently the companies were not enlisted for twelve months as the *Texas Gazette* of March 10, 1835, states General Smith had given orders for the re-enlistment of the companies commanded by Captains, Walker, Travis and Henry.

According to the Post Returns, Fort Clark, February 1855, "February 20, 1855, Headquarters Department of Texas, Capt. Henry's Company C, Capt. Walker's Company B and Capt. Travis' Company E to proceed to Ft. Clark to be mustered out of service by Bvt. Maj. Chas. Ruff, Mounted Rifles." After being mustered out of service Captain Henry and most of his company joined up with Captain Callahan at Uvalde and participated with Callahan in the burning of Piedras Negras, Mexico, in October 1855. Captain Travis (son of Col. Travis of Alamo fame) was commissioned in the Army's new Second Cavalry Regiment and by the time that unit had marched to Texas, Captain Travis was court-martialed out of the

U.S. Army. Captain Walker name reappears as a colonel of 8th Texas Cavalry in the Civil War.

Post Return, Fort Clark, Texas, February 1855

Texas State Gazette, Austin, Texas, August 26, 1854, November 4, 1854, January 6, 1855, March 10, 1855, Lena Clara Koch, Federal Indian Policy in Texas, 1845-1860, SWTQ, Vol. XXIX, No. 1, July 1925, pgs. 28-29

Col. Harold B. Simpson, *Cry Commanche, The 2nd U.S. Cavalry in Texas, 1855-1861*, Hill Jr. College Press, Hillsboro, 1979, pgs. 58-59

Lower Road
1855

The Indians on the Lower Road (San Antonio-El Paso) were exceedingly troublesome and killed a great many people all along the road. Although the Lower road had been in operation since June 1849, there was no real Protection to the travelers from Fort Inge (Uvalde) to the "Post Opposite El Paso" El Paso then was the Juarez of today, El Paso del Norte; the post as established on the Coon's Ranch). In 1852 Fort Clark was added and then in 1854 Fort Davis, but here was almost 300 miles of treacherous Indian country between and it was no wonder that the graves in the old cemetery at Fort Clark held unknown occupants. Both Forts Clark and Davis in the earliest years were garrisoned by infantry. Another reason for troubles on the Lower Road with Indians is that the road cut through two branches of the Old Comanche Trail to Mexico; at Comanche Springs (later Fort Stockton), and near Howard's well.

The Department of Texas ordered Lt. Col Henry Bainbridge, (Mounted Rifles Regiment), Commanding Officer of Fort Clark, to detail Brevet Major Charles Ruff and Company I, Mounted Rifles, to form a mobile detachment for six months duty patrolling the Lower Road concentrating on the most troubled area, Eagle Springs, between Fort Davis and Fort Quitman (established at later date). Fort Clark equipped a wagon train consisting of twenty-five six-mule teams to haul the necessary supplies, since there were no relay stations in between a herd of spare horses and mules had to accompany. In addition to Company I, Lieutenant J.E.B Stuart, a doctor (Basil Norris), a guide (James Cloud), a carpenter for wagon repairs (W. J. "Jeff" Maltby), and thirty-seven teamsters.

The mobile garrison departed Fort Clark in May 1855 and headed up the Lower Road the 538 miles to Eagle Springs. In July the Mounted Rifles started cleaning up the area around Eagle Springs. Captain Ruff reported killing as many as 13 Indians in several engagements in the area.

When he felt he had the area under control, the mobile unit traveled up the remainder of the road to El Paso then returned to Eagle Springs. After two months, the mobile garrison moved down the road to the vicinity of Fort Davis and camped at Barrilla Springs some thirty miles between Fort Davis and Leon Holes (12 miles west of the later Fort Stockton).

When the mobile garrison started to move south from Barilla Springs, they spied two lone horsemen coming to meet them. One of the horsemen was George McClellan, a civilian government wagon master, and the other was one of his teamsters. McClellan reported to Bvt. Maj. Ruff, that he had been sent from Fort Clark with nine six-mule teams and wagons loaded with supplies to be delivered to Fort Davis. The day before he had reached Leon Holes about noon and turned his mules loose to water and graze with two men to herd them. Evidently, the Indians saw them coming to Leon Holes and secreted themselves and when the mules wandered off a little distance from the wagons the Indians dashed in between the mules and wagons and drove the mules off.

Ruff and his mobile unit proceeded to Leon Holes with McClellan and his teamster. The guide, James Cloud, investigated the area and found that there were four bands of Indians (Comanche) and that they were driving as many as 1,000 head of mules and horses per band, making some 4,000 head in all, besides the fifty-four mules taken from the government train. Ruff and his sixty-five well-mounted, well-armed, U.S. Riflemen, and guide, followed the Indians for a day and then returned to the mobile camp with no contact. "Jeff" Maltby and the thirty-seven teamsters requested that Capt. Ruff permit them to pursue the Indians to Horse Head Crossing of the Pecos River where they were sure the Indians would rest for several days while watering their huge herd. They were upset on Ruff's refusal but Ruff's orders were to protect the Lower Road and from Captain Ruff's military records, he probably wanted to make the contact with the Indians more than any of his mobile garrison. The mobile garrison completed its assignment and returned to Fort Clark in December 1855. This detachment most probably assured the Indians the Lower Road would be protected and they could expect military escorts along with those traveling the road. However, it in no way stopped the hit-and-run tactics of the Indians whenever the opportunity presented itself.

=====

Maltby, W. J. *Captain Jeff or Frontier Life in Texas with the Texas Rangers*, Texian Press, Waco, pp. 135-136

Jeb Stuart
1855

James E. B. Stuart known as Jeb became a cadet at West Point, July 1850 and graduated July 1, 1854, assigned to the Mounted Rifles, Major John R. Simonson's regiment on the western frontier (Texas). Stuart traveled by ship from New York to New Orleans but was held up by an yellow fever epidemic and did not join his regiment until December 1854. From 1854 until May 1855 Jeb Stuart participated in the field scouting against the Apache Indians which were endeavoring to do away with the Lower Road (San Antonio–El Paso). By May 1855 he was promoted to First Lieutenant and transferred to the newly formed 1st Cavalry Regiment. Stuart was to become a dashing and daring Confederate Cavalry General and he was caught in a melee (1864) with Custer's Michigan Cavalry and shot down by a dismounted Sergeant in blue.

In 1880 H. B. McClellan of Lexington was preparing to write the story "I Rode with Jeb Stuart" which as later published in the *Civil War Centennial Series*. For an earlier background on Jeb Stuart he wrote to Major General J. S. Simonson, Retired. Major Simonson was the Commanding Officer of Fort Clark from May to December 1855. At the time of Jeb Stuart's joining Fort Clark, Lieutenant Colonel Bainbridge was Commanding Fort Clark and the senior officer of the Mounted Rifles at Fort Clark. Major Simonson was the Squadron Commander at that time for the four companies of Mounted Rifles.

Remember that General Simonson is replying some 26 years later.

"Sir—In reply to your inquiry for information as to Gen. (J.E.B.) Stuart's services in the expedition against the Apache Indians in the years 1854 and 1855, I have to state that Stuart, then a Second Lieutenant, joined my command at Fort Clark, Texas, in December 1854 and continued with it until May 8, 1855, when he was relieved to take advantage of his promotion to the First Cavalry. In the order relieving him I gave expression to the estimation in which he was held in complimentary terms, highly creditable to his character as a soldier and a gentleman. My order-book is lost, and I have no copy of that order. A copy was furnished Lt. Stuart and may be among his papers.

Lt. Stuart was brave and gallant, always prompt in the execution of orders, and reckless of danger or exposure. I considered him at that time of the most promising young officer in the U.S. Army. The expedition continued on duty in mountains and valleys of western Texas on the El Paso Road and borders of the Rio Grande, until Oct. 1855. A large portion of country little known at that day, was explored, and the Mescalero Apaches were made to flee across the Rio Grande into Mexico. It would take a volume to contain the history of that expedition,—its scouts, marches, skirmishes and privations. I enclose here-with slips containing a communication of Lt. Stuart to the Jeffersonian, a paper printed in Staunton, Va. It gives a full description of the difficulties and privations encountered in one of the scouts.

These slips were pasted in, and cut from my morning report book. Lt. Stuart wrote another communication which was printed in some paper in Virginia or Texas, giving an account of a fight, at the crossing of the Peacus (Pecos) River, with a band of Comanche Indians, by a portion of the troops of this expedition. Very Respectfully, Your Obedient Servant, J. S. Simonson, Maj. Gen. (Ret.)."

"Camp Stuart, Texas
Maj. Simonson's Command
Feb. 15, 1855

Dear Sir:

On the 6th instant this command, of the operation and character of which you learned something in a former letter from Ft. Clark, was divided into parties, one of which under command of the Major, started on the trail of a more numerous party, leading toward the Sierra Guadalupe. A few notes on this scout, through unsuccessful as regards to finding Indians, yet embracing an extensive region of which but little was previously known, may not be a void of interest to the readers of the Jeffersonian.

The narrow trail led in the direction of a very rugged range of mountains, a circumstance which determined the substitution of pack mules for wagons. The trail continued for about ten miles through a narrow ravine, surrounded by precipitous ridges of a species of red sandstone, which cropped out so frequently as to leave no space for vegetation except here and there a bunch of cactus of a singular variety.

This ravine was soon headed by a high mountain, up whose steep side the trail wound its serpent way. Hardly had we reached the summit when a furious storm set in, first by a few preliminary drops, then in torrents of rain and hail. Welcomed as a change from six inches of dust to a refreshing shower, this time it came most inopportunely for the command all of whom were well drenched with rain and benumbed with cold. Our march continued in this way for several miles, the storm so blinding us that we could scarcely discern the ground; when suddenly, not only had we debouched upon a level plain, but every vestige of the storm had vanished save a few raindrops which lingered on the grass. All nature rejoiced at the change, and the gorgeous splendor of a rainbow which hung in the west was interpreted as an omen of success to the scout. Thus you see that in Texas, instead of having to follow the circuit of the seasons for variety in climate, we can have May and December in one day in Feb. We were obliged to camp without water, a circumstance by no means uncommon with this expedition, for its operations have been very much circumscribed on account of the great scarcity of water.

Next day we started early in the march, having a bright day and a better road than before. Proceeding thus over a diversified track, alternately rough and smooth, now a ridge with scrubby pine, then a ravine skirted upon a tableland that seemed better clad with vegetation than any of the preceding, we were suddenly checked by finding ourselves on the crest of a stupendous precipice. Up to this time we had led our horses over the rough places from choice; it now became a matter of necessity for the weight a man on his horse would undoubtedly have precipitated both many hundred feet below. To look at the mountain from its base, any sane man would pronounce it impassable, for it seemed a vertical ledge of rock; yet, strange to say, the Indian trail transversed its side in a zigzag manner to the base. The descent was extremely slow, and those in the rear of the line had ample opportunity to survey prospect before them. I was raised in the Blue Mountains of Virginia but never have I beheld anything to compare to the grandeur of the scenery from that Comanche Pass. The ridge on which we stood extended in a straight line as far as the eye could reach north and south, sloping gradually toward the rear, but in front rising in a huge column of solid rock, or vertical ledges, to a height of two thousand feet above the level plain at its base, which extended twenty-five miles across and sixty miles in a longitudinal direction. The other side of this broad valley was terminated by a similar range, rising to an equal height, but not so precipitous or continuous. To the north, the gray and rugged peaks of the Sierra Guadalupe limited the weary vision. In the center of the valley, a beautiful lake covered with ice; but it proved to be a dry salt lagoon, perfectly white with incrustations of niter and salt. Long before the rear-guard had begun the descent, the advance had dwindled away over the plain to a mere speck in the distance. Before sundown, however, we were discussing our frugal fare on the verge of the salt lagoon. In the immediate vicinity were several pools of salt water and one of sculpture.

Next day the trail, instead of keeping the valley, passed up a narrow and steep gorge, nearly opposite the other pass, obstructed at every point by huge boulders, often six feet in diameter and almost spherical. It was evident that these difficult passes were selected on purpose to elude pursuit, for the road today was, if possible, more difficult than that of the day before. We soon began the ascent of another ridge, where the trail scarcely furnished footing for the animals. One mule on which the surgeon had packed the entire dispensary of the command in two panniers, lost his footing and rolled over and over to the base of the cliff, all below taking care to give him a wide berth. Thanks, however, to the efficiency of the doctor's medicine, both the mule and panniers escaped injury. Not far from the summit of this ridge we came upon the deserted Indian Village. Their dismantled lodges were in perfect preservation, and enough was left to show they had not been gone more than ten days, the circumspect manner in which their camp was laid out would have done credit to more scientific heads. It was carefully guarded against surprise by a system of flankers and advanced posts which occupied the prominent knolls around it. The main camp was concealed from superficial observer by a dense cluster of pines. Each lodge, formed for a family, was constructed by bending a series of twigs after the manners of bows of an ordinary wagon, the sharpened ends being driven into the ground, and the system connected at the top by a ridge piece, over all was thrown brushwood and straw in quantities sufficient for shelter.

We camped near the village, and started early the day for the Guadalupe Mountains, still about thirty miles distant, leading our horses the greater part of the way. There we met with a party of 8th Inf. commanded by Major James Longstreet, on a mission from El Paso similar to our own. He reported that some ten days before, his guide (a Mexican) had ridden some distance in advance of the party, and was found dead on the roadside. He was killed by a small party of Indians who being on foot, could not be pursued. From this point to the Delaware Creek, along the road from El Paso to Fort Chadbourne, having the strong hope of finding a hostile party there. We were, however, again destined to be disappointed for that clear and lovely stream seemed never to have been polluted by the Redman's presence.

Our bivouac that night was lighted in a deep and narrow valley or arroyo, clothed in luxuriant grass (probably near the Delaware Creek). We had scarcely let our horses to grass when there came down the hollow a gust of wind which scattered our fire over the grass like a tornado, setting the whole prairie in a blaze in a few moments. It swept, apparently at one breath, over the entire camp, consuming bridles, saddles, blankets, caps, overcoats, and everything else that met its devouring grasp. Many of the horses were badly singed, nor did the men escape much better, for many lost their caps and had their beards closely singed. None of those encamped in that arroyo escaped without some loss. The deplorable condition of the command caused us to steer a straight course for Camp Stuart. We descended into the same broad valley by a different, and less obstructed canon from the other,in bottom of which was dry bed of a stream. At places this bed was flat slate like rock, on which were found some singular specimen of aboriginal drawings. It was done with a deep substance not unlike Indian red. The characters were distinctly marked, and those which I examined particularly represented three warriors, one on horseback with his bow drawn, and two other on foot, similarly equipped. Their arrows being directed up the canon, suggested the idea that at the time they were made three warriors had gone in that direction, leaving this drawing to indicate that fact to others of their tribe. They are pretty good draughts men in the human figure, but make a very grotesque representation of the horses. Next day we arrived in camp, which really seemed like home to us, and our floorless, chair less, and comfortless tents looked luxurious after a week's shelter beneath the broad canopy of heaven.

This camp was name in honor of Capt. Stuart* of South Carolina, formerly in the Mounted Rifles, and has here-to-fore been the rendezvous of the expedition; the Major expects, however, in a few days to move it to the Guadalupe Springs, so as to operate from that point toward the Sacramento Mountains, where the Indians must be, if anywhere in this section of the country. The party dispatched below the Presidio have not yet been heard from. They have not had time to return, as it is some distance below Fort Davis, which is about one hundred and ten miles below this place. If they succeed in jumping the Indians in that quarter, you will be apprised of the results by

Yours Truly, Jeb Stuart"

=====

Post Returns of Fort Clark, December 1854, January-February 1855

H. B. McClellan, "I Rode With JEB Stuart," *Civil War Centennial Series*, Indiana University Press, Bloomington, 1958, pp. 10-15

*Stuart, James. S.C., Cadet M.A. 1 July 1842,Bvtd. 2nd Lt. Mtd. Rifle 1 July 1846, 2nd Lt. 9 Oct. 1847, Bvtd. 1st Lt. 20 Aug. 1847 for gal. and mer. con in battle of Contreras and Churubusco. Capt. 13 Sept. 1847 for gal. and mer. con battle of Chapultelpec. died 18 June 1851 of wds. recd. 17 June 1851 in action with Inds. near Rogue River, Oreg.

"I Married a Soldier or Old Days in the Old Army"

Lydia Spencer Lane

(Company E, Mounted Rifles replaced Company I, May 25, 1855, at Fort Clark.) On June 12, 1855, Lt. William Lane joined Company E, Mounted Rifles having been a recent graduate of the Military Academy. December 12, 1855, Lt. Lane transferred to Company H, Mounted Rifles and in April was stationed at Fort McIntosh (Laredo).

"During the summer of 1856, the Regiment of Mounted Rifles was ordered to New Mexico, and we were soon on the move again, after having been about two months at Fort McIntosh. We left July 15 (1856) to join the troops at Fort Clark, from which point they were to begin a march of nearly one thousand miles. This would take them far into the fall of the year to accomplish, being obliged to travel slowly to save the animals as much as possible through the hot weather. We arrived at Fort Clark on the 22nd of July (1856) and remained until the 27th, when everything being ready, we left with one of the three columns into which the regiment was divided, each column being two or three days' travel apart. We had quite a comfortable "outfit" for a lieutenant and family, owning a pretty little ambulance and a fine pair of large gray mules as one could wish to see ... There were several ladies besides myself with the command, but we saw very little of each other those awful hot days. We broke camp, usually at day-light each morning, and tents were again pitched at noon, when we had little desire for anything but to get under shelter and stay there until the sun went down. Then after enjoying the cool breeze, which nearly always came with the night in Texas, we were ready to retire ... There were several army posts along our route, and to arrive at one was as pleasant variety in the irksomeness of the long days. Camp Lancaster (Fort Lancaster, Oak Creek at Pecos Crossing) was the first we passed, August 2, 1856—and was the worst station I had seen in Texas, but the ladies I met at the post seemed cheerful and contented. On August 12, we reached Fort Davis, where the quarters were bad, but the Surroundings were very beautiful.... We made what was called a very quick journey to Fort Bliss (El Paso) from Fort Clark, arriving August 27 (1856), two days less than a month on the road ... Fort Fillmore, on the Rio Grande, was forty miles from Fort Bliss, and in New Mexico ...

(October 1859) In the fall, my husband applied for a years leave of absence, he had been on the frontier for five years, and thought he would like a change ... We found Fort Clark much improved since we had lived there, in the little shanty in the chaparral. General French was in command (Lt. Col. John Magruder and Maj. John Simmonson were in command on the previous visits to Ft. Clark), and entertained us most kindly.

All army women, from the wife of commanding general down to wife of a second lieutenant, are treated with so much courtesy and politeness by army officers that they do not like anything that has the least appearance of a slight or infringement of their rights. They never grow old in garrison, and always received attentions to which no women in citizen life is accustomed when no longer young. I have seen gray-haired ladies at an army post dance at the hops with as much enjoyment as the younger ones, and they are always invited by the men, young and old, to do so as matter of course. After

Colonel Lane was retired, and we lived in the East and North, it took me sometime to understand that I need not look for the numerous courtesies to which I had always been accustomed at an army frontier post, and that if I went out at all, I must join the army of "wall flowers," and expect nothing."

=====

Lydia Spencer Lane, *I married a Soldier or Old Days in the Old Army*, Philadelphia: J. B. Lippincott Company, 1893

Devil's River 1857
(John B. Hood)

Second Lieutenant John Bell Hood (commander), Delaware Scout John McLoughlin, 1st. Sergeant Joseph P. Henley and twenty-five troopers of Company G, Second Cavalry, were preparing on July 5th, 1857, to leave Fort Mason on an extended scout with thirty days of supplies. Prior to departure Lt. Hood was briefed on orders from Washington regarding a band of Tonkawa Indians who would be enroute on the frontier to the Texas Reservation near Camp Cooper. Indian Affairs had instructed these Indians that when encountering U.S. troops that they were to raise a white flag and soldiers would not restrict their passage to the reservation.

After about 10 days, the detachment discovered an Indian trail, apparently about two or three days old. The indications were that the Indians were headed to Mexico via the headwaters of the Devil's River. By July 20th the trail indicated that this band had joined up with others and were several days ahead of Hood's detachment.

Hood decided to abandon the trail since they were fairly close to the Rio Grande and the Indians were probably safely crossed over to Mexico. Also his command was in desperation for water but the steep embankments were presenting an obstacle to reaching the water. While paralleling the Devil's

River seeking an approach to the water a group of Indians were discovered on a parallel range of mountains waving a white flag.

Hood was convinced these Indians were either Tonkawas or a hostile bunch endeavoring by ruse to throw him off his guard, entrap, and massacre the entire command. At this time only 17 of his men were available for action as the remainder had halted in rear because of the exhausted state of their horses. Hood's small detachment crossed over a mound and when within about two hundred yards, the flag, seemingly a sheet, was still waving aloft and a few Indians were lounging about with every appearance of a party desirous of peace.

The ground in that vicinity was rough and partially covered with a growth of Spanish bayonets which afforded a secure place of concealment. The troops continue the advance, still mounted, and when they were within about twenty or thirty paces of the mound occupied by the Indians, four or five of them advanced towards the troopers with the flag. Suddenly, they threw it on the ground and fired upon the troopers. Simultaneously from a large heap of dry grass, weeds, and leaves to the immediate front there appeared a blaze of flame some thirty feet in height. With a furious yell the warriors instantly rose up around the detachment, while others charged down the slope seizing some of the trooper's horses reins. Hood was shot in left hand with an arrow which passed through the reins and the fourth finger, pinning his hand to the bridle. Hood jerked the arrow out to free his hand. The hand to hand fight continued until all pistol shots were expended.

Then the troopers fell back, dismounted, and reloaded. While they were reloading, a mourning howl arouse beyond the burning heap and these sounds of sorrow revealed that there would be no renewal of the assault. Two troopers were killed; Private Thomas Ryan and Private William Barry. Four besides Lt. Hood were severely wounded; Privates John Davit, William W. Williams, Thomas W. Tirell and John J. Kane.

The Indians were Comanches and Lipans but the troopers had managed to kill nine of them (one a chief). Ten or twelve of the Indians were wounded. The Indians after picking up their dead, and with night fall approaching, disappeared through the underbrush toward the Rio Grande.

Lt. Hood continued his march toward the Devil's River, even more desperate to obtain water for his men and animals. About 10 P.M. he reached the stream where his exhausted, bloodied column bivouacked for the night. Hood dispatched a messenger to nearby Camp Hudson to obtain supplies and medical treatment for the wounded.

Next Day, Lieutenant Theodore Fink and a detachment of the First Infantry from Camp Hudson arrived bringing supplies and medical aid. Lt. Hood and troopers fit to travel, rode east to Fort Clark, arriving on July 27. After rest and medical treatment they returned to their command at Fort Mason.

=====

J. B. Hood, *Advance and Retreat, Personal Experiences in the U.S. and Confederate States Armies.* pp. 8-14

Richard M. McMurry, *John Bell Hood, and War for Southern Indians*, pp. 17-20

Harold Simpson, *Cry Comanche*, pp. 91-93

U.S. Army General Orders No. 14, November 13, 1857

Captain Charles C. Gilbert
First Infantry Regiment
1858

Captain Gilbert deserves recognition in the history of Fort Clark as he was garrisoned at Fort Clark from October 18, 1858, until March 21, 1859. During those months he was the senior officer present and thus was the post commanding officer. In addition to the above listed reasons, as history would have it he was one of 34 officers who served Fort Clark prior to the Civil War and later became one of the general officers in the war. In his case he served with the Union forces.

Charles Champion Gilbert was born March 1, 1822, at Zanesville, Ohio. During the period of July 1, 1842, to July 1, 1846 he was a cadet at the Military Academy. Upon graduation he was promoted in the Army to Brevet Second Lieutenant and assigned to the Third Infantry. He served in the War with Mexico, 1846–1848. September 27, 1846, he was promoted to Second Lieutenant and transferred to the First Infantry. He was engaged in the Siege of Vera Cruz, March 9-29, 1847, and remained garrisoned at Vera Cruz 1847–1848. Later in 1848, the end of war with Mexico he was at Mexico City.

At the end of the Mexican War, he was transfered back to the United States and garrisoned at East Pascagoula,

Mississippi. Due to the U.S. Army's Requirements in the Treaty of Guadalupe Hildago and responsibility to Texas for Indian protection, Lieutenant Gilbert and First Infantry were transferred to Texas. He served in frontier duty at Ringold Barracks (Rio Grande City) 1848–1850 He was then assigned to the Military Academy for period 1850–1855 as the Assistant Professor of Geography, History, and Ethics. This assignment came on top of his promotion to First Lieutenant on June 10, 1850.

September 1855 he was released from the Military Academy and returned to his regiment which was on frontier duty at Fort MacKavett, Texas. December 1855 he was promoted to Captain and became the commanding officer of Company B, First Infantry at Fort MacKavett where he remained until 1856. He transferred to Fort Chadbourne, then on to Fort Duncan, Texas in July 1856. August 1856 he was on an Indian Scout from Fort Duncan to Devil's River. He and his company were engaged in the Pursuit and Surprise of three parties of Comanche Indians near the mouth of the Pecos River, August 30th. Capt. Gilbert and his Company B remained garrisoned at Fort Duncan until October 18, 1858, when they transferred to Fort Clark.

While Captain Gilbert was garrisoned at Fort Clark he had in his possession a trophy of war he had acquired while in Mexico. It was a Mexican silver presentation mug believed to have been manufactured in 1820. Captain Gilbert had a monogram removed and new inscription put in its place. This inscription was engraved in a decorative cartouche on front of the mug which reads:

Presented to
Mattie P. Gilbert
By Her Father, Fort Clark
Texas Dec.12th 1858

A later inscription was added below cartouche which reads:

Katherine Gilbert Gresham
Oct. 17, '83

June 1991, this mug was in the hands of Antique Silver Dealer, Houston, Texas, who felt it should be in the Old Guardhouse Museum and notified the museum of this rare artifact and the history surrounding it. The price of such an artifact makes it beyond the reach of finances of the Old Guardhouse Museum. Sad commentary since this gift was given by Capt. Gilbert some 6 years and 5 months after the founding of Fort Clark.

After March 21, 1859, Captain Gilbert and Company B marched to Camp Cooper, Texas. Later they were garrisoned at Fort Cobb, Indian Territory until 1861. With the pending Civil War they were again transferred, this time to Fort Leavenworth, Kansas.

As a Union Officer he served during the Rebellion of the Seceding States (Civil War) 1861–1866. His first action in that war came in an engagement at Dug Spring, August 2, 1861. Following that engagement he was involved in the Battle of Wilson's Creek, August 10, 1861, where he was severely wounded. His wounds resulted in his being on sick leave August 20–September 21, 1861. After his return to duty he was appointed acting Inspector-General of the Department of the Cumberland September 21 until November 18, 1861. Later he was assigned the Inspector-General Department of Ohio until March 11, 1862. He was engaged in the engagement of Pittsburgh Landing, Tennessee, and April 7, 1862, was in the Battle of Shiloh. For his services in Battle of Shiloh he was appointed Brevet Major for gallant and meritorious services. Two days later he was involved in the Siege of Corinth and after May 30th, 1862, was in the operations in North Alabama and Louisville, Kentucky. Due to the military necessity during the period of September 1–27 he was acting Major General in command of the Army of Ohio. He was appointed September 9, 1862, Brigadier General, U.S. Volunteers, the rank he held until March 1863. On September 1, 1862, he was brevetted a Lieutenant Colonel in regulars for Gallant and Meritorious services at the Battle of Richmond, Kentucky.

He was charged with 3rd Provisional Corps, Army of Ohio during the period of September 29–October 1862, at which time he was engaged in the Battle of Perryville which resulted in another brevet in the regular service, that of Colonel for Gallant and Meritorious services in the Battle of Perryville, October 8, 1862. He held many assignments for the remainder of the war in the northeastern United States and evidently he was not engaged in combat for the remainder. In September 1866, he reverted to his regular rank of Major and he was assigned to 28th Infantry. On July 8, 1868, he was promoted to Lieutenant Colonel and transferred to 7th Infantry Regiment then garrisoned at Jacksonville, Florida. In May 1869 his regiment was transferred to Fort Bridger, Wyoming. Later the regiment was at various forts in Montana then on to Fort Snelling, Minnesota, October 1, 1879. Col. Gilbert was in command of a Battalion in the Ute Expedition to June 1880. He was on sick leave of absence until Jan. 22, 1881.

Again he was promoted in the regulars, this time to Colonel and transferred to 17th Infantry Regiment, May 19, 1881. Although he held the command of this regiment, his health and age began to affect his services as during this next period he was granted two extensive sick leave of absences. March 1, 1886, Colonel Gibert was retired from active service, being 64 years of age.

In 1894 a Congressional Act conferred commissions on certain officers for distinguished services with the thanks of Congress. Charles C. Gilbert was so listed which cited him as a colonel retired but granted him the commission of Brigadier General in Volunteers for gallant conduct at Springfield, Missouri, and Pittsburgh Landing, Tennessee, 9 September 1862. He as an old soldier who faded away in 1903.

=====

Gen. Cullum's Biographical Register of the Officers and Graduates of the United States Military Academy, The Riverside Press, Cambridge 1891, Number 1292

Harold A. Hamner, Captain Second Texas Mounted Rifles, Commanding Officer, Fort Clark, 1861

So far Harold Hamner's earlier life remains somewhat of the mystery. Perhaps that is due to the fact he didn't stand out so prominent among his peers as he did in later life. Hamner's historic notoriety first appears in the community of Jacksborough (Jacksboro, 1890), Jacks County in 1858. H. A. Hamner and Isaac R. Worrall were co-editors of the newspaper *The Whiteman*. *The Whiteman* was published from 1858 to July 1860 as a weekly newspaper. Hamner, the chief editorial writer, made bitter attacks on Sam Houston and his policy for frontier defense. The paper had a large circulation in the Jacksboro area because it was distributed by the California Stage Line. Also because of its sensational style which appealed to the frontiersmen. Hamner's press was destroyed by fire July 29, 1860. He claimed that it was purposely destroyed and since it was such a vitriolic sheet, Hamner was probably correct. As critic of policy for frontier defense he became tagged as an "Indian Hater." It was noted while in Jacksborough about 1859 he enlisted and commanded the Jack County Volunteers. This unit was on call for Indian depredations or invasions in Jack and surrounding counties.

Hamner moved from Jacksboro to Weatherford after the fire and joined forces with John R. Baylor at Weatherford. They started on September 13, 1860 publishing *The Whiteman*. Evidently, before these two joined forces in the publishing business, they were acquainted by their bond as "Indian Haters." When John R. Baylor was discharged as a Indian Agent at the Brazos Agency he managed to gather a large force of men in the surrounding area to drive the Indians out of Texas. In this force was the volunteer ranging company that was commanded by Harold A. Hamner. "About two weeks before the 'Reservation War' a noble young man named Holden was killed and scalped about halfway between the two Indian reservations. His slayers were trailed into the Comanche reservation. It was either Peter Garland or Captain Hamner who was in command of a group of men doing the trailing and they came to a camp of Indians. The pursuers were all mad and asked no questions but commenced firing and killing friendly Caddoes. This hastened the war with the reservation Indians. This war was waged by what the Indian agents chose to call a mob of frontier citizens. Even later when Baylor gather his force of "Buffalo Hunters," he found support in Hamner. John Baylor, George Baylor and Harold Hamner, besides being Indian Haters, were some of the first advocates in Jack County for secession of Texas.

On January 31, 1861, H. A. Hamner wrote from Weatherford to Allison Nelson, member of the Secession Convention. "My Friend, Ere this reaches you, I will be on my way to seize Camp Cooper and hold the same subject to the order of the convention. I am aware of the responsibility and trust, I will sustained by the convention. I would have been off three weeks sooner but for the want of cooperation here. Hoping to hear from you while in Austin. I am respectfully, H. A. Hamner." This was two weeks before the Convention moved to take over the forts of Texas, this hot spur launched a movement in Parker County against Camp Cooper, 100 miles away.

Robert H. Ward, a member of the Secession Convention, in early February 1861, located Colonel William C. Dalrymple at the old Comanche Reservation near Camp Cooper. Col. Dalrymple was commander of the State Militia, with six companies of mounted rangers, who were temporarily headquartered there. Captain H. A. Hamner's company was one of the six. Hamner previously had been authorized by Governor Houston to raise a company of rangers for frontier defense against the Indians. Col. Dalrymple with his expedition of 228 men forced Captain S. D. Carpenter, First Infantry, to surrender Camp Cooper with force of approximately 180 men. Camp Cooper was surrendered February 21, 1861, by the commanding officer, Capt. Carpenter.

Later, Colonel Henry McCulloch troops went to Camp Cooper to accept the surrender of the post. "We arrived on March 7th. The Camp had already been surrendered to troops in the old State Service which had been under Governor Houston. However, it was promptly turned over to Colonel McCulloch, who left me (Buck Barry) in command of the place."

It is difficult to understand how Governor Houston could have enlisted Captain Hamner and his "Buffalo Fighters" as rangers for the Frontier since Hamner was such a critic of Houston. However at that time, Governor Houston had within the state a total of a thousand or more Texas Rangers in active service, the largest force that Texas had in the field at one time. Evidently, the state ranger force was soon dissolved and Captain Hamner was free to return to Weatherford. Hamner was again authorized to enlist another company which probably embodied many of the men from the previous ranging company. This authorization was for state service for one year in Colonel Ford's Second Cavalry Regiment. Naturally since Lieutenant Colonel John R. Baylor commanded a portion of this state unit it follows logically how Harold Hamner was selected to muster a company at Weatherford. The authorization for this company to Captain Hamner was by order of the Committee of Public Safety, Secession Convention and not that of Governor Houston. He had no sympathy with seceding and later resigned because of it.

On May 17, 1861, Ford's regiment of Second Cavalry was mustered into state service for one year and Lieutenant Colonel Baylor's portion of that regiment was designated the "Second Mounted Rifles," Provisional Army of Texas. May 23, 1861, this regiment was mustered into the Confederate Service as the Second Texas Mounted Rifles. In the Confederate Service, Captain H. A. Hamner's company was designated Company H, Second Texas Mounted Rifles. About June 1, 1861, Companies A, B, D, E, and H, Second Texas Mounted Rifles under the command of Major Edwin Waller, left Camp Leon, near San Antonio for the upper Rio Grande posts and later Arizona. Enroute on the march to El Paso, Company H was left at Fort Clark. The other the troops were left at Camp Hudson, Fort Lancaster, and Fort Davis. While the troops of Second Texas Mounted Rifles marched gloriously to their duty stations, Lt. Col. Baylor rode in an Overland Stage to El Paso. The other portion of Ford's regiment (four companies) went with Colonel Ford earlier to the lower Rio Grande.

When Captain H. A. Hamner and Company H, Second Mounted Rifles were detailed to command and maintain Fort Clark in early June 1861 they found the fort under the command of Captain T. T. Teel and his Battery B of First Texas Artillery. Captain Teel had arrived at Fort Clark, March 5, 1861, with his company of the Texas Provisional Army (formerly a company of the Charles Beckley Castle, Knights of Golden Circle). May Day 1861, Captain Teel and his company were sworn in the Army of Confederate States of America. Upon the arrival of Captain Hamner and Company H, Captain Teel and his Battery B of First Texas Artillery joined in the march with the other companies of Second Mounted Rifles to El Paso. After the arrival of Captain Hamner and Company H at Fort Clark, Lieutenant Colonel John R. Baylor arrived via stage. He then decided to relieve his brother George who was the First Lieutenant in Company H. George became the Adjutant to John R. Baylor and rode the stage with him to El Paso (Franklin).

In the initial assignment of the posts of the Second Mounted Rifles, Companies C and F were omitted. They were brought into the Army of the Confederate States from companies of the Texas Provisional Army previously on duty in the northern Nueces Strip. Company C was a company Captain William C. Adams had been directed by Colonel McCullough to form and take possession of Fort Inge and Camp Wood for the state of Texas. Later Camp Wood was garrisoned by Captain Richardson's "W.P. Lane Rangers," another company of Texas Provisional Army. In late June 1861, the "W. P. Lane Rangers" at Camp Wood were sworn into the Army of the Confederate States by a designated officer as Company F, Second Texas Mounted Rifles. On June 25, 1861, Captain W. C. Adam's company of the Texas Provisional Army had been transferred to Fort Clark and leaving Fort Inge with only a detachment of Company F. Here at Fort Clark Captain W. C. Adam's company was sworn in as Company C, Second Texas Mounted Rifles.

After Captain W. C. Adams and his company were sworn into the Confederate army, they moved to a camp on Piedras Pinto (Pinto Creek) between Fort Clark and Del Rio. During the period of June 30th and July 17th, 14 men and boys were added to Adam's company. July 17th, 1861, Captain Adam with Company C commenced the march to Fort Lancaster were they arrived July 28th. By August Company D was occupying Fort Bliss (El Paso), but later Company C along with Hawthorne's (formerly Sgt. in Teel's state company) and McAllister's (formerly Teels state Company) companies occupied Fort Bliss. In August, Baylor heard of the disastrous engagement with Indians of Lt. Reuben Mays (and a detachment of Company D), August 11th, near Ft. Davis. Baylor transferred Company C (Capt. Adams) and Company H (Capt. Hamner) to Fort Davis to reinforce the remaining eighteen men of Company D. On August 31, Captain Adams led most of his command out of Fort Lancaster and proceeded to his new assignment in Davis Mountains. At about the same time Captain Hamner (Company H) left Fort Clark . Captain Hamner would join Adams and the small detachment from Walker's company (D) at Fort Davis early in September. To prevent Hamner's post (Ft. Clark) from remaining vacant, Baylor ordered Captain Richardson (Company F) to place detachments at Fort Inge and Fort Clark, apparently Camp Wood was no longer considered essential as were the posts located on the Lower Road.

Captain Hamner during his first period at Fort Clark (June–August 30,1861) was able to engage in his favorite past time of "Indian Hating." A mixed band of Apaches, Lipans, and Mescaleros, from the Pecos River area attacked the Mexican town of Resurrecion. Several of the inhabitants of the town were killed and five children were carried off as captives. In order to render assistance to the town Captain Hamner with detachment of company H, made an unauthorized entry into Mexico and accompanied some of the citizens of Resurrecion in pursuit of the Indians. The pursuit was discontinued after a few leagues without results. As an aftermath of this aid to Mexican citizens, Captain Hamner convinced Lieutenant Colonel Baylor that aid should be offered to the Mexican border with their Indian problems. Baylor sent Hamner to Mexico as Special Commissioner with letter to the Governor and Military Command of Coahuila to propose combined actions against the tribes of hostile Mescaleros, Lipans, and Comanches. The Mexican authorities spurned this offer. Although the Mexican authorities were smart in spurning any offer of these two "hot spurs." It appears that the Mexican's practice at this period was to avoid involvement with the Confederate Army. The Mexicans had prior experience with the slave catching practices of the Knights of the Golden Circle. They were leery of the Knights of the Golden Circle's involvement in the Texas units of the Confederate Army.

Near the end of September 1861, Lieutenant Colonel Baylor ordered Captain Hamner and Company H from Fort Davis to return to Fort Clark. October 5, Company H made a reappearance at Fort Clark and relieved Captain Richardson's Company F who in turn departed for Fort Lancaster. This return to Fort Clark must have presented an opportunity to Captain Hamner to gain some public relations as the *Bellville Countryman* of November 13, 1861 had a short article that "Captain H. A. Hamner, Commander of Fort Clark, lamented that his troopers were near naked, and without shoes and socks." This of course was the condition of all Confederate troops on the Rio Grande. It easy to visualize the Confederate Army in neat gray uniforms. However, the Second Texas Mounted Rifles were deplorably short of clothing and very few had uniforms, they looked more like rag tag farmers and their weapons weren't a great deal better. However, Captain Hamner's appeal in the newspaper brought some results as the ladies of Jackson County set about collecting clothes and blankets to be sent to the regiment.

One can't help wondering why Captain Hamner and his company were returned to Fort Clark when Indian and the war problems at this time were taking its toll on Lieutenant Colonel Baylor and the remainder of Second Mounted Rifles, particularly, the units from Fort Davis to Arizona. Perhaps, the next documented activities of the "Hot Spur" Captain Hamner has some bearing. Captain Hamner was reported to have visited Eagle Pass in 1861. The report indicated that he came to Eagle Pass for the express purpose of eliminating some Union sympathizers. According to the writer of the report, Jesse Sumpter, the four Union sympathizers were Aleck Oswald, Charles Groos, Green Van, and Jesse Sumpter.

Captain Hamner's plan was to get the four of them drunk and murder them. Captain Hamner brought one of his most confidential men with him (probably George Hagler as George Baylor had been transferred by this time) and Edward Braden of San Antonio as his ambulance driver. Hamner only succeeded in getting Green Van and Aleck Oswald to the saloon for a spree as Jesse Sumpter begged off the invitation and Van disliked Hamner's actions, so he took an early departure. Hamner during the spree shot Oswald when he wanted to leave and then tried to effect an speedy escape but his ambulance wrecked. Hamner then abandoned the ambulance and driver, Braden and with his confident man went up the river to John Levin's ranch. There they borrowed horses and returned to Fort Clark. Captain Hamner managed to escape arrest for the killing of Oswald since the only government authority in that part of the country was the Confederate military. Sounds as if Hamner took Baylor tactics. Perhaps Hamner had heard of his commander, Baylor's recent killing of Robert Kelly in Mesilla, Arizona.

Captain Hamner and Company H, Second Mounted Rifles remained Fort Clark until their enlistment was to expire, May 1862, then returned to San Antonio where they were discharged from Second Mounted Rifles. However, with the civil war in full swing so most of the Second Mounted Rifles reenlisted in other Texas units to fight until the end of the Civil War. Harold A. Hamner became a major in Griffin's Battalion Texas Infantry.

Additional Information concerning Confederate Army activities at Fort Clark was developed by later research of the Confederate Records. June 1861 until May 1862, Company H and/or Company F, Second Mounted Rifles were garrisoned at Fort Clark. May 10, 1862, Captain John Carolan and Company H, Woods 32nd Regiment of Texas Cavalry remained at Fort Clark until December 1862 when they were ordered to join their regiment.

Later, October 1862, Captain Joseph Taylor with Company G, Woods 32nd Regiment of Texas Cavalry had reported to Fort Clark by detachments. The first 50 man detachment commanded by First Lieutenant John R. Kelso arrived from Fredericksburg. The second detachment commanded by Captain Taylor arrived from Camp Clark (near New Braunfels). Captain Taylor's Company G remained at Fort Clark until December 1862 when they were ordered to join their regiment.

Another Company of Woods 32nd Regiment, Company I, commanded by Captain A. Stevens, arrived in Fort Clark from Camp Frio in late October or November 1862. Company I departed Fort Clark in December 1862.

During the early part of 1863 all remained of the Confederate Army at Fort Clark was Doctor David P. Ramseur, an Assistant Surgeon, and a Hospital Steward at Fort Clark. Woods 32nd Regiment of Texas Cavalry was sent to the lower Rio Grande valley to counter reported raids by Cortina but they might have been more effective had they remained in

Fort Clark area as a threat to the Indians which had returned to the area.

As for the recorded history of Harold Hamner, he disappeared from view like his earlier life. It took the hostile Indians and Secession to make him an historical subject and glory or popularity can be so short lived.

=====

B. P. Gallawy, *The Dark Corner of the Confederacy.*
John M. Elkins, *Indian Fighting on the Texas Frontier.*
Clayton Williams, *Texas Last Frontier.*
J. J. Bowden, *The Exodus of Federal Forces From Texas.*
Stephen Gates, *Recruiting Confederate Cavalry in Texas.*

1. Information furnished by W. Paul Burrier, Sr., researched for the Battle of the Nueces.

Trevanion T. Teel
1861

Commanding Officer Ft. Clark during the Secession Period Teel was born at Pittsburgh, Pa., on August 18,1824. By 1841 he was licensed to practice medicine in Missouri. At the outbreak of Mexican War he joined the Second Indiana Volunteer Regiment and was elected as a first lieutenant. He participated in the battle of Buena Vista and served until the completion of the Mexican war.

After the war he was mustered out of the volunteer regiment and moved to Lockhart, Texas, where he settled and began the practice of law. In 1856 he moved to San Antonio where he continued his law practice and was recognized as a criminal lawyer.

In 1854 the Knights of the Golden Circle was organized in New York and spread to Texas. It was a secret organization with highly fantastic dreams of establishing a strong slave empire within a circle of 2,400 miles in diameter around Havana, Cuba as its center. In the early 1850s San Antonio was a hot bed on the slavery issues. After the Seminole Chief (Wildcat) Coacoochee established in 1850 the Seminole Indian and Seminole Negro-Indian military colonies in Coahuila, Mexico. San Antonio took a specific interest in Mexico. Teel was a strong partisan of the Knights of the

Golden Circle and belonged to the San Antonio's Charles Beckley Castle.

It was under semi-military discipline with various lodges in the State of Texas. The secrecy of its operation prevents full knowledge of Teel's participation much less the organization's full participation in the filibustering against Mexico from 1855 (Capt. Callahan's Raid) through 1860. The Knights of Golden Circle were a strong advocate in the Secession movement and its para-military discipline furnished the state of Texas with it's provisional army to take control of the Federal Military Posts. Teel was a mustering Officer for a San Antonio company of the Knights of the Golden Circle.

An act of the Texas Secessionist Convention, Committee of safety, on February 14, 1861, called Teel's Company and other companies of the Knights of the Golden Circle into state service. February 15, 1861 Teel's Company joined hundreds of Texas volunteers and the units secretly assembled at Sea Willow Creek, a few miles north of San Antonio On February 16th, Teel, as the mustering officer, mustered his company into the State (Texas)Provisional Army, Infantry Company to serve six months (February-July 1861). After mustering the company into state service, he complied with Colonel Ben McCulloch's call to arms. Colonel McCulloch was assembling the newly formed Provisional Army of Texas into a combat unit for the capture of the historic Alamo and the Department of Texas, U.S. Army. The Headquarters of the Department of Texas was surrounded by the participating units of the Texas Provisional Army at daylight. With over a 1000 armed Texans surrounding the Alamo commissary and arsenal buildings with only little over a company of U.S. Army to resist such a demand to surrender all Federal Government property in the State of Texas.

General David "Bengal Tiger"Twiggs surrendered to the commissioners of the Committee of Safety. The U.S. Troops were permitted to retain their clothing, etc., and were marched out that evening to encamp at the San Pedro Springs, there to remain until transportation was furnished to convey them to the coast. The Federal Posts in Texas were ordered to evacuate their garrisons, as soon as preparations could be made and marched out of Texas by way of the coast. They were to turn over all government property to the authorized Texas state agent with exception of those items authorized to be carried by U.S. Troops evacuating. Those items being: issued arms, clothing, camp and garrison equipage, quartermaster stores, subsistence, medical, hospital stores and such transportation as necessary for efficient and orderly movement.

Capt. Teel's company was at Camp Leon (San Antonio) by February 21st making preparation for state deployment to garrison a few of the surrendered Federal posts. Colonel Ben McCulloch ordered Teel's Company to prepare for transit to the Rio Grande. Colonel McCulloch's provisional army consisted of some 400 men and Teel's company initially consisted of 109 so he was ordered to garrison: Fort Clark, Fort Duncan, Fort Lancaster, Camp Hudson, and Fort Stockton. Teel was relieved of the posts of Fort Inge and Camp Wood as they were assigned to Capt. William (Bill) C. Adams' company from the Uvalde Castle (lodge).

March 5th, Teel's company took departure from Camp Leon heading west on the Lower Road (San Antonio-El Paso). The company had dwindled in the number of men to 96 or less, by departure but they marched as a company westward as far as Uvalde where Lt. Jordan W. Bennett and 15 privates departed for their post of Fort Duncan (Ft.Inge-Ft.Duncan road). At Fort Clark Capt. Teel and 18 privates departed the company in order to man their post. The march continued for the remainder of the company up the lower road to Camp Hudson where Sergeant T. L. Wilson, a Corporal and 15 privates departed to garrison their assigned post. At Fort Lancaster, Lt. John C. Moody, one corporal and 15 privates departed for their assigned post. Sergeant Coleman Denman, one corporal and 15 privates were remains of the company which marched to Fort Stockton. Remember this March was made in 1861 through Indian country that after the civil war became Indian battle fields.

When Captain Teel and his detachment arrived at Fort Clark they proceeded down the Las Moras Creek for about two miles where they erected "Camp Las Moras." At Fort

Clark Companies H, K & D, of the Third U.S. Infantry were garrisoned and Teel's small detachment needed the separation to prevent conflict with the Federal troops. The three companies were commanded by Brevet Major W.T.H. Brooks, Captain George Sykes, and Lieutenant William Bell. These three would later become Union Generals.

Doctor J. H. Lyons, the appointed agent for the Committee of Safety, had previously arrived at Fort Clark. He had commenced the arduous task of inventorying public property to be transferred from U.S. Government to State of Texas. Captain Teel joined with Dr. Lyons to assist in the acceptance and inventory of the surrendered property. Teel's detachment remained at Camp Las Moras.

March 18th Dr. Lyons, with Capt. Teel's aid, had completed the inventory with their Federal counterparts. With the inventory complete, the post and its command were ready to be transferred to the State of Texas. Teel arranged with the Federal Officers for a formal change of command ceremony (March 19th (see Teel's letter reporting the change of command).

March 19th until March 29th, Capt. Teel and his small detachment occupied themselves with garrison duties that mostly involved sentry duties. At this time Capt. Teel had to respond to an appeal from the area ranchers on Indian depredations and he with his detachment, and perhaps area volunteers, went on an Indian Scout. He intercepted the Indian trail on road to Fort Duncan and trailed the Indians to the crossing of the Rio Grande where they crossed near the mouth of Piedra Pinto (Pinto Creek), a short distance below Villa Nuevo. Teel visited with Mexican authorities and attempted to establish a cooperative relationship on the Indian problems. This he reported to Governor E. D. Clark who had replaced Governor Sam Houston.

March 31st, the Federal evacuation of post of El Paso began with Lt. Col. I. V. D. Reeves and 135 men of the Eight Infantry. As they headed south on the Lower Road at Fort Quitman, they acquired Lt. Z.R. Bliss and company. At Fort Davis, Major James Bomford and Company joined thus increasing to six companies. At Fort Stockton, Lt. Edwin W. H. Reed and company C, joined the march to the evacuation port. This march by the Federals had added costly time to the State of Texas surrender agreement. March 16th Texas became part of the Confederate States of America and by April 11th, the Confederates had sent Colonel Van Dorn to Texas to command Confederate troops of Texas and to capture Federal Troops within that state.

Lieutenant Colonel I.V.D. Reeves with eight companies of Eight Infantry and six companies of First Infantry were continuing their march to Indianola and by May 6, 1861 they camped near Fort Clark Captain Teel issued rations to the teamsters accompanying this contingent of Federal troops. What Colonel Reeves did not know that Capt. Teel was under orders from Colonel Van Dorn to follow the Federal Forces as a rear guard to San Antonio with his artillery and there they would be met by Colonel Van Dorn and elements of the Confederate and Texas Armies.

May 9, Colonel Van Dorn with 1300 troops confronted Lieutenant Colonel Reeves at Adams Hill, San Lucia Springs. At first Colonel Reeves was tempted to fight but when he discovered that at his rear flank was Captain Teel with his small artillery company. He was also flanked on both sides by Texas Partisan Rangers, so he elected to surrender instead.

The Federals became Prisoners of War. May Day 1861, Captain Teel and approximately 60 men of his company of Provisional Army of Texas were mustered into the Confederate Service as Light Company B, First Regiment of Artillery.

Early in June, Captain H.A. Hamner and Company H of Texas Second Mounted Rifles relieved Captain Teel and his company of Light Artillery of command and garrison of Fort Clark.

Captain Teel's Company B, Light Artillery went to El Paso and joined General H.H. Sibley's Army of New Mexico. When Sibley was defeated at Glorietta, New Mexico, Captain Teel made the retreat to El Paso and assisted in burying their cannons along the retreat to El Paso. Captain Teel returned in retreat along the same path that he took from San Antonio. He continued to serve during the civil war and after the war he became a noted criminal lawyer in El Paso.

=====

Camp Las Moras (2-4 miles) downstream of Las Moras Creek from Fort Clark was established by Captain Teel's detachment of Provisional Army of Texas to prevent trouble with Union Army 3rd U.S.Infantry-3 companies). After Teel's Company took command of Fort Clark the camp area became an iterate camp for transient government freighters and visiting detachments of the Frontier Regiment enroute between Camp Nueces and Camp Elm Creek.

Secession Convention Records, Texas Archives (RG-10)

T.T. Teel, "Sibley's New Mexican Campaign. Its objects and causes of Failure." *The War Of The Rebellion*, Vol. 1 of 4 volumes, Century Company, New York.

Martin H. Hall, *The Confederate Army of New Mexico*, pp. 19-39, and *Sibleys New Mexico Campaign*, pp. 42.44.53n, Univ. of Texas Press, Austin, 1960.

Harry M. Henderson, *Texas in the Confederacy*, Naylor Company, San Antonio, pp. 123-127.

J. J. Bowden, *The Exodus of Federal Forces from Texas, 1861*, pp. 66.

Company Headquarters Fort Clark, Texas March 19, 1861

President O. M Roberts
Secession Convention
Austin, Texas
Sir:

    I have the honor to report that this Post was surrendered today at 10 O'clock A.M. and that the detachment under my command occupy the garrison, and are in full possession of all public property at this time.

    I regret to report that Company K (3rd Inf.), Federal Army set fire to the quarters occupied by them, which quarters were wholly destroyed. Another, Company H (3rd Inf.), broke all the windows, doors, partition walls of their quarters, mutilated and destroyed the iron camp bedsteads, burnt the water casks or tanks belonging to their quarters, attempted to set fire to the building.

    On the night of the 17th ultimate, some of the soldiers of the Federal Army attempted to fire the dwelling of one of the citizens (Dr. Ramuer). They threw large faggots upon the roof but the inmates discovered it in time to prevent much damage. At his request on the night of 18th, I stationed a sentinel at his house to protect his property and family. On previous night some of the soldiers of the Federal Army attempted to ravish his wife and daughter. After the sentinel was posted no further molestation took place.

I would further report that Dr. Lyons and myself had understanding with the Federal Officers on the 18th that they should have two brass field pieces to fire a salute when the Federal Flag was to be taken down, and that immediately the State Flag (Texas) was to be run up, and we were to fire a salute.

Lt. Bell (3rd Inf.) was in command today of the two pieces, and as soon as the salute of the Federal Army was over they lowered their flag and cut the halliards and pulled it out of the pulleys at the top, to prevent us from hoisting our colors. Upon reaching the flag staff with my detachment, I sent up four of the men to the cross top and with a large rope, lowered the topmast, run the halliard through the pulley, hoisted it to its proper position, and run up our colors with a salute of the guns before the Federal Troops were out of sight.

I cannot close this report without mentioning Capt. Sykes (3rd Inf.) of the Federal Army. This gentleman did all in his power to have the fire extinguished, and saved the houses near the burning building, and it was only by his energy and prompt action, that many other buildings were saved. No other officer or company aided in the least.

Dr. Lyons and myself were upon the grounds as soon as the fire was discovered and did all we could to arrest the conflagration. The detachment under my command (18) were at at the Camp (Las Moras) at that time. If all of my company had been here there would have been a conflict. With 18 men I could do nothing with the 4 companies, I had to do the best I could, that was to protest against such conduct. Dr. Lyons can better inform you as to the damage of the fire and mutilation of public property.

I respectfully beg leave to call your attention to the fact that conditions of this post that it is impossible to give it adequate protection with the small force under my command. The stables and forage and corrals are on the other side of the river, Las Moras. The Q. Master and Comming Stores are some distance apart, the ordinance at different points, the magazine at another place. It requires eight men to stand guard at one time, and to properly mount the guard for twenty-four hours it takes 24 men, 1 com. officer, 1 segt., or corpl.

The whole detachment has been on duty all of the time since the 17th and it is a pleasure to report to you that as yet I have heard no complaints, the men are willing to do all they can & are under my good discipline.

Dr. Lyons, the agent, does all he can to assist me in the duties of the post devolving upon me, and I am much indebted to that gentleman for his counsel & advice, and shall still draw upon his long experiences in affairs to aid me. My company numbers 96 men, all on duty at the different posts.

       Respectfully,
       Trevanion T. Teel
       Capt.
       Comdy. Com.

To: President Of The Convention
Hon. O. M. Roberts

=====

Texas Adjutant General's File, Texas State Archives RG-10

Chaplain Elijah Guion 1864

Elijah Guion like his opposite, Chaplain D. Eglinton Barr, both appeared in the post Civil War colored infantry regiments and each tried desperately to improve the morale and education of the black soldiers in Texas as part of the Federal Occupation Army. Elijah Guion was listed as a dissented rector of the Episcopal by Bishop of Louisiana, Leonidas Polk. Now Leonidas Polk was a very influential Episcopal Bishop in Louisiana and he can be listed as having the influence on a number of army chaplains. Actually six were commissioned in the army for religious training from the Bishop's recommendation to fill the need of the six black U.S. Army Regiments formed after the civil war. These chaplains spent the majority of their time attempting to improve the educational standards of the black soldiers.

A word in favor of Leonida Polk, the Episcopal Bishop of Louisiana, seems appropriate at this point since he was so instrumental in furnishing chaplains to colored regiments in the army's of both the Confederate and Union. It is also interesting to note during the Civil War Polk was a lieutenant general in the Confederate Army. He acquired this position as he was educated at West Point and attended the academy at same time "the President (Jefferson Davis), the two Johnstons, Lee and Magruder.[1] After graduation from West

Point he served a short time in an artillery regiment but resigned to enter the church. During the war General Polk commanded a Confederate force at the battles of Perryville and Belmont, as well as at Shiloh and Murfeesborough.[2] General Polk was killed at the battle of Kenesaw Mountain, Georgia, June 14, 1864.[3] He failed to live to see the influence he had through his appointees in raising the education level of color soldiers in U.S. Army but that may have been influenced by the fact that prior to the war he possessed seven hundred slaves. He also argued the Civil War was about states' rights not slavery.

Elijah Guion ministry of 15 months was primarily devoted to the First New Orleans Volunteers. Guion was appointed to serve First New Orleans Infantry February 27, 1865, and he was honorably mustered out of service June 1, 1866. While in service with First New Orleans he held services for troops at the regimental headquarters, camp of distribution, and the "police jail." After his discharge he was appointed chaplain, July 28, 1866, for the U.S. Forty-First Color Infantry Regiment. This unit was one of four color infantry regiments authorized by Congress in July 1866 to increase the army for its occupation duties in south. The Forty First Infantry was assigned Brevet Major General Randal S. Mackenzie, one four "boy generals" in the Union Army.

After U.S. Forty-First Color Infantry Regiment was formed they were shipped from New Orleans to Galveston, marched to San Antonio and reported for duty to the Department of Texas. The first duty in Texas was at Fort Ringold (Rio Grande City). Since the Indian depredations were in the north and west of Texas, the Department of Texas transferred the Forty-First Infantry to Fort Clark, March 1868.

At Fort Clark Chaplain Guion was discouraged by what he found. Fort Clark had suffered since 1856 without improvements and very little repair if any. The Confederates only occupied Fort Clark from March 19, 1861, until August 1862 with more destruction to the fort than improvements. Although at the commencement of the civil war there were three palisado log barracks, Company K, Third Infantry managed to burn one of those and another company attempted in bitterness to fire theirs only to damage the inside. Chaplain Guion found he had no facilities for school or religious programs and it appeared there would be none for a long time. Moreover, while the regimental headquarters was located at Fort Clark, the companies were scattered at other Texas forts and many miles apart. The stay at Fort Clark was relatively short. January 1869, Colonel Mackenzie was appointed commander of the Military District of the Pecos and transferred with most of the Forty-First Infantry Regiment to Fort MacKavett.

In October 1869, the Army was required by Congress to cut back its forces this resulted in consolidations of 38, 39, 40 and 41 Infantries. The 38th and 41st were consolidated into the 24th Infantry Regiment. Somehow Chaplain John N. Shultz of the 38th Infantry was assigned to the new 24th Infantry. The 39th and 40th were consolidated into the 25th Infantry and Chaplain Guion (41st) became unassigned and declared a supernumerary. Thus he was assigned to Galveston where he served until December 1870. At that time he was assigned to the Tenth Cavalry in the Indian Territory (Fort Sill) . He served with Tenth Cavalry until he died January 17, 1879.

=====

1. Lt. Col. Fremantle, *Three Months in the Southern States, April-June 1863*, New York, John Bradburnn, 1864, p. 140.

2. *Ibid*, p. 148.

3. Francis Heitman, *Historical Register & Dictionary of the U.S. Army*, Washington, GPO, 1903.

4. Earl Stover, *Up from Handymen, The U.S. Army Chaplaincy, 1865-1920*, pp. 13-14.

5. William G. Muller, *The Twenty Fourth Infantry*, Ft. Collins, The Old Army Press.

Elm Creek
1864

Capt. Joshua Cox in 1864 lived on Elm Creek, seven miles east of Fort Clark (near the present rest stop on Highway 90). Capt Joshua Cox was a nephew of old man William Cox, who had such a successful fight with the Indians on the West Prong of the Nueces in 1865. Capt. Joshua Cox was an old settler and experienced Indian fighter in his own right.

Capt Joshua Cox and friend, Nilus Cantrell, were out on a horse hunt when nine Indians charged them. The Indians tried to use a tactic to take the two white men with two of the Indians charging directly at the men while the other seven tried to encircle them. Being experienced Indian fighters, Cox and Cantrell charged at the two coming head-on and at nine yards from the targets both men fired at the two charging Indians. Each hit their Indian who wheeled and retreated with the white men in pursuit but the Indians disappeared over a bank. The other seven Indians seeing the determination of the Indian fighters, made a hasty retreat as soon as the firing began.

One of the two wounded Indians was shot through the body and the shot had also broken his left arm. He still managed to take off his shirt, and tied it tightly around his body. In this condition he managed to ride for six miles to a waterhole, and dismounting there, tied his horse to a tree, and laid down by it and died. On the seventh day after the fight his body was discovered and the nearly starved horse was still standing by. The horse was stolen from William Pafford of Brackettville. Pafford operated an eating establishment in Bracketville for the Texas Militia and Confederate Soldiers stationed at Fort Clark during the early part of the secession of Texas and civil war.

The head and shoulders of another Indian was found by cowboys in the Anacatchi (Anachua) Mountains some few miles south of the original engagement site and these remains were supposed to be the Indian shot by Cox since the other was identified as having been shot by Cantrell. The Indian's horse was also discovered by the cowboys and it had a short piece of rope around its neck when discovered.

=====

A. J. Sowell, Texas Indian Fighters, Austin, State House Press, pp. 604-605

Fort Lancaster
1864

When Captain R. H. Williams, his detachment of rangers, and Edward Westfall returned from their pursuit of the Indians at the Pecos, they rejoined Major Hunter's command at Pecan Springs. Pecan Springs was approximately halfway on the Lower Road between old abandoned Fort Hudson and Beaver Lake, which was at the headwaters of Devil's River. Beaver Lake is no longer in existence as it was wiped out in the 1955 flood.

To their surprise, they found a Mexican company of soldiers under the command of a Captain Pattinia. This was probably the only time there was an international command trying to clean up the Rio Grande border of Indians. Major Hunter maintained the overall command and the next day moved the command from Pecan Springs to Beaver Lake. The command camped at Beaver Lake upon arrival at 2 P.M., halting early since that was the last water until they reached Howard's Well, some fifty miles north.

About an hour after camp had been set up, the picket-guard came riding in to report that a small party of Indians were seen driving a band of horses. They were headed in the direction of Beaver Lake, and would pass the head of the ravine in which the camp had been placed. The camp was hidden from the riders' view, so Captain Williams took twenty men to the entrance of the ravine and took cover for an surprise ambush, a real welcoming party. When the party driving the horses came in full view of Captain Williams, he realized they were not Indians but ten white men.

The Captain quickly ordered his men to line up across the entrance to the ravine and when the ten men rounded a corner to enter into the ravine, Captain Williams ordered them to halt. The ten men abandoned their horse herd, wheeled about and bolted. Captain Williams and his detachment mounted immediately and gave chase. The ten men beat a hasty retreat to a mott of trees and dismounted. Captain Williams whipped out a handkerchief as a flag of truce and then rode up to the mott of trees and called for their surrender. Presently the leader of men stepped to the front and demanded Captain Williams identify his command. At about the same time, Major Hunter with his fifty men, rode up and the ten men surrendered without further ado. Williams reported to the Major that they were either "bush whackers" or Confederate deserters but he had accepted their surrender. They became unwillingly a part of the international command.

Major Hunter had the command depart camp the following morning but he detached a 20-man detail to ride on ahead to clear out Howard's Well which would be the only water in the next 100 miles and it would be vital that water be available when the command arrived. It had been a common practice of the Indians all during the Civil War to make the water holes along the Lower Road unusable for the soldiers and other travelers. Their primary method was to fill the springs or waterhole with carcass of sheep or other animals to make the water un-potable for horses and humans.

Captain Williams and his 19 man detail arrived at Howard's Well at sundown but it took his detail until 10 P.M. to clear the spring. Evidently, the spring had a good flow such that they could start watering the horses and stock immediately. It took them the rest of the night and midday of the next to complete the watering. It had to be complete too, as they had another 50 miles to travel before intercepting Live Oak Creek above Fort Lancaster.

Actually Major Hunter was more or less making his own trail on this leg as he was leaving the Lower Road to intercept Live Oak Creek above Fort Lancaster. He was hoping to surprise either Indians or Federals between Fort Lancaster and the Pecos River crossing. Major Hunter sent Captain Williams with a small party to reconnoiter Fort Lancaster or as Captain William's termed it, "to spot the Major's imaginary 'Feds.'"

Captain Williams' report of the reconnoiter was that there were no living creatures at the Fort. The Indians had burned everything about it that was consumable, leaving nothing but the walls standing, bare and gaunt. This is why so many of Texas Indian Forts that were abandoned appeared with only chimneys standing like tombstones in a graveyard. Fort Lancaster had been turned over by the U.S. Army to the Texas Militia in March 1861 and completely abandoned after Sibley's Army of New Mexico had finished straggling in retreat down the Lower Road in August 1862.

Major Hunter kept his international command camped at the confluence of Live Oak Creek and Pecos River for two days.

The Command returned to their previous camp at Piedras Pintas (Pinto Creek) some seven miles west of Fort Clark.

=====

R. W. Williams, *With the Border Ruffians*, p. 396.

Border Ruffian
1864

As the civil war wore on, the Indian attacks on the frontier increased. Early in the war, the Comanche had united with the Cheyennes in a war on the Union Army in the West. In time that lost its appeal and they were back to their old haunts in west Texas and northern Mexico. In the meantime the Kickapoos in their endeavor to escape the Civil War, tried to return to eastern Mexico which they had left in 1851. Being treated as hostiles by the Texas Militia guarding the frontier, they had declared war on Texas and all it stood for. With such renewed activity, the Mescalerous and Lipan Apaches in Mexico wanted a piece of the action.

All the Confederates possible were drawn from Texas and engaged in the last ditch stand of the Confederacy. Left to guard the frontier were few ill equipped Texas Militia Ranger companies with too few men and too many miles to effectively scout, much less stop, the incursions. The Confederate government along with the state government considered it more important that these companies should be rounding up all the deserters and draft dodgers that were capitalizing on the Indians raids in frontier portion of Texas. Conditions were in such a state on the frontier that settlers, not all ready slaughtered by the Indians, were fast abandoning their ranches for more protected communities.

Many of those living in Brackett City and vicinity had moved into Fort Clark although the Confederate Army had abandoned it as a post in 1862. The main military operation at Fort Clark was the hospital which treated settlers and rangers in the region.

Captain R. H. Williams had a small company of Rangers and maintained a camp in the vicinity of old Camp Wood in the latter part of the Civil War. Williams received orders to join forces with Major R. H. Hunter with the expectation that they were going up the Lower Road from Fort Clark to the vicinity of the Pecos and abandoned Fort Lancaster to fight Union Militia from California who were trying to penetrate Texas from the west.

The rendezvous for the Texas Militia Forces was at Piedra Pinta (Pinto Creek) a camp seven miles west of Fort Clark and utilized in 1854–1855 as a Texas Temporary Indian Reserve for hostile Indians (primarily Lipans and Tonkawas). Early in January 1864 the command under Major Hunter departed Piedra Pinta. The second day's march took them well beyond the farthest settlements. That night they camped at San Felipe Springs (Del Rio) prior to crossing the Devil's River (Rio Diablo). The third day's camp was after crossing the Devil's River where the rangers saw Indian paintings in the caves and many black bear in the ravines.

Going up the Lower Road at slow pace to conserve the animals, they paralleled the Devil's River. The next camp was by a big water hole called "Yellow Banks," so named because of the color of the water. At this spot they found the remains of a recently slaughtered horse. The Comanche esteemed horse marrow as the greatest delicacy, often killing a horse for marrow only.

The fifth day's march lay over the portion of the Lower Road, so called "Deadman's Pass," due to the steep narrow defile in the mountains where the Indians in 1850 lay in wait to massacre the teamsters returning from a supply trip to the post opposite El Paso. A few miles beyond Deadman's Pass they came close to the Devil's River, which they had actually been paralleling. A few miles beyond they came to abandoned Fort Hudson which was near the second crossing of the Devil's River. Here they set up camp for the night and discovered that the Fort was in complete ruins (abandoned in August 1862 by Company F, Second Texas Mounted Rifles). Everything except the adobe walls, which wouldn't burn, had been burned by the Indians. Capt. Williams stated that in wandering around the ruined Fort, he came to a little graveyard, the last resting place of some dozen brave fellows who had once guarded this solitary, far-away outpost of civilization. What Williams didn't know was that in those graves were some of Lt. John Hood's men who had the battle on the Devil's River with white flag-waving Comanches.

After the camp at the Fort Hudson ruins the command marched along the Devil's River to the Pecan Spring where they camped the next night. Williams defined the Pecan Spring as a noble basin of clear blue water. Because of fresh Indian signs, he detached 16 rangers with Edward Westfall of Leona Creek as trailer, to follow the Indian trail. Westfall was nearly killed by Indians along with his employee, French Louie, many years previous. The trail lead across some rough country westward to the Pecos River. Williams claimed Pecos is a corruption of the Mexican (Spanish) name for the stream, (Rio Puerco or Pig River). Probably so named for the dirty color of its water and muddy character of its banks.

The Pecos River current ran strong and deep, and about 150 yards wide. After some prospecting up and down stream, they found a place where the banks shelved on both sides. About 15 yard of swimming had to be done to cross safely. That night they camped in a mott of trees. Before dawn they were surrounded by 150 Comanches. The Ranger detachment held their fire for over two hours as the Indians taunted them. The Indians were afraid to charge them in the protection of the trees. As evening approached the Indians gave up the hope of a fight and retired. At dusk the Rangers withdrew in the direction of the Pecos River. Six days later they returned to the command camp at Pecan Spring.

=====

R. H Williams, With the Border Ruffians, pp. 325-334

Anacacho
1865

In 1865 Henry Shane settled on Chicon creek thirty miles west of Uvalde, at the foot of the Anna Catchi (Anacacho) Mountain (19 miles south of Brackettville). One day he started to the Cameo Ranch. On the way he had to pass the San Miguel Ranch. This was an old-time Mexican Ranch with a rock wall all around it, with an entrance through a gate. When Shane arrived at this place he could see no one stirring and the entrance gate was open, an unusual condition. Shane dismounted and went in, but could see no signs of life except a little dog. On a smooth piece of sheet iron which lay upon two rocks were several loaves of bread which had not been turned and were burned on the underside. The fire was still burning under the loaves of bread. Shane thought something was wrong, but he could see no one, so proceeded on his way.

About 300 yards from the ranch he had to cross Sauz Creek and here he found a dead Mexican. It was evident he had been killed by Indians, as the body was full of arrows, and nearby was his horse, which had also been killed. It would seem that the Mexican was trying to get to the ranch, pursued by the Indians, who first killed his horse and then him. When Shane got out of the Sauz Bottom and up on a ridge he discovered a horse tied some distance off. By this time in life Shane had learned enough about Indians not to approach the horse, so he very carefully skirted the horse and continued his journey. Before he lost sight of the tied horse he saw an Indian near the horse and soon five others came into view. They came in pursuit of Shane, but he was mounted on a good horse and made an escape from them.

Shane next came to a ranch where there was a crowd of excited Mexicans, some of whom were from the same ranch as the slain Mexican. The Mexicans explained to Shane that the ranch owner was away from the ranch when it was attacked. The Indians cut him off from the ranch and killed him when he made a run to get inside the walls.

=====

A. J. Sowell, *Texas Indian Fighters*, Austin, State House Press, pp.495-496.

West Prong of Nueces 1865

William Cox moved in 1861 to Brackett and after the Civil War, 1865, moved his family to the west prong of the Nueces River. In this new settlement, besides William Cox and family, was his son Henry and his family, and John Bingham and his family. They all lived in tents near each other. Two months passed before any signs of Indians were noticed. Henry Cox's tent was about fifty yards from his father's and John Bingham's a short distance on the opposite side of William's.

As is usual on the frontier during a long period of quiet and peace, the settlers became careless, and when the Indians did come they were poorly prepared to receive them. On the eventful morning in question Henry Cox was at his father's tent, and his family were at their own, fifty yards away. No close watch was being kept, and the Indians came over the hills and into the valley near the camps before any one discovered them. The war party was twenty-five in number, and all on foot. Mrs. Bingham was the first to see them, and exclaimed, "Lord, God! Look at the Indians!" At this time they were about 100 yards from the tent of the elder Cox. William Cox heard the announcement of the Indians, and at once seized his old flintlock rifle (muzzle loader) and went out to make a fight and defend his family as best he could.

Another mistake, however, had been made by the old man

as he had fired his gun at a turkey that morning and neglected to reload it. Standing, however, in full view of the approaching and now yelling savages, he began hastily to load, but he was hit by an arrow in the knee before he could do so. Reaching down he pulled it out, but the spike (point) remained in the bone. Henry now came to his father's assistance, but without his gun, it was in his tent. Old man Cox coolly finished loading his gun, and together the Coxes charged. A shot from the old rifle wounded one Indian badly and he ran into a mott of timber close by. At the first discovery of the Indians the elder Cox shouted for all of the settlers to concentrate at his tent. A little 4-year-old girl of Henry Cox made a run to get to her grandfather's tent, but was caught by the Indians who were retreating from the old man and Henry. They all headed for the mott of timber the wounded one had headed for. During this exchange, John Bingham and his wife attempted run to the tent and both were shot and wounded by bullet or the same ball as they were both wounded in the legs. In spite of their wounds the Binghams made it to the Cox's tent.

A couple of the Indians began to plunder the tent of Henry Cox, and got his gun. Henry's wife had previously made her escape to her father-in-law's tent with one of her children. Somehow, in the excitement the mother had failed to notice her 2 year old underneath a wagon near the tent. William Cox had started to retreat back to his tent when he spied the little 2 year old stranded underneath the wagon. He threw all caution to the winds, made a run and rescued the little girl.

Bingham had no gun, the Indians had Henry's, and the old man had to fight the battle alone. The brave old man was totally equal to the occasion. He would ram another ball home as fast as he could, fire again hitting an Indian every shot. He killed one just as he was coming out of Henry's tent with his arms full of plunder. The Indians certainly did not know the almost unarmed condition of the white men, as they could have made a charge enmasse and overpowered them at once. The Indians dreaded the ominous crack of the old rifle, and were soon all out of sight in the bottom, but still in rifle range. The war chief had a whistle, which he would sound when he wanted his men to come closer. Old man Cox wanted to kill him, and watched his chance to do so, believing that his death would put an end to the battle and the balance of the party would make their departure. Cox had the chief located by the sound of his whistle, behind a tree in the brush, but very close to camp. His warriors seemed to be further back, and he wanted them to come and charge. Finally he turned to give a blast and exposed part of his body. At that instant the rifle cracked from the tent and the chief fell dead in his tracks.

This shot sealed the fate of the little captive girl. She was at once put to death in retaliation for the slain chief. She was killed with a lance, and her screams could be heard as the cruel blade entered her little body. It was about 10 A.M. when the chief was killed, and soon after that the Indians took their departure in silence, up the river in the timber, hid from view. When they left the valley they came into view going up a mountain, and the white men watched them until they disappeared.

Old man Cox and Henry then went into the mott where the Indians had been, fearing for the safety of the child and not seeing her with the Indians. In the mott they saw the trail where the chief had been dragged, and followed it until they found his body dumped in a waterhole. They pulled it out and scalped his corpse then came back, but on the way found the body of the little girl. That evening a sad burial took place and survivors made preparation for flight. During all this time old man Cox was limping around with the arrowhead still in his knee.

The Indians had taken all their horses, and nothing was left but one yoke of oxen to convey these three families. The next morning, however, the start was made for Brackett, the wounded and small children in the wagon and the balance on foot. After a great many hardships they succeeded in arriving at Fort Clark for medical treatment for the wounded.

It was later learned that three of the Indians shot in this battle died on the retreat. Their corpses were found on the retreat trail.

=====

A. J. Sowell, Texas Indian Fighters, pp. 602-605. (Doctor Ramur must of still been at Post Hospital at this time. He was reported to have been at Fort Clark 1860-1865.)

Donald Jackson
Acting Assistant Surgeon
U.S. Army
1866

Fort Clark not only had outstanding officers of line and field that served at Fort Clark but several of the staff officers were worthy of note. Several were chaplains and at least three were surgeons. One who deserves much consideration was Donald Jackson who first appeared on the scene of Fort Clark when the post was reoccupied after the Civil War. On December 10, 1866, Captain John Wilcox and Company C, 4th Cavalry reoccupied the post while Acting Assistant Surgeon Jackson with Company C was to take charge of the post hospital. The stone hospital Jackson fell heir to on Fort Clark had been built in 1856 and surrendered along with the remainder of the post by the U.S. Third Infantry to the Provisional Army of Texas on March 19, 1861. At the time of surrender the hospital was under the charge of Acting Assistant Surgeon David P. Ramseur.

Doctor Ramseur operated the hospital from 1861 until the end of the war in 1865. No recorded information has yet been located to fill in the status of the hospital and its operation from the latter part of 1865 until Doctor Jackson made his appearance December 10, 1866. It sure would be interesting to know what Captain Wilcox, Doctor Jackson and Company C of the Fourth Cavalry found at Fort Clark when they arrived after a 135 mile march from San Antonio.

Since the latter part of the Civil War this portion of Texas had found the area being overrun with Indians and others: deserters, bandits, and horse thieves. In spite of the poor state of quarters and other buildings on the post they had little time to get settled before their mission put them in the field on scouting parties. Doctor Jackson may well have been the post doctor but he was expected to accompany all scouting parties in case any of the soldiers were wounded on the scouts. The next week after their arrival, December 17, they made their first scout with a party of 35 soldiers. This scout left the post and scouted north of the Nueces River but returned on December 23 with no Indian contact after traveling 100 miles. However, that very night information was received at the post that a marauding band of Indians were encamped on Mud Creek (the 18 mile creek). A scouting party consisting of Captain Wilcox, Acting Surgeon Jackson, and 40 troopers marched to Mud Creek a distant between 20-30 miles northwest of the post and found the Indians. After attacking the Indians they routed them, wounding two and capturing 12 horses, 2 mules, 1 rifle, a package of bed clothes, and some female wearing apparel. The scouting party returned to the post the night of 24 December after having traveled a distance of 50 miles.[2]

There was very little rest between scouts as the Indians remained active in West Texas in spite of the army regarrisoning many of the main forts. The next major scout of Capt. Wilcox and Dr. Jackson took place March 12, 1867, and is best indicated in the letter Brevet Major General Griffin sent from the District of Texas:

Headquarters, District of Texas
Galveston, Texas
March 28, 1867

Brevet Major General Hartsuff,
Assistant Adjutant General
Fifth Military District
New Orleans, Louisiana

General:

I have the honor to enclose a copy of an official report, dated 21st instant, from Capt. John A. Wilcox, Fourth U.S. Cavalry, Commanding Fort Clark, Texas of a recent encounter with a large band of Indians encamped in the valley of the Pecos, some 20 miles from Lancaster.

I recommend that Capt. Wilcox, Acting Assistant Surgeon Jackson, Sergeants Lugden and Griffin, Corporals Bruner, Duval, and Lee, be especially commended for bravery and coolness exhibited by them, and that the force under Capt. Wilcox in this scout be complimented in General Orders.

The trying position of Capt. Wilcox and his men 6 days without rations opposed by a force of some fifteen hundred Indians. With limited ammunition and his command mounted on almost unserviceable horses, deserves warm commendations.

Few officers would have been able to extricate themselves from the difficulties which Capt. Wilcox and his little band of 30 men were placed.

I would especially invite attention to the reference made by Capt. Wilcox to the Mexican guide, Patino, killed in the fight at Indian camp no. 1.

During the time Capt. Wilcox has been at Fort Clark he has made six scouts, resulting in disposing of hostile bands which infest this section.

I have the honor to be General, very respectfully
    Your obedient servant.
    Charles Griffin
    Brt. Maj. Gen. Commanding[3]

Like his predecessor, Dr. Ramseur, Dr. Jackson found himself in contact with the civilians of the area. For those in the surrounding territory of Fort Clark the hospital and medical skill came in handy in medical emergencies. Although the army viewed their hospitals and doctors to serve the medical needs of army personnel, humanitarian needs dictated the treatment to civilian emergencies. Since the doctor had to be the judge under the circumstances as to whether medical treatment was in the realm of the local facilities, more than likely he felt it was necessary rather than endeavoring to refuse it. Some times the doctor found himself involved in more than just medical treatment by his contacts with local civilians.

Two such occasions with Dr. Jackson are displayed by recorded records. One is when Dr. Jackson entered into a partnership with A. O. Strickland of the Dolorous Ranch, Brackettville; W. C. Adams, rancher in Nueces Valley; James H. Taylor, Leona Valley, Uvalde; Randolph Pafford of Brackett City; and Joseph Ney to form the San Felipe Irrigation and Manufacturing Company. In 1868 Dr. Jackson was also involved in clerical duties as result of his medical practice and he wrote a letter to Governor of Texas E. M. Pease. In this case Dr. Jackson was acting as agent for William B. Hudson who had ransomed a boy from a Comanche camp on the Pecos River.

        Fort Clark, Texas
        May 8th, 1868

Honorable E. M. Pease
Governor of Texas
Austin, Texas
Sir:

I have the honor to forward the Enclosed Affidavit for the man Hudson who was instrumental in rescuing the boy "Francis M. Buckelew" from the Indians. I saw the boy at Fort Clark, as Hudson was taking him home to his friends last year (1867).

The account he then gave of his being with the Indians corresponded with what is set forth in the accompanying document.

I have reason to think that Hudson had to give a ransom for the boy, but do not know positively. At Hudson's request, and believing that he is entitled fairly, to remuneration for the services he has rendered the State, I take the liberty of now addressing your honor, respectfully calling your attention to the previous communications on this subject.

Mr. Hudson desires to be addressed through me at this Post in any future communications.

I have the honor to be, very respectfully,
> Your obedient servant,
> Donald Jackson
> Acting Assistant Surgeon
> U.S. Army.[4]

To summarize the case of Francis (Frank) M. Buckelew, he and two sisters as orphans were brought to this country by their uncle Berry Buckalew, Sr. Frank and his sisters lived on Judge Davenport's ranch in Sabinal Canyon. Frank as a boy of 12 years was sent to hunt on the ranch for a bell that was lost by an oxen. While hunting for the bell he was captured by Comanche Indians and taken to their camp on the Pecos River (Probably the same Comanche Camp on the Pecos River that Dr. Jackson and the scouting party destroyed). He lived 11 months as a captive but as a young boy he displayed wits and courage that saved his life and gained the respect of his capturers. He occupied his time making arrows for the Indians and accompanied them to Mexico when they traded their wares. Frank was spotted by Hudson with the Indians and he offered a Mexican $150 as reward for the delivery of the boy to him.

This the Mexican did and Hudson accepted the delivery of boy on Texas side of the Rio Grande. Hudson in returning the boy to Sabinal Canyon stopped by Fort Clark where Dr. Jackson examined Frank who looked much like an Indian with his garb and sunburned skin. Frank later became a Methodist preacher in Bandera County.[5]

February 1868, Capt. Wilcox and Company C, Fourth Cavalry were transferred to Fort McIntosh and Company G, Ninth Cavalry replaced it. Also in March 1868 a major portion of 41st Infantry appeared at Fort Clark. All the while Dr. Jackson remained the post surgeon although the 41st Infantry also had a doctor assigned. None of this prevented Dr. Jackson from having to accompany major Indian scouts. The next recorded scout with Dr. Jackson's participation was commenced January 3, 1870.[6]

Captain John M. Bacon, 9th Cavalry, set out from Ft. Clark to scout the Pecos River from the Lancaster Crossing to its mouth. In his command was First Lt. (Brevt Capt.) Charles Parker, Lt. Francis Snelling Davidson, Acting Assistant Surgeon Donald Jackson and detachments from Companies G & L, 9th Cavalry, in all about 100 men. On January 16, the soldiers spotted an Indian encampment five miles ahead, but the Indians, seeing the approach of the troops, hastily fled in the direction of Johnson's Run (between Beaver Lake & Howard's Well). The troops gave chase for fifteen miles but when night came the Indians scattered like quail.

Their encampment, which according to a letter in the San Antonio Herald, consisted of about fifty lodges, "with the usual covering of dressed hides, thousands of pounds of dried meats, about 100 animals, horses and mules, a large number of them with packs of provisions, clothing, cooking utensils, hatchets, bows and arrows."

The troops destroyed all the captured property that could not be sent to Ft. Clark. Capt. Bacon continued his scout some distance farther before returning to Ft. Clark, February 6, 1870.[6]

Dr. Jackson as post surgeon inherited other duties besides treating the sick and wounded, such duties as; Indian fighting, sanitary inspections, maintaining Records, and corresponding with the Surgeon General's Department. We find in 1870 Dr. Jackson was required to submit to the Surgeon General's Department a report on Fort Clark and its medical conditions this was issued as the Surgeon General Annual Report No. 4.

His report indicates some rebuilding of Fort Clark since the Civil War. "Two buildings were erected last year (1869) for barracks, but are not quite completed; each measures 120 x 20 by 15 feet clear; they are of limestone rock, and have square gable roofs, which are shingled. In front of each are three doors and two windows; on one side of each is one window, and in the rear three windows and one double door, from one end of each is set off a space of 20 feet, which is again divided into two rooms—the first sergeant's, the rear, the commissary, and quartermasters sergeants storeroom."

"There are five buildings at present used as officers quarters; three on the northwest side, framed, grass covered, square or gabled roofed buildings. The space between the posts of the frame are filled with light logs, lying horizontally, and fitting into grooves in the post; these were put in 1854–1855, and are 18 by 50 by 10 feet. On the south side of the rectangle are two stone buildings, with shingled roofs; built in 1857, the other just completed; the latter, now occupied as headquarters, is intended for two sets of quarters. The building formerly used as headquarters with a porch in front and rear, a hall, 8 ft. wide, through the center, and two capacious rooms on either side and one in the end, with a fire place in each." Dr. Jackson's report contained a lot more than this summary about the buildings. Dr. Jackson's 1870 Report also contained a comment, "There is, west of the post, at the San Felipe Creek and Rio Grande, 30 miles distant on the El Paso and San Antonio road, a small settlement containing about a dozen families.

"This settlement was known as San Felipe due to the name given by the Spanish explorers to the spring and creek which became a most important watering spot for travelers."

In 1871 the first meeting of the San Felipe Agricultural, Manufacturing, and Irrigation Company. This was important since the company is credited with the founding of San Felipe del Rio which later became the city of Del Rio, Texas. It is also important to this paper because one of the first members of this company which later became a corporation, was Doctor Donald Jackson of Fort Clark. However, Dr. Jackson failed to live to see the importance of this company on establishing the community that now exist on the former company land.

His wife, a widow, sold the ownership share held by former Dr. Jackson. Although a business partner, Jackson was still required to maintain his army career. His next venture with a large troop contingent was in 1873 he became part of Colonel Mackenzie's force that made the raid on Remolina. During the early morning raid on May 17 two of the soldiers were wounded. One was mortally wounded, Private Peter O'Rouke, and although Dr. Jackson tried to attend to his wounds, he died on the battle field. Another, Private Fair received a severe arm wound which required Dr. Jackson to amputate the arm on the battlefield. Several of the Indians captured were also wounded including the Chief who was lassoed. Dr. Jackson's treatments of the wounded delayed the departure from the Mexican battlefield which caused some anxiety for fear Mackenzie's forces would be engaged by Mexican soldiers.[9]

Dr. Jackson continued to attend the wounded on the long horse back trip to Fort Clark.

Dr. Jackson was finally promoted by the army to Assistant Surgeon, November 10, 1874,[10] after some rough 8 years of frontier medicine. What probably aided even such a slow promotion was in 1873 the army had 64 vacancies for doctors. In 1874 Congress gave the army help by authorizing both promotions and hiring of more contract surgeons.

Doctors during this period could become a commissioned officer if they would elect to accept the army as a military career. Since Dr. Jackson came into the army from Texas and being a partner in the San Felipe Company, maybe he was considering leaving the army in the future.

In May 1875, Dr. Jackson found he had to author another major report for the Surgeon General's Circular No. 8, but this time he was to co-author with Captain Passmore Middleton, M.D., who was also garrisoned at Fort Clark. This report of 1875 in the Fort section reflected on all the building that had taken place on post during 1873-1874 period which was for Fort Clark a major rebuilding effort.[11]

The later part of 1875 Dr. Jackson was transferred to another frontier post. By April 26, 1876, he was transferred back to Fort Clark only this time it was for medical treatment but he died September 22, 1876.[12]

Evidently, his transfer back to Fort Clark was due to the fact Captain Passmore Middleton was the post surgeon although the hospital was then staffed also with Assistant Surgeon Thomas Bannister, 8th Cavalry surgeon, and Acting Assistant Surgeon W. S. VanDyson, 10th Cavalry Surgeon. Captain Middleton had served since 1861 and for service in the Civil War was commissioned an officer in the Medical Department.

Dr. Middleton remained in the service until 1891.

=====

1. U.S. Army Post Returns, Fort Clark, Texas, December 1866.
2. *Ibid*, Events Section.
3. Letters sent District of Texas, 1865–1867, NA, RG 393, MC 1165 Roll 1.
4. Dorman, Winfrey & James D. Day, *Texas Indian Papers, 1860–1916*, Austin, Texas State Library, 1961, pp. 261-262.
5. A. J. Sowell, *Early Settlers and Indian Fighters of Southwest Texas*, Austin, State House Press, 1986, pp. 587-590.
6. *San Antonio Herald*, February 14, 1870; Clayton Williams, *Texas Last Frontier*, Fort Stockton and the Trans-Pecos, 1861–1895, College Station, Texas A&M Univ. Press, 1982, p. 121
7. Surgeon General's Report, Circular No. 4, Washington, GPO, 1870, p. 220.
8. Mrs. John M. Jones (ed.), *La Hacienda, Del Rio*, Val Verde Historical Society & Whitehead Museum, p. 468-469.
9. Ernest Wallace, *Ranald S. Mackenzie on the Texas Frontier*, Lubbock, West Texas Museum Association, 1964, pp. 102-103. Ernest Wallace, Ranald S. Mackenzie's Official Correspondence Relating To Texas, 1871-1873, Lubbock, West Texas Museum Association, 1967, pp. 167-169.
10. Francis B. Heitman, Historical Register and Dictionary of the United States Army, Washington GPO, 1903, p. 567.
11. Surgeon General's Report, Circular No. 8, Washington, GPO, 1875.
12. Francis B. Heitman, Historical Register and Dictionary of the United States Army, Washington GPO, 1903, p. 567. U.S. Army Post Returns, Fort Clark, Texas, April 1876.

Post War
1866

1864 was a bad year in Texas for Indian depredations. The few Frontier Rangers were almost constantly in the saddle. Try as they might, the Rangers were too few and the area too large to control. By April 1865 Texans had started the trek from the battlefields to home and the Indians were aware also that the war was over. This told them that there would be more men and fewer unprotected and defenseless ranches. The Indians began slacking off on the raids from the previous year but the Indian Wars were many years from being over. For Texas, the first thing that happened was that General Grant sent General Sheridan and 50,000 troopers to the Rio Grande as a bluff and deterrent to Maximillan. Until the French threat passed little thought or concentration could be given to the Indian menace so the frontier continued to suffer even though the war was over.

The year 1866 brought little relief from the Indian menace to the frontier. In July 1866 the peacetime strength of the Army was set at five regiments of artillery, ten of cavalry, and forty-five Infantry. Each artillery and cavalry regiment was composed of 12 companies and each infantry of 10. Provision was made for 1,000 Indian Scouts but it would be 1870–1872 before Fort Duncan and Fort Clark would benefit from that provision. The army was organized into 19 territorial departments and five geographical divisions.

Major General John M. Schofield (Served Ft. Clark as an Lt. in Artillery.) described the military establishment thus scattered over such a vast area as a "police force and not an army." Despite its smallness and dispersion, the Army had to perform three important missions: 1. Elimination of the threat posed by the government of Emperor Maximilian in Mexico; 2. Occupation of the Southern States; 3. Supression of the dissident Indians and restoration of order on the Western Frontier. These may have been the three important missions but General Sheridan, who as commander of Military Division of the Gulf, had control of approximately 50,000 troops for service in Texas, didn't see the Indian problem as important as protecting the Texas freedmen.

The Fifth Military District was formed to administer the occupation and defense of the Frontier. Colonel J. J. Reynolds found he had too few men for too large an area to be the least bit effective against the Indians. It was not until 1871, when General Sherman came to Texas for a first hand evaluation of the Indian problem, that it rated the first priority with the Army.

=====

American Military History 1607–1953, U.S. Department of the Army, Govt. Printing Office.

James M. Merill, Spurs to Glory, p. 196

Government Mail 1867

Henry Brucks arrived as a small child with his parents in the vicinity of Quihi in 1847. Shortly thereafter he was captured and remained a captive of the Indians for over a year. Through the efforts of an Indian agent, he was returned to his family. By 1867, Henry Brucks was a guard for the United States Army Mail between Fort Clark and Fort Stockton. The U.S. Mail was under government contract to Major Ben Ficklin and his stagecoach company.

Due to the poor frequency between the west and east bound runs, the Army started its own mail service between the posts to improve the communications between the posts and to combat the Indian menace. The Army Mail Service was operated by two men, Holiday and Cook, who would each depart on the same day from the two posts and past enroute on the Lower road between the two forts.

In March 1867, Cook's party had departed Fort Stockton enroute to Fort Clark and at Live Oak Creek went into temporary camp. This camp was a few miles above Fort Lancaster. The purpose of the camp was to rest the mules three hours prior to continuing the run. At the camp the mules were unhitched from the coach and a man was sent with them a short distance to water them in the creek. Evidently Indians were in hiding and observing the white men's operation. With perfect timing, the Indians rushed the man with the mules and captured the mules before many shots could be fired at them. This left Cook and nine men with a coach and the U.S. Mail but no "mule power." Under the circumstances the pioneers knew to stay with the coach and be alert as the Indians might return, so Cook's party spent the night at the camp with the coach.

When morning came so did the Indians. They came in all directions but Cook and his nine men were a match for them but Cook decided the numbers would soon overwhelm them. They began a gradual retreat through the roughest country backing towards the mountains while holding the Indians at bay. Now perhaps the reader is wondering why Fort Lancaster didn't play a part in this Indian battle. Fort Lancaster had been closed during the Civil War (1862) and not reopened, so no help was to be had from Fort Lancaster. Only Forts Clark and Stockton covered this wide expanse on the Lower Road. Cook's party had a Mexican, Big Joe, who didn't have the stomach for a good Indian fight. He found a hole in the side of one of the hills and hid in it while the rest of party continued retreating and fighting.

Big Joe's hideout was secure from the Indians and it gave him a commanding view of the mail coach near the creek. He watched the Indians rob the mail and burn the coach, then depart the area. Big Joe felt the Indians had overcome Cook's party when he could no longer hear any firing. Being all alone he had only one choice, walk the Lower Road toward Fort Clark and hope if he met anyone enroute it would be Holiday and his crew.

Big Joe must have been quite a walker because the next day he met Holiday's coach near the Painted Cave on the Devil's River. Big Joe told Holiday the happenings to Cooks' party and begged Holiday not to proceed or they would all be killed. Holiday, even at that day, was instilled with the famous mail motto and stated the mail must be delivered or they would die in the attempt. He told Big Joe he better go with them. At that time Joe thought maybe safety was in numbers but, after riding a short distance on the coach, he jumped out. "I can't go; you will all be killed, boys; just like they killed our men." Once again Big Joe struck out on his own and Holiday proceeded. Near abandoned Camp Hudson at the second crossing of the Devil's River, Holidays' crew halted to rest and water the mules. After Bruck was relieved of guard duty he heard somebody talking up on the road and in English. He soon discovered it was Cook and his men. They were tired and hungry. Holiday's crew shared some food with them while they heard the story of the fight.

Cook described the fight. Knowing their ammunition was in short supply they thought they had better retreat to more a secure position. Before they started their retreat Big Joe had decided he had no stomach for the operation and had retreated into a cave in the mountain. They made a gradual retreat into a gorge full of cedar and once they were in the "cedar fort" the Indians gave up pursuit.

After resting up and getting a bite to eat, Cook's men started by foot for Fort Clark while Holidays' crew and the mail started for Fort Stockton. Holiday knew the roads perfectly and was aware of a little used road which cut off some eight miles but because of having to transcend a very steep hill it was seldom used by wagons and coaches. Since Holiday was sure the Indians would be laying in wait for him on the known road, he took the other route and late that night he could see fires burning which he was sure was the Indian's camp waiting for him to come via the other route. Needless to say, both Cook's and Holiday's crews reached their respective forts, one on foot and one with the mail.

=====

A. J. Sowell, *Texas Indian Fighters*, Austin, State House Press, pp. 368-373.

June 1869

On June 7, a military force from Fort Clark commanded by Colonel Ranald Mackenzie, 41st Infantry, and Captain John M. Bacon, Ninth Cavalry with a detachment of troops from Companies G, L, and M, Ninth Cavalry, scouted above the mouth of Pecos for some fifty miles. Here they encountered about 100 Lipan and Mescaleros Apaches. Mackenzie's force also had several civilian volunteers and two guides attached. The first charge by the military force killed two Indian braves. The second charge, the Indians scattered to the adjoining escarpments and fled downriver. During the engagement one trooper was also killed. Mackenzie ordered the rancheria destroyed and the troop endeavored unsuccessfully to pursue the Indians.

=====

AGO Chronological List of Actions, &c., with Indians, Jan. 1847 to Jan. 1891.

Army Navy Journal, October 9, 1869.

Clayton Williams, *Last Texas Frontier*, Ft. Stockton, & Trans Pecos, p. 41.

Seminole Negro-Indian Scouts Interred at Seminole Indian Scouts Cemetery Brackettville, Texas

	Date of Death
Bowlegs, John	March 17, 1890
Bowlegs, John (II)	July 3, 1937
Daniels, Caesar	June 19, 1919
Daniels, Elijah	January 12, 1908
Daniels, Jerry	January 29, 1925
Daniels, John	July 5, 1923
Dixie, Joe	August 1, 1941
Factor, Dembo	July 15, 1891
Gerry, Williiam	June 1907
Grayson, Renty	May 31, 1929
Giner, Dallas	May 20, 1888
Gordon, Sam	March 22, 1905
Halls, Morell	May 13, 1929
Jefferson, Sam	July 14, 1934
July, Benjamin	September 14, 1912
July, Fay	August 6, 1940
July, Chas (Cabo)	November 5, 1879
July, Sampson	May 16, 1918

July, Carolina	April 13, 1884
Kibbetts, George	unknown
Kibbetts, John	September 7, 1878
Kibbetts, Robert	April 26, 1905
McClain, Adam	September 12, 1950
Payne, Aaron	January 27, 1879
*Payne (Paine), Adam	January 1, 1877 (MOH)
Payne, Davis	1879
Payne, Titus	1878
Perryman, Ignacio	May 20, 1933
Perryman, Isaac	September 12, 1918
Perryman, James	September 26, 1930
Perryman, Pompey	January 5, 1923
Phillips, John	June 14, 1880
Phillips, Joseph	August 13, 1936
Remo, Joe	March 10, 1930
Shields, Archibald	June 7, 1907
Shields, John	April 10, 1928
Thompson, Joe	May 17, 1918
Thompson, John	September 7, 1883
Thompson, Prymas	March 13, 1906
*Ward, John	May 24, 1911 (MOH)
Warrior, Bill	April 10, 1903
Warrior, Carolina	January 31, 1917
Washington, Sam	October 1, 1933
White, Lewis	unknown
Williams, Bill	July 8, 1914
Wilson, Benjamin	September 16, 1918
Wilson, Billy	July 22, 1952
Wilson, Isaac	January 26, 1918
Wilson, Jasper	1898
Wilson, Kelina	September 7, 1873
Wilson, Tony	April 1903
Wilson, Tony (II)	April 1, 1938
Woryer, Henry	September 12, 1931

Other Medal of Honor Recipients with Headstones
Factor, Pompey, death unknown—may be interred in Mexico
Payne, Isaac, January 12, 1904—interment not certain.

(Revised March 21, 1991)

Seminole Negro-Indian Scouts, 1872

After the completion of the Civil War and the haunts of slavery and slavers had became only a bad dream, the older Seminole Negroes began thinking about returning to the Seminole Nation in the U.S. where they still had relatives. This was further accentuated when Robert Kibbetts escorted a party back to the U.S. Indian Reservation. Of course, old friends and relatives were happy to see this party after some 17 years and invited all the Seminole Negroes to return. This was the message Robert Kibbetts delivered to the colony at Naciementos on his return. John Kibbetts had a conference on the return of the tribe with John Horse and the headmen. Kibbetts was appointed to have a conference with the commanding officer at Fort Duncan (Eagle Pass, Texas) in regards to such a move.

March 17, 1870, John Kibbetts had a conference with Captain J. C. DeGress, 9th U.S. Cavalry, then the commanding officer at Fort Duncan. Kibbetts explained that his and John Horse's groups of Seminole Negro Indians at both Laguna De Parras and Naciementos wanted to return to Seminole Nation, U.S. Indian Territory. He also stated he felt sure that the Kickapoos also wanted to return.

Captain DeGress felt positive any reduction in Indians in Mexico would be a relief for the U.S. Army and he undertook the necessary action as he saw it for the moment. He wrote letters to the U.S. Customs and Immigration authorities to pass the Indians who would enroute to U.S. Indian Reservation. He instructed Kibbetts to have the Seminole Negroes come to the Fort Duncan Reservation where they could encamp until transportation for both groups would be ready. Captain DeGress then prepared a letter to Commander, Department of Texas at San Antonio, explaining the conversation and the action he had taken and also requested the commander's approval.

The Department of Texas granted Captain DeGress approval for his actions and stated that if the Seminole Negroes Indians returned before transportation could be arranged, they were to be furnished camping grounds and rations. The rations of course were to be regular army rations but the army would be reimbursed from the Office of Indians Affairs which had appropriated funds for this purpose. Now the army was assuming that recent funds appropriated by Congress ($25,000) for transportation and feeding displaced U.S. Indians from Mexico at the reservation would apply in this case (proved much later a mistake). The Assistant Judge Advocate General, Department of Texas forwarded Captain DeGress' letter along with an endorsement to the War Department. The War Department seemed to have more concern about the Kickapoos because their immediate response was to direct the Department of Texas to verify the seriousness of the Kickapoos' desire to return. By this time the commanding officer at Fort Duncan had changed and Captain F. W. Perry had replaced Captain Degress who had to retire from the army. The Department of Texas notified Captain Perry to determine the Kickapoos desires. He first responded by stating, "the Seminole Indians whom I am directed to receive from Mexico turned out to be Negroes. I am informed that the Lipans and Kickapoos will not avail themselves of the invitation to come upon a reservation this side of the Rio Grande."

In the interim time until Captain Perry received the order to effect the meeting with the Kickapoos, his correspondence of May 17, 1870, was forwarded to the War Department. This prompted a response from the War Department, "the

Secretary of War authorized the employment of such a number of Indian-Negroes as may be found useful as scouts provided no more than 200 are kept in service which is your Department's quota." This was based on a 1866 law passed by Congress authorizing the U.S. Army to enlist Indians to serve as auxiliary to the army as scouts. The Department of Texas in turned notified the newest commanding officer at Fort Duncan, Major Zenas Bliss, 25th Infantry, that he is authorized to enlist twenty (20) Seminole Negro Indians or such a number as shall be found fit for service. The scouts to receive pay and allowance as Cavalry soldiers. 'Kibbutz', or the head man will receive the pay of a sergeant, and approval granted to locate the Seminole Negroes Indians on Elm Creek under control and protection of military authorities of Fort Duncan. (Note—to the army they were Seminole Negro "Indians" so they could qualify under the Congressional Appropriation).

August 1870, Major Bliss had enlisted the first 7 in the Seminole Negro Indian Detachment at Fort Duncan. He continued enlisting until he had his assigned quota of 20 by the first 1871. In October 1871, Elijah Daniels and his tribe of Creek Negro Indians from Nueces River, and earlier Matamoros, Mexico, arrived at Fort Duncan and 13 of this group were enlisted which was permitted under a new quota.

May 20, 1872, the Seminole Negro Indians were initiated as army scouts in an Indian engagement. On duty with Lieutenant Gustauvs Valois and detachment of 9th Cavalry, they encountered a war party of Comanches on La Pendencia Creek.

Later in 1871 John Horse (Gopher John) led his band of approximately 150 Seminole Negro Indians from Laguna de Parras, Coahuila to Fort Duncan where several were enlisted in the Fort Duncan Detachment. (Note John Horse was not enlisted in the Seminole Scouts although John Kibbetts was at the age of 62 which was also the age of John Horse.) With the two bands of Seminole Negro Indians and the tribe of Creek Negro Indians, the Elm Creek Reservation was becoming overburdened. A transfer to Fort Clark Military Reservation was ordered for August 7, 1872, and the establishment of a Seminole Negro Indian Detachment at that post. Seventeen Seminole Negro Indian Scouts were transferred to Fort Clark from Fort Duncan and their family members also moved. Fort Clark also enlisted 5 scouts during the month from the group that transferred from Fort Duncan. Second Lieutenant Thomas S. Mumford, 13th Infantry, was ordered as first commanding officer of Fort Clark's Detachment and there were 22 scouts in the detachment at that time.

During the first 8 months of the Fort Clark Detachment, the number of scouts remained at 22 but the commanding officers changed rather frequently. September 1872, Lieutenant Mumford was relieved from command and replaced by Lieutenant G. W. Raddyke, then next came a Lieutenant Gerhard but he only lasted a month (January 1877). Lieutenant Cranston was next but by February he was replaced by Lieutenant Raddyke for a second try at commanding. Lieutenant Raddyke relinquished the command to Lieutenant Leopold Parker, 4th Cavalry, who was also Fort Clark Post Adjutant and Post Signal Officer.

May 1873 was a high point in Fort Clark's history and the detachment of the Seminole Negro Indians Scouts. Colonel Ranald Mackenzie and 4th Cavalry regiment commenced an invasion of the Mexican border to assault Indian villages at Remolina. Colonel Mackenzie assembled his force at Las Moras Crossing of the Rio Grande. Among the various companies of the 4th Cavalry was Lieutenant Leopold Parker with 18 Seminole Scouts from Fort Clark and Lieutenant John Bullis with 16 Seminole Scouts from Fort Duncan. Colonel Mackenzie had also appointed Lieutenant Parker as adjutant for the 4th Cavalry and the Colonel desired that Parker be free from all other duties. On the spot he ordered Lieutenant Bullis as the commanding Officer of the Seminole Scouts and both detachment were consolidated for the raid. In Colonel Mackenzie's report after the raid he stated, "I also wish to mention Lieutenant Bullis with the Seminole Scouts who charged under the command of that gallant officer very well." Mackenzie had welded an Indian fighting detachment together the likes of which southwest Texas and the Indians were to know and respect from 1873–1881.

The many battles with Indians fought by the Seminole Negro Indians Scouts has been documented and written for public appreciation. The neglected battle is the one fought by the U.S Army and the Office of Indian Affairs, a bureaucratic war between the War Department and the Interior Department over the Seminole Negro Indians. Initially the Seminole Negro Indians where invited to Fort Duncan Military Reservation until transportation could be arranged to move them to the U.S. Indian Reservation. The U.S. Army never had an appropriation to feed much less transport Indians to the reservation. It was rather common knowledge at the time that Congress had made two successive appropriations so that the Bureau of Indian Affairs could transport U.S. Indians from Mexico to the Indian Reservation and subsist them. The Army believed this would be available to cover the subsistence and transportation of the Seminole Negro Indians but the Bureau of Indian Affairs had other ideas. The Army issued rations to the Seminole Negro Indians expecting reimbursement and the Quartermaster filed religiously the adjustments. When the reimbursements failed to arrive, the Army made an inquiry only to be informed that the appropriation was for subsistence in the Indian Territory and not at the forts in Texas. After more letters to the Office of Indian Affairs, the Army was informed they were not authorized to bring U.S. Indians out of Mexico.

After years of more correspondence trying to defeat the red tape the Army got a crowning blow. John Jumper, Principal Chief of the Seminoles, at the Seminole Nation stated, "these Negroes ... fled their owners and took refuge in Mexico ... Mexico gave them a reserve ... they became citizens of Mexico ... they have no rights here ... our citizens may have individually invited them to come here ... as a nation we have protested against their coming." The bureaucratic war was lost and the Army's only recourse was rely on the 1866 law that allowed them to enlist Indians as Scouts. So the only subsistence the army could legally furnish was that for the enlisted scouts but there were so many family members on the reservations that any means possible became the recourse from starvation. The Army was bound with no land to give them and they could only live on the reservation as long as they actively enlisted in the scouts. If a scout terminated his enlistment by law he was to move his family off the reservation. The Army was stuck with no way to send these Seminole Negro Indians back to the U.S. Indian Reservation much less to aid the family suffering from the lack of subsistence. At one point there were 44 scouts with their wages of $13 per month trying to feed and clothe over 150 family members. Little wonder they were accused of stealing and killing four cows belonging to a rancher which Lieutenant Bullis paid for out of his own pocket to Inspector Ballantyne.

In spite of the hardships, poverty, disappointments and racial problems of their families as well as those they endured as soldiers, the Seminole Negro Indians Scouts earned a prominent place in the history of the Indian Wars. In 1875 three scouts: Sergeant John Ward, Trumpeter Isaac Payne, and Private Pompey Factor were awarded the Medal of Honor for rescuing Lieutenant Bullis from Comanche Indians. For action in the Red River War of 1874 Adam Paine (Payne) was awarded a Medal of Honor. May 1876, Chief John Horse and Titus Payne were ambushed on the Fort Clark Reservation and Payne was killed. Military duties and engagements continued for the Seminole Negro Scouts over the year 1870–1881. In 1881 the last Indian depredation was committed in the Military District of the Nueces. It was not necessarily good news for the Seminole Negro Indian Scouts because it eliminated the army's need for them but worse—Lieutenant Bullis was ordered to return to his unit, the 24th Infantry. During Bullis' command the Fort Clark Detachment of Scouts had a very low rating due to desertions, and court-martials, but a fast response time for the call to arms.

After Lieutenant Bullis' departure, the command of the scouts was rotated through many young army second lieutenants until September 1892. Then the Seminole Negro Indians Scouts were transferred to Fort Ringold, Texas, to serve with 3rd Cavalry and to check the stealing of cattle in lower portion of Texas.

Most of the scouts families remained living on Fort Clark Military Reservation and the scouts except for furloughs were at Fort Ringold or with field service for 7 years. March 1899, the six Seminole Negro Indian Scouts were transferred back to Fort Clark. With no hostiles to track over the countryside, there was no military need for the scouts. However, the Army was always fortunate in finding garrison duties—mending fences, patrolling perimeters, and more menial jobs—these all went to the scouts to justify their existence.

After the Spanish-American War until World War I, Fort Clark had a period of survival to maintain the post from being closed and also justifying the need to maintain the Seminole Negro Indians Scouts. In the period of 1908–1910 the army was under pressure to close Fort Clark but the internal political problems of Mexico and the need to enforce the U.S. Neutrality Laws gave new life blood to the post. The closure pressure brought forth the order to disband the Seminole Negro Indian Scouts Detachment. Each time Fort Clark gained a stay on closure, the order for disbandment of the scouts detachment would be held in abeyance. By 1912, the abeyance of the termination order brought about other conditions. "Sixteen Seminole Negro Indians Scouts are authorized at Fort Clark. As their place are vacated by death or other causes they are not to be filled, and only those now in the service may be reenlisted. The organization will therefore in due course of time cease to exist. "At this period the army reported the Indian Settlement on the Fort Clark Reservation consisted of 43 men, 49 women, and 150 children, all closely related.

The year 1914 was final decision time for the U.S. Army, all Indians Scout Detachments formed as a result of the Act of 1866 would be terminated and those in the service who desired to enlist in the regular army would be permitted to do so. (The regular army service would be enlistment in the 9th or 10th Cavalry Regiments). From the War Department this order filtered to the command level at Fort Clark.

The painful duty of writing the command order for the final disbandment of the Seminole Negro Indian Detachment fell upon Captain Sterling P. Adams, 14th Cavalry. Then the Post Adjutant and Commanding Officer of the Seminole Negro Indian Scout Detachment. Within the parameters authorized, he prepared the "To Whom It May Concern" order to the best military possibility of absorbing the shock of the document and with an attempt to recognize the past faithful service. Since the post was not under eminent orders to close, there was no plot of land the U.S. Army could give the families. Since this was the strongest desire harbored since leaving the U.S. Indian Reservation, the Seminole Negro Indians 53 families were in a state of shock in spite of the tone and consideration offered in their final removal from the reservation. Few discharged scouts ever gave any consideration to the fact that no other army personnel upon termination of service were allowed to remain on the army reservation or given land by the army. The make-shift houses were destroyed as the discharged scouts or family members departed the post and the irrigated garden plots formerly tended by them was allowed to be reclaimed by mother nature.

History seems to have hid from view the service, the accomplishments, and what their service meant to West Texas and Mexico. The Seminole Negro-Indian Scouts have only recently been receiving the recognition that has long been denied because it was hidden by more current events until the scouts were no longer remember but now it is history and accounts for why this area was kept from being reclaimed by hostile Indians.

Headquarters Department of Texas San Antonio, Texas

May 12, 1875

GENERAL ORDERS NO. 10

The following report of a scout made by First Lieutenant J. L. Bullis, 24th Infantry, Commanding Scouts at Fort Clark, Texas is published to this command

Fort Clark, Texas
April 27, 1875

Lieutenant G.W. Smith, 9th Cavalry,
Post Adjutant.
Sir:

I have the honor to render the following report of a scout, made in compliance with verbal instructions received from the commanding officer of the post, the object of which was to find out if a large party of Indians were camped on the lower Pecos or Rio Grande, Rivers, or between them.

I would say that I left the garrison on the 16th day of the present month with but three Seminole Scouts, as I desired to leave but little or no trail and not to be seen. We accompanied Co. A, 25th infantry (enroute to Fort Stockton), as far up as

Beaver Lake, a distance one hundred miles, and during the time we kept our horses upon corn transported with the Infantry train. We left the company on the morning of the 22nd Instant and marched west, toward the Pecos. We saw signs of Indians on Johnson's Run, a dry arroyo that runs into the Pecos, on the east side. We marched this day about fifty miles and went into camp, after dark, at a water hole in a rock, grass good.

The following morning (the 25th Instant) we left camp at 4 o'clock and marched south for about eighteen miles and crossed the Pecos about a mile above the mouth, at an Indian crossing; we then marched southeast for about six miles and went into the country between the Pecos and the Rio Grande we did not see any fresh Indian signs, but plenty of old, nearly all of which went toward the shallow crossing of the Rio Grande, known as Eagle's Nest Crossing. We left the spring at 1 o'clock P.M. and marched east for about three miles and struck a fresh trail going northwest toward the settlements, and was made, I judge, by seventy-five head or more of horses. We immediately took the trail and followed it briskly for about an hour, and came upon a party of Indians, unobserved, attempting to cross the Pecos to the west side. We immediately dismounted and tied our horses, and crept, back of a bush, up to within about seventy-five yards of them (all of which were dismounted except a squaw) and gave them a volley which we followed up lively for about three-fourths of an hour, during which time we twice took their horses from them, and killed three Indians, and wounded a fourth. We were at last compelled to give way, as they were about to get around us and cut us off from our horses. I regret to say that I lost mine with saddle and bridle, complete and just saved my hair by jumping on to my sergeant's horse, back of him. The truth is, there were twenty-five or thirty Indians in all; and mostly armed with Winchester guns, and they were too much for us. As to my men, Sergeant John Ward, Trumpeter Isaac Payne, and Private Pompey Factor, they are brave and trustworthy, and are each worth a medal, the former of which had a ball shot through his carbine sling, and the stock to his carbine shattered. Relative to the Indians,

I would say that, in my opinion, they were Comanches, and were from Mexico.

After the fight we marched about twelve miles and went into camp at Paint Creek, grass and water plentiful and good. We marched this day fifty-six miles.

The following morning (the 26th Instant) we left camp at sunrise and took the main road to Fort Clark where we arrived at 3 P.M.; we marched this day forty-three miles. Total distance marched three hundred and twenty-six miles.

       I remain, Sir,
       Your obedient servant
       John L. Bullis
       1st Lieutenant, 24th Infantry
       Commanding Scouts

Words commendatory of the energy, gallantry, and good judgement, displayed by Lieutenant Bullis, and the courageous and soldierly conduct of the three scouts who composed his party are not needed. The simple narrative given by himself explains fully the difficulties and dangers of his expedition. His own conduct, as well as that of his men, is well worthy of imitation, and shows what an officer can do who means business.

BY COMMAND OF BRIGADIER GENERAL ORD:
       J. H. Taylor
       Assistant Adjutant General

Headquarters 4th U.S. Cavalry
Fort Clark, Texas
May 23, 1873

To the Assistant Adjutant General
Department Of Texas

Sir:

    I have the honor to submit the following report of a scout just made against the Kickapoo and Lipan Indians. At about 11 o'clock on the night of the 16th instant I received reliable information of the location of a camp of a party of Kickapoo and Lipan Indians who have been depredating in this part of Texas frontier. I at once ordered Company A, B, C, E, J, M, 4th Cavalry to concentrate early the next morning at a point on the Las Moras River about 12 miles distant from the post, where Captain Wilcox, 4th Cavalry, was encamped with his Company C. Companies A and B, 4th Cavalry were encamped on Pedra Pinto Creek about seven miles northeast of the Post. Companies E and M, on Elm Creek about twelve miles east of the post and I Company being at the Post, all of the Companies being about 15 miles apart. On the morning of the 17th I left the post with Company I and 18 Seminole Scouts and proceeded to the camp of Captain Wilcox.

    After getting the command together, including Lt. Bullis,

24th Infantry, and 16 Seminole Scouts from Fort Duncan, which was accomplished at about 1 P.M. on the 17th instant, the command marched at once for the Indian camp and reached it at 6 A.M. on the following morning, having marched about seventy four miles from Captain Wilcox's camp.

The command had a sharp skirmish for a few minutes and killed nineteen (19) Indians whose bodies were found, captured forty (40) women and children and Costelletos, the principal chief of the Lipans, and sixty five ponies. The ponies have been divided among the three guides, who looked up the camp, as the reward for the danger they fared in their hazardous undertaking.

The following officers were present:

Capt. A. B. McLaughlins, 4th   Capt. Clarence Mauck, 4th
Capt. John Wilcox, 4th   Capt. E. B. Beaumont, 4th
Capt. Wm. O. Connel, 4th   1st Lt. W. O. Hemphill, 4th
1st Lt. G. A. Thurston, 4th   1st Lt. C. L. Hudson, 4th
1st Lt. D. Lynch, 4th   2nd Lt. O. U. Budd, 4th
2nd Lt. R. G. Carter, 4th   2nd Lt. M. G. White, 4th
2nd Lt. G.A.P. Hatfield, 4th   2nd Lt. J. W. Martin, 4th
2nd Lt. John Bullis, 24th Inf.   Lt. & Adjutant L.O. Parker,
also Acting Surgeon Donald Jackson, U.S.A.

All of these officers acted handsomely and deserve consideration and the soldiers showed after their terribly hard ride a creditable eagerness to attack.

It was the good fortune of Capt. McLaughlin with his Company I, 4th Cavalry, to be in on the advance of the column and I feel called on to mention the gallant manner which himself and Lt. Hudson led the company of men which acted gallantly to the extent of rashness.

I also wish to mention Lt. Bullis with the Seminole Scouts who charged under the command of that gallant officer very well.

I wish it understood in making special mention of these officers that others probably acted as handsomely, but from leading the advance they attracted more notice, more especially. In the Indian fight officers a men soon got so scattered in pursuit of Indians that it is perfectly impossible to give each his proper credit.

I mention Lt. Hudson this time and should have done so before for gallantry on the north fork of the Brazos. He is a very gallant officer but inclined to be a little rash.

I also wish to mention Lt Parker, my adjutant, and Dr. Jackson for gallantry and good conduct.

I also feel called upon to mention especially Capt. Clarence Mauck, 4th Cavalry, who was sent for by me when I received news that the precise locality of the camp had been determined, he at that time was quite ill and was asked whether he thought he could stand a hard trip. Capt. Mauck said that if there was any prospect of his company going into a fight he could and would, and acted throughout handsomely.

I was obliged on account of the rapidity with which the column marched on the night of the 17th, I abandoned almost all of my packs and for two days the men were entirely without rations except a little bread in their pockets, yet there was no complaining.

Should it be decided to mention any of the officers, I wish that all of them may be mentioned, as otherwise it is perfectly possible that injustice may be done, but those whom I have specially mentioned are those who from their positions more particularly attracted attention.

My loss was three men wounded. Private Peter Corrigan, Company D, 4th Cavalry, who happened to have been on detached service was attached to Company I, 4th Cavalry, was mortally wounded. Private Wm. Pair of Company C, 4th Cavalry, a splendid old soldier who has served in the regiment, lost his right arm near the shoulder. Private Leonard Krapper, Company E, 4th Cavalry, slightly wounded in the face, is now doing duty. No horse gave out on the scout, and only horses lost were two shot in action and one or two which died from overheat in the chase. The name of men deserving special notice will be sent in after when the different company reports are received. I have omitted to state that three villages averaging from fifty to sixty lodges were destroyed.

They appeared to be well supplied with stores including ammunition.

In closing this report I wish to express my great appreciation to Lieutenant Colonel Shafter, Commanding Fort Duncan, for his cooperation to me and his support he has given me throughout.

I have the honor to be respectfully
>your obedient servant.
>Ranald S. Mackenzie

Military Telegraph System 1875

The remainder of Indian Wars period after the Civil War left the army almost ineffective due to the slow and poor communications. It was most urgent if the army was going to become effective in the stopping the Indian forays that its communication system must be improved. Not only were the authorities learning too late about the raids but the coordination between posts were held up because they were depended on a horseback courier system.

The army resorted to heliograph system at Fort Davis. This was a signal system using movable mirrors to transmit the Morse code. Doctor Albert Meyer was stationed at Fort Davis in 1854 and he became interested in the heliograph system. He later switched from medicine to signaling and he became the father of the Army's Signal Corp. However, the heliograph system had as big a drawback as did the courier system. The Heliograph System was depended on line of sight, a distance limitation. The courier system was limited by the time requirement.

Samuel F. B. Morse had invented the telegraph system and in 1844 he constructed a line between Baltimore and Washington. By 1860 there were some 50,000 miles in operation and the civil war proved the telegraph system as a method of more rapid communication. When it fell the lot after 1866 for the army to protect the Lone Star State frontier against Indians and Mexican raids and depredation, they begged the Secretary of War for a telegraph system. He of course was at mercy of Congress who had to make the necessary appropriations and as far as they were concerned it was peacetime. Not the time for expenditure of large sums of money. More than 6 years of pressure on Congress because of the Indian problem before they began to see communications had to be speeded up if control was ever going to succeed. Finally on June 3, 1874, an act was approved granting the Secretary of War authority to construct and operate a telegraphic line in the Lone Star State. This bill designed the route and provided the sum of $100,000 to begin the work.

Army Special Orders No. 43, March 22, 1875, 1st Lieutenant A. W. Greely, an officer of Chief of Signal Office, was placed in charge of construction of the military lines of Texas. (A. W. Greely was later a Brigadier General. He commanded the Greely Expedition 1881–1884 to establish Artic Station and he was missing in the Artic for an extended time.) By June 1875 the north-south line, Ft. Sill to Ft. Brown, Brownsville, was partially completed with a Ft. Clark–San Antonio connection. The plans called for extension to the western garrisons. On November 10, 1875, when the line had been completed from Denison to Ft. Concho, Captain Daniel Hart, 25th Infantry, was ordered to take thirty men and construct the telegraph line from Ft. Stockton to Ft. Concho.

Ft. Clark ordered 2nd Lt. William Pauling, 10th Infantry, to be officer in charge of construction for the Fort Clark link of the telegraph system. Lt. Pauling under the supervision of J. C. Van Duzer, a civilian Superintendent of Construction, commenced construction June 11, 1875. This was the initial line for Fort Clark and connected it to San Antonio, the Headquarters of Department of Texas, which was completed September 22, 1875. This branch line ran through Uvalde, Sabinal, D'Hanis, and Castorville with each town having its own station and a soldier operator assigned who was a member of the army signal service. On June 24, 1875, Sergeant I. R. Birt, Signal Service, established the office at Fort Clark in order to keep Lt. Pauling in communication with his post while installing the line to San Antonio. When the line was completed September 22 to the Headquarters, Department of Texas, its office was connected to Western Union Telegraph system and Army Telegraph of Texas was now hooked up as part of a international system. This branch line from Fort Clark–San Antonio was 124.32 miles long, cost about $12,000, or $96 per mile.

After completing the line to San Antonio, Lt. Paulding returned to Fort Clark and he was assigned a detachment from Fort Clark to commence building the telegraph line to Fort Duncan (Eagle Pass). This line was 41.36 miles long and completed November 25, 1875. On November 30, Lt. Pauling was given a detachment of 30 men from Fort Duncan to continue construction on to Laredo (Fort McIntosh). When Lt. Pauling completed the line Ft. Duncan–Fort McIntosh on February 2nd, He was surprised to learn that the line Ft. Brown (Brownsville), Ringold Barracks to Fort McIntosh was already completed by a detachment from Ft. Brown. The line from Fort Clark–Fort Duncan cost $3,900 or $95 per mile. Thus the military districts of Lower Rio Grande and Nueces were all connected via a direct line to Headquarters of Department of Texas (San Antonio). Cozy, as each fort knew what the other was telling the general.

Now that story should end with happy ever after but not so. The Indians soon learned the singing wire wasn't singing their praises so they proceeded from time to time to cut the wires. Also, the telegraph poles were sometimes the best firewood and most conveniently located. So the poles were chopped down and burned by ruthless people passing through. On September 22, 1875, as an example, the Rio Grande Telegraphic lines were damaged about 13 miles above Brownsville when two poles were pulled up and the wire cut in 8 places. Another example dated December 1875, the telegraph system between San Antonio and Ft. Clark, the most thickly settled area through which the telegraph lines ran, was damaged five or six times. The Army finally offered a reward for detection and proof of causes of damages to the lines.

=====
Ellis Tuffly (ed), Lt. A. W. Greely's Installation of Military Telegraph Lines in Texas, *Southwestern Historical Quarterly*, LXIX, July 1965, No. 1, pp. 66-85.

Chaplain D. Eglinton Barr
1876

Fort Clark was not only blessed with outstanding officers of the line but it also had its share of staff officers who gained some historic recognition. Chaplain D. Eglinton Barr was probably the most noted of the chaplains who served at Fort Clark. Barr served at Fort Clark while attached to the Twenty-Fifth Infantry Regiment. The Twenty-Fifth Infantry Regiment was garrisoned at the post from March 1871 to April 1872.

Barr was born in Scotland but immigrated to the United States. In 1860, Bishop Leonidas Polk appointed him rector of the St. Johns Protestant Episcopal Church, Baton Rouge. At that time Bishop Leonidas Polk was resident bishop for the Diocese of Louisiana, having previously been the missionary bishop of Arkansas and Indian Territory. During the Civil War Polk became Lieutenant General in the Confederate Army.

When the Civil War broke out, Reverend Barr had to flee to New Orleans because of his Union sympathies. In September 1864, Barr was captured at his home in New Orleans by a rebel scout and taken behind Confederate lines. There he was accused of furnishing information to the Federals, of being both a "Lincoln Yankee" and a chaplain to a black Federal regiment (which of course he was). For three months he was held a prisoner, and his money, property and private papers were confiscated. He was also court martialed and almost hanged, but he finally escaped and returned to New Orleans. Upon his returned he was re-elected as regimental chaplain by the officers of the 81st U.S. Colored Infantry Regiment. Thus he served the 81st Infantry until the end of the war when the regiment was discharged in September 1865. He was honorably discharged as chaplain.

On July 28, 1866, Barr was commissioned to serve as chaplain in the 39th U.S. Colored Infantry which was one of four colored infantry regiments to be established after the Civil War in New Orleans. Barr served with the 39th Infantry until April 29, 1869, when the 39th and 40th Colored Infantry Regiments were consolidated into one regiment which was redesignated the 25th U.S. Colored Infantry Regiment. It might be interesting to note that after the Civil Wars and during the following Indian War period chaplains were only assigned to the colored infantry and cavalry regiments which meant that upon the consolidation of 38th-41st and 39th-40th regiment the army had two surplus chaplains. Of course Barr was luckier than his counterpart in the 40th regiment.

The commanding officer of the 25th Infantry Regiment was Colonel George L. Andrews who served in the Civil War and he was noted as a taskmaster. Colonel Andrews thought the level of education of the soldiers in the 25th Infantry was terrible. He assigned Chaplain Barr to establish a school for the soldiers of the 25th regiment. Barr began a school for the enlisted men, holding evening classes in his quarters for those whose duties made it impossible to attend during the day sessions.

When the 25th regiment was transferred to Fort Clark, Barr found the conditions similar to those encountered by Chaplain Guion in 1868. Fort Clark had no facilities for a school or religious programs. The worst of it all was there was none indicated for the near future. Although there was an indication of a rebuilding program for Fort Clark but it had been delayed due to the yellow fever epidemic in Texas. However, the 24th and 25th Colored Infantry Regiments soldiers were obligated to live in tents year around while attached to Fort Clark. The limited barracks at the post until 1873 were assigned to the Cavalry units. Whether due to the

Colonel's orders or Barr determination, the absence of facilities did not stop his programs and he continued classes in the open air, the stables, the mess hall, or his quarters.

Attendance by the enlisted (colored) soldiers were irregular because of the poor facilities and the duty demands. Barr found himself so busy with schools he had little time for his appointed activities. In addition to the soldiers' school, he conducted school for the children of the post and community. The commanding officer also mandated all non-commissioned officers to attend the post school. The Colonel believed a sergeant should at least know how to read and write in order to perform minimal administrative duties. Chaplain Barr continued to develop educational programs for the men and children under trying conditions at Fort Clark and later on the transfer of 25th Infantry to Fort Davis. That is until he became involved in a controversial event.

Unfortunately research has failed to positively set the date and time for all the circumstances that evolved in this event. Chaplain Barr was reported to be required for the services of a funeral but he failed to appear. By consequences, Colonel Andrews had lost his first wife within this time frame and from his actions this was perhaps the funeral Chaplain Barr failed to hold services for. Colonel Andrews was determined that Chaplain Barr was too drunk to perform services for the funeral but the Chaplain maintained he was sick and under medication. Colonel Andrews was furious and gave Barr the ultimatum, resign or be court-martialed. Barr still claimed that he was ill with a high fever and was in no condition to perform at the funeral but for the record he resigned, September 2, 1872, at Fort Davis.

When Chaplain Barr's resignation became public, he received a letter of appreciation for his work in public education from the Department of Education of the State of Texas but it didn't help him get reinstated. Barr immediately regretted his action of resigning and proceeded to obtain a number of affidavits declaring he was not drunk at that time. One of the affidavits was completed by the post surgeon stating he was under treatment at his quarters during the time charged. Even though Barr kept insisting he should be reinstated both the War Department and President Grant refused to review his cause stating he had in effect removed himself from the service by resignation.

Chaplain Barr holds local recognition in Brackettville as one of the founders of the St. Andrews Episcopal Church besides his education endeavors for the local children as well as those at Fort Clark.

=====

D. E. Barr letter to Adjutant General Townsend, Washington D. C., selected ACP, D. E.Barr, RG-94, National Archives.

Arlen L. Fowler, *The Black Infantry in the West 1869-1891*, pp. 93-94, 109 Westport, Greenwood Publishing Corporation, 1871.

Earl F. Stover, *Up from the Handy Men: The U.S. Army Chapaincy, 1865-1920*, Office of the Chief of Chaplains, Dept. of U.S. Army, Washington 1977, pp. 13-15.

Kickapoo's War 1876

The Kickapoos in two large bands returned to Mexico during the Civil War. There were at that time Mexican Kickapoos who had come with Wild Cat and the Seminoles in 1850 but failed to return to Indian Reservation in U.S. with their brethren in 1851. After the Civil War, they lived peaceable in a place near Santa Rosa Mexico called the "El Nacimiento," an Indian reservation established by the State of Coahuila in lieu of a military colony. This reservation was actually established for the Seminoles and consisted in two sections, Indios and Mascogos. During the Civil War or earlier, Governor Santiago Vidauri of the States of Coahuila and Nuevo Leon had started a quasi-revolution against the Supreme Government of Mexico and took over the Nacimiento Reservation and sent the Seminole Negro Indians to El Parras military colony. Later the Federal Government restored Nacimiento as an Indian Reservation and the Kickapoos occupied the Indios section.

Chief Machemanet of the Southern Kickapoos with about 600 followers left Kansas in autumn of 1862 for Mexico but at Little Concho River in Texas they were treated as hostiles by the Texas Militia. This mistake caused Texas to lose 16 "rangers" and a declaration of war by this band. Chief Papequah and a large following left the Pottawatomie Agency in Kansas, December 1864 and were attacked by Captain Buckner Berry and his Texas Militia for hostile Indians at Dove Creek. Those of Papequah's band who finally reached Mexico and were also at war with Texas. Now most of the Southern Kickapoos had joined the Morelos Kickapoos. Most of these migrant Kickapoos settled at Nacimiento some 110 west of the Rio Grande (Piedra Negras) and they were protected for their "war on Texas."

At Nacimiento they were under the protection of the government of Coahuila and especially supervised by the loyal authorities of Musquiz (Santa Rosa). Texas consisted of many isolated ranches that provided many unprotected Texans for the Kickapoos to take their vengeance out on. They also stole horses and cattle for their own commissary. Due to the wealth of animals they managed to capture, they found the militia and officials in state of Coahuila ready customers for their excess. Later their raiding took on more commercial aspects and a Santa Rosa business man by the name of Jesus Galan began to profit from their war on Texas. He established a trading house near the village of Nacimiento. The stolen cattle and the horse herds were often delivered to Galan and a payment made, generally in form of voucher for purchases in Galan's General Store. Each Kickapooo warrior receiving his share of the proceeds.

Between the raids the warriors received goods on credit at Galan's store. Cattle worth $15-20 a head in Texas were purchased from the war parties by Galan for $3. Later he sold them to cattle buyers from Santa Rosa and Saltillo for $5.

The Kickapoos raiders had become so efficient and audacious by 1877 that they were actually taking "commercial orders" from interested parties in Mexico for the delivery of particular types and numbers of the animals.

The various bands of the former Texas Lipans in Mexico had received punishment from Colonel Mackenzie, Lieutenant Colonel Shafter, and Lieutenant Bullis so often in previous years they were reluctant to raid on their own. The warriors so inclined teamed up with the Kickapoos. However, the Mescaleros remained isolated in the mountains and operated independently of the other two tribes.

Maybe this better explains why the Texans demanded the return of Colonel Mackenzie and the 4th Cavalry in March 1878 at Fort Clark.

=====

Greer, James K., *Buck Barry, Texas Ranger & Frontiersman*, pp. 186, 196.

Gallaway, B. P., editor, *The Dark Corner of the Confederacy*, pp.130-131.

Gibson, A. M., *The Kickapoos*, pp. 208, 209, 216, 217, 210, 211.

Statement of William Schuchardt, Washington, Jan. 14, 1878, 45 Congress 2nd Session, House Report No. 701, pp. 35-36.

Wm. Schuchardt, U.S. Consul Agent letter to Hamilton Fish, Sec. of State, Consular Dispatches, Micro M299, Roll 1, RG59.

Riot in Brackett 1876

January 1876 the 8th Cavalry Regiment with Colonel John I. Gregg, commanding reported to Fort Clark after a march from New Mexico. The families of the members of 8th Cavalry were required to remain in camp for ten days waiting the departure of the 9th Cavalry from main post of Fort Clark. Attached the 8th Cavalry was Captain Oremus B. Boyd whose wife became one of the early descriptive writer about Fort Clark.

She states that finally they moved into a very comfortable little house built of limestone, and charming as to the exterior. Even in the month of February vines were growing rapidly, and beginning to cover the verandas with a beautiful green. Ft. Clark was different from other posts in ways no one seemed sure but made a lasting impression on all.

This arose partly from the fact of there being an insufficient number of Quarters, and mainly from the position of the post being such that troops were sent there to be held in readiness for any emergency—which was generally at this period supposed to be an impending war with Mexico.

The Boyd's first home at Fort Clark was a pretty little house (remember they were built in 1873-1874) so they were only 2-3 years old. Originally each duplex only had three rooms downstairs and three upstairs with a detached kitchen) the rooms were double parlors on the ground floor, a front and back stairs, two large bedrooms and bath above. The purpose of a detached kitchen was supposedly for fire safety.

"We had no furnishings for months, and simply used our camp equipage until carpet and etc., could be sent for." In the two years the Boyd's were garrisoned at Fort Clark, they were required to move to different quarters due to the "ranking process" that offered senior officers the privilege of ordering juniors to give up the quarters that the senior desired. This ranking privilege was referred to "Tumbling Bricks" and caused the Boyds to move 3 or 4 times in the 1876-1878 period.

Not only were the quarters a problem to Mrs. Boyd so were the servants. Her first colored cook, a huge, strapping creature, who seemed a very giant in strength and stature. Her last colored cook was so surly she was equally afraid of him. When he left the Boyds' employment he moved to the little town of Brackett. After only a few days had passed, he murdered a woman, and to hide his guilt, burned the house. Circumstantial evidence was so strong that he was captured and imprisoned in the little jail (Old Kinney County Jail), which was constructed of heavy stone and was the only decent building in town.

The murdered woman had been the widow of a white soldier, and his comrades in arms (10th Infantry Regiment) were determined to avenge her. One night, under the cover of the darkness, a number of soldiers stormed the jail. The jail was well guarded, and the thick doors seemingly impregnable, but the mob did affect an entrance.

At Fort Clark the garrison was greatly alarmed, for the town was so near they could hear the firing and tumult. The ladies were doubly frightened, because each one's husband had been summoned to march at the head of his troops and quell the disturbance.

The jail had been forced before the arrival of the troops from Fort Clark; but the soldiers, though carefully searching every cell, had been unable to find the prisoner. After vowing vengeance on the authorities for having removed him, they assembled outside, where they vented their wrath and disappointment by firing against the heavy stone building. When the cavalry companies reached the scene, and in their turn began to fire, every soldier disappeared, escaping under the cover of darkness and confusion. The soldiers found their way back to the fort, where at roll-call all answered to their names as innocently as possible.

The first officer who entered the jail was Captain Boyd, who was at once told by the sheriff that the murderer was secreted on its second story roof, which, unknown to the soldiers, had a stone coping six feet high that well concealed him. A more pitiable object was never seen by Capt. Boyd; for expecting every moment would to be his last he was praying and groaning, and had the tumult outside been less he would have been quickly discovered.

"The sequel proved the soldiers to have been right in not trusting to the course of the law, for in Texas no crime but that of horse-stealing was considered deserving of hanging: the murderer was only imprisoned, but fortunately for him, he was taken to another county."

=====

Mrs. Orsemus B. Boyd, *Cavalry Life in Tent & Field*, pp. 248–260

Sabinal Canyon
1876

In the fall of 1876, the Indians made their last raid through the Sabinal (Uvalde) canyon. The War party first struck the settlers on the main Frio River, and then like a wave of destruction through the valley, and then made a circuit of many miles towards the Rio Grande. This path of destruction accounted for sixteen persons meeting their death at the hands of the warriors and lost to the settlers of some 200 horses.

The war party came to Sabinal Canyon on the 10th of September, stole many horses, and then turned southeast below the foot of the mountains, playing havoc as they went. The Sabinal settlers gathered quickly and were soon joined by scouts from the Frio Canyon settlers. From Sabinal were: James Thigpen, Phil Hodges, Albert Harper, C.S. Jones, J.H. Simpson, James Watson, Jack Kelly, and a German schoolteacher named Lirch. From the Frio settlers were: Henry Patterson, John Patterson, Riley Patterson, Joe Van Pelt, William Nichols, and Capt. Joe Richarz. The group elected as their leader Henry Patterson and their trailers; Phil Hodges and John Patterson.

For the first day and night the trail led southeast, and on this route the Indians killed a Mexican who was herding sheep for Henry Shane. On Squirrel Creek they killed and scalped another Mexican herder. Then they headed on a south course for sixty miles and killed six men in the lower part of Frio County. Then they started a westward swing towards the Rio Grande where they managed to kill another eight, to make their total 16 in all. When the trail turned west to the Nueces River, Captain Patterson concluded he would have to change his tactics to overhaul the war party before they reached the Rio Grande. Indians when being pursued had a great advantage over the pursuing party. When night came the trailers had to stop, while the Indians could keep on. This was one reason why so many raiding bands got out of the country and in their sanctuary of Mexico. The Captain now decided to try a night ride, thinking that if he would go straight west, guided by a bright star in that direction, it would throw him south of the trail, and then when daylight came he could turn north and intercept the trail of the Indians. One reason why he thought this plan would work was because the Indians generally traveled northwest and crossed into Mexico at the mouth of the Devil's River (San Felipe-Del Rio Crossing). This time, however, the Indians acted the opposite and turned south. The settlers failed to find the trail as they anticipated when daylight came. Finding that the marauders had eluded them, the party now turned and went to Uvalde to procure fresh horses and more provisions, intending to strike the trail again and follow it into Mexico. At Uvalde, eight of the men left and went home.

Since the company was now reduced to twelve men, they thought it advisable to telegraph to Fort Clark and request soldiers to meet them at some point west of the Nueces River. The soldiers were allowed to cross into Mexico (hot pursuit policy) after Indians, but the citizens were not. Captain Patterson telegraphed Fort Clark for the soldiers and designated the meeting place as the "Anna Catchi" (Anachua) Mountains, about twenty five miles west of the Nueces. The settlers determined to continue the pursuit were: Henry Patterson, John Patterson, Riley Patterson, Joe Van Pelt, Jim Highsaw, Jack Grigsby, William Wall, John Kittinger, William Nichols, Jim Thigpen, Albert Harper, and Phil Hodges. The Commanding Officer (Col. Mackenzie) sent Lieutenant Oremus Boyd with a detachment of soldiers. The soldiers met the settlers at the mountains designated.

Lieutenant Boyd had strict orders from General Mackenzie about crossing the Rio Grande, and all had to act accordingly. So it was agreed that the citizens would cross as soldiers with Patterson as their commanding officer and the total command under Lieutenant Boyd.

With command set as to policy and with forty nine in all, they set out for the Santa Rosa mountains (120 miles from border) in Mexico. The soldiers had a Seminole Negro Indian Scout along for a guide and trailer, but the first night out he lost his horse and he had to walk back to the post. So the guide and trailer for the command fell to Capt. Patterson. The day before the command got to the river another large Indian trail came and joined the one they were following. A consultation was held, and it was decided to halt there, and Lieutenant Boyd would send to Fort Duncan (Eagle Pass) after more men, as the Indians now greatly outnumbered their command. About twenty men came from Fort Duncan, and it was supposed that they brought whiskey along, for that night the soldiers got on a spree and one of their numbers was badly wounded by the accidental discharge of a gun. The man who caused the shooting was tied up all night by his thumbs by order of Lt. Boyd. The wounded man was sent back to Fort Duncan for treatment and the balance went on to the Rio Grande. The Rio Grande was badly swollen by recent rains and could not be crossed. Some of the men were so anxious to go over they made an attempt to swim it, but came near being drowned and had to desist.

The Indians, unfortunately, had crossed over before the river rose. Their place of crossing was opposite "La Villa Nueva" (new town) referred to as the Maverick (Sycamore) Crossing. Unfortunately this ended the pursuit and the war party was safely in Mexico and would not have to pay for the depredations they had committed. So often this was the frustrated ending to trailing of war parties by both the settlers and the soldiers.

=====

A. J. Sowell, *Texas Indian Fighters*, Austin, Statehouse press, pp. 503-507.

U.S. Army's Seminole Negro-Indian Scouts

After 1857 and the death of Coacoochee (Wildcat), the Seminole Indians wanted to return to the U.S. Indian Reservation and they found the Bureau of Indian Affairs only to glad to accommodate them. The bad part of this was it meant leaving their friends and former slaves, the Seminole Negroes, behind since slavery was still in existent in Texas. The Seminole Negroes could not chance the danger of capture to serve as slaves between the U.S.–the Mexican border and those in the Indian Territory who would attempt to capture and sell them into slavery. So their choice was determined for them as remaining and continuing service for Mexico by fighting the hostile Indians. Another severe setback was handed to the Seminole Negroes was when they were informed that the Mexican Governor of the state of Coahuila had terminated and sold the Naciementos Indian Reservation. The Governor supposedly came to the Seminole Negroes aid when he offered them the opportunity to move to the Las Parras military reservation about 150 miles south of Naciementos.

The Civil War was in progress in the United States, the hostile Indians were playing havoc on the defenseless ranches in Texas and they began again to cross the border into Mexico. This kept the Seminole Negro warriors busy and in 1862–1863 El Naciementos was reestablished as a Federal Indian Reservation which presented an opportunity for the Seminole Negroes to return. The reestablishment of the Federal Reservation was due primarily to the return of Kickapoos and the governor learning that it was a federal not a state reservation. During the Civil War to dodge participation with either side, North or South, Chief Machemanet's and later Chief Papaquah's tribes of Kickapoos emigrated to Mexico. Both tribes were mistaken by Texas Militia as hostile Indians and were attacked enroute. After severely whipping the Texas militia, they collectively declared war on Texas. When the opportunity presented itself for the Seminole Negroes to return to their old home at Naciemento part of the tribe was desirous. So those wanting to return to Naciementos formed under Sub chief John Kibbetts and returned. About 150 remained with John Horse at Las Parras.

After the completion of the Civil War, and the haunts of slavery and slavers had became only a bad dream, the older Seminole Negroes began thinking about returning to the Seminole Nation in the U.S. where they still had relatives. This was further accentuated when Robert Kibbetts escorted a party back to the U.S. Reservation. Of course old friends and relatives were happy to see this party after some 17 years and invited all the Seminole Negroes to return. This was the message Robert Kibbetts delivered to the colony at Naciementos on his return. Sub chief John Kibbetts had a conference concerning the return of the tribe to the U.S. Indian Reservation with John Horse and the headmen. John Kibbetts was appointed to have a conference with the commanding officer at Fort Duncan (Eagle Pass, Texas) in regards to such a move. March 17, 1870, John Kibbetts had a conference with Captain J. C. DeGress, 9th U.S. Cavalry, then the commanding officer at Fort Duncan. Kibbetts explained that his and John Horse's groups of Seminole Negro Indians at both Lagua De Parras and Naciementos wanted to return to Seminole Nation, U.S. Indian Territory. He also stated he felt sure that the Kickapoos also wanted to return.

Captain DeGress felt positive any reduction in Indians in Mexico would be a relief for the U.S. Army and he undertook the necessary action as he saw it for the moment. He wrote letters to the U.S. Customs and Immigration authorities to pass the Indians who would enroute to U.S. Indian Reservation. He instructed Kibbetts to have the Seminole Negroes come to the Fort Duncan Reservation where they could encamp until transportation for both groups would be ready. Captain DeGress then prepared a letter to Commander, Department of Texas at San Antonio, explaining the conversation and the action he had taken and also requested the commander's approval.

The Department of Texas granted Captain DeGress approval for his actions and stated that if the Seminole Negroes Indians returned before transportation could be arranged, they were to be "furnished camping grounds on the reservation and rations." The rations of course were to be regular army rations but the army supposed it would be reimbursed from the Office of Indians Affairs which had appropriated funds for this purpose. Now the army was assuming that recent funds appropriated by Congress ($25,000) for transportation and feeding displaced U.S. Indians from Mexico would apply in this case (proved much later a mistake). The Assistant Judge Advocate General, Department of Texas forwarded Captain DeGress' letter along with an endorsement to the War Department. The War Department seemed to have more concern about the Kickapoos because their immediate response was to direct the Department of Texas to verify the seriousness of the Kickapoos' desire to return.

By this time the commanding officer at Fort Duncan had changed and Captain F. W. Perry had replaced Captain Degress who had to retired from the army. The Department of Texas notified Captain Perry to determine the Kickapoos desires so Brevitt Major (Captain) Perry invited Willliam Shuchardt, U.S. Consul Agent at Piedras Negros, to accompany him to Naciementos to consul with the Kickapoos. Both of these men reported afterwards that Mexican authorities prevented their meeting with the Kickapoos. They did see John Kibbetts and he assured them the Seminole Negroes still intended to come to Ft. Duncan and would be ready to move shortly. Somehow this meeting has been misconstrued that Captain Perry went to Naciemento to recruit the Seminole Negroes and that he made a treaty with them. Neither Captain Perry nor William Schuchardt were Indian Affairs Representatives besides the fact the United States only makes treaties with nations and the Negroes at Naciementos did not represent any Indian Nation. Captain Perry did learn that, "the Seminole Indians whom I am directed to receive from Mexico turned out to be Negroes. I am informed that the Lipans and Kickapoos will not avail themselves of the invitation to come upon a reservation this side of the Rio Grande."

In the interim time until Captain Perry received the order to affect the meeting with the Kickapoos, his correspondence of May 17, 1870 was forwarded to the War Department. This prompted a response from the War Department, "the Secretary of War authorized the employment of such a number of Indian–Negroes as may be found useful as scouts provided no more than 200 are kept in service which is your (Texas) Department's quota." This was based on a 1866 law passed by Congress authorizing the U.S. Army to enlist 1000 Indians to service as auxiliary to the army as scouts. The Department of Texas in turned notified the newest commanding officer at Fort Duncan, Major Zenas Bliss, 25th Infantry, that he was authorized to enlist twenty (20) Seminole Negro Indians or such a number as shall be found fit for service. The scouts to receive pay and allowance as Cavalry soldiers. 'Kibitz,' or the head man will receive the pay of a sergeant, and approval granted to locate the Seminole Negroes Indians on Elm Creek under control and protection of military authorities of Fort Duncan. (Note—to the army they were Seminole Negro "Indians" so they could qualify under the Congressional Appropriation.)

August 1870, Major Bliss had enlisted the first 7 in the Seminole Negro Indian Detachment at Fort Duncan. He continued enlisting until he had his assigned quota of 20 by the first 1871. In October 1871, Elijah Daniels and his tribe of Creek Negro Indians from Nueces River, and earlier Matamoras, Mexico, arrived at Fort Duncan and 13 of this group were enlisted which was permitted under an new quota.

May 20, 1872, the Seminole Negro Indians were initiated as scouts in an Indian engagement. On duty with Lieutenant Gustauvs Valois and detachment of 9th Cavalry, they encountered a war party of Comanches on La Pendencia Creek. Later in 1871 John Horse (Gopher John) led his band of approximately 150 Seminole Negro Indians from Laguna de Parras, Coahuila to Fort Duncan where several were enlisted in the Fort Duncan Detachment. (Note: John Horse was not enlisted in the Seminole Scouts although John Kibbetts was at the age of 62 which was also the age of John Horse.) With the two bands of Seminole Negro Indians and the tribe of Creek Negro Indians, the Elm Creek Reservations was becoming overburdened. A transfer to Fort Clark Military Reservation was ordered for August 7, 1872 and the establishment of a Seminole Negro Indian Detachment at that post. Seventeen Seminole Negro Indian Scouts were transferred to Fort Clark from Fort Duncan and their family members also moved. Fort Clark's detachment further enlisted 5 scouts during the month from the group that transferred from Fort Duncan. Second Lieutenant Thomas S. Mumford, 13th Infantry, was ordered as first commanding officer of Fort Clark's Detachment and there were 22 scouts in the detachment at that time.

During the first 8 months of the Fort Clark Detachment, the number of scouts remained at 22 but the commanding officers changed rather frequently. September 1872, Lieutenant Mumford was relieved from command and replaced by Lieutenant G. W. Raddyke, then next came a Lieutenant Gerhard but he only lasted a month (January 1877). Lieutenant Cranston was next but by February he was replaced by Lieutenant Raddyke for a second try at commanding. Lieutenant Raddyke relinquished the command to Lieutenant Leopold Parker, 4th Cavalry, who was also Fort Clark Post Adjutant and Post Signal Officer.

May 1873, was a high point in Fort Clark's history and the detachment of the Seminole Negro Indians Scouts. Colonel Ranald Mackenzie and 4th Cavalry regiment commenced an invasion of the Mexican border to assault Indian villages at Remolina. Colonel Mackenzie assembled his force at Las Moras Crossing of the Rio Grande. Among the various companies of the 4th Cavalry was Lieutenant Leopold Parker with 18 Seminole Scouts from Fort Clark and Lieutenant John Bullis with 16 Seminole Scouts from Fort Duncan. Colonel Mackenzie had also appointed Lieutenant Parker as adjutant for the 4th Cavalry and the Colonel desired that Parker be free from all other duties. On the spot he ordered Lieutenant Bullis as the commanding Officer of all the Seminole Scouts and both detachment were consolidated for the raid. In Colonel Mackenzie's report after the raid he stated, "I also wish to mention Lieutenant Bullis with the Seminole Scouts who charged under the command of that gallant officer very well." Mackenzie had welded an Indian fighting detachment together the likes of which southwest Texas and the Indians were to know and respect from 1873–1881.

The many battles with Indians fought by the Seminole Negro Indians Scouts has been documented and written for public appreciation. The neglected battle is the one fought by the U.S. Army and the Office of Indian Affairs, a bureaucratic war between the War Department and the Interior Department over the Seminole Negro Indians. Initially the Seminole Negro Indians where invited to Fort Duncan Military Reservation until transportation could be arranged to move them to the U.S. Indian Reservation. The U.S. Army never had an appropriation to feed much less transport Indians to the reservation. It was rather common knowledge at the time that Congress had made two successive appropriations so that the Bureau of Indian Affairs could transport U.S. Indians from Mexico to the Indian Reservation and subsist them. The Army believed this would be available to cover the subsistence and transportation of the Seminole Negro Indians but the Bureau of Indian Affairs had other ideas. The Army issued rations to the Seminole Negro Indians expecting reimbursement and the Quartermaster filed religiously the adjustments. When the reimbursements failed to arrive, the Army made an inquiry only to be informed that the appropriation was for subsistence in the Indian Territory and not at the Forts in Texas. After more letters to the Office of Indian Affairs, the

Army was informed they were not authorized to bring U.S. Indians out of Mexico.

After years and years of more correspondence trying to defeat the red tape the Army got a crowning blow. John Jumper, Principal Chief of the Seminoles, at the Seminole Nation stated, "these Negroes ... fled their owners and took refuge in Mexico ... Mexico gave them a reserve ... they became citizens of Mexico ... they have no rights here ... our citizens may have individually invited them to come here ... as a nation we have protested against their coming." The bureaucratic war was lost and the Army's only recourse was rely on the 1866 law that allowed them to enlist Indians as Scouts. So the only subsistence the army could legally furnish was that for the enlisted scouts but there were so many family members on the reservations that any means possible became the recourse from starvation. The Army was bound with no land to give them and they could only live on the reservation as long as they actively enlisted in the scouts. If a scout terminated his enlistment by law he was to move his family off the reservation. The Army was stuck with no way to send these Seminole Negro Indians back to the U.S. Indian Reservation much less to aid the family suffering from the lack of subsistence. At one point there were 44 scouts with their wages of $13 per month trying to feed and cloth over 150 family members. Little wonder they were accused of stealing and killing four cows belonging to a rancher which Lieutenant Bullis paid for out of his own pocket to Inspector Ballantyne.

In spite of the hardships, poverty, disappointments and racial problems of their families as well as those they endured as soldiers, the Seminole Negro Indians Scouts earned a prominent place in the history of the Indian Wars. In 1875 three scouts: Sergeant John Ward, Trumpeter Isaac Payne and Private Pompey Factor were awarded the Medal of Honor for rescuing Lieutenant Bullis from Comanche Indians. For action in the Red River War of 1874 Adam Paine (Payne) was awarded a Medal of Honor. May 1876, Chief John Horse and Titus Payne were ambushed on the Fort Clark Reservation and Payne was killed. Military duties and engagements continued for the Seminole Negro Scouts over the year 1870–1881. In 1881 the last Indian depredation was committed in the Military District of the Nueces. It was not necessarily good news for the Seminole Negro Indian Scouts because it eliminated the army's need for them but worse–Lieutenant Bullis was ordered to return to his unit, 24th Infantry. During Bullis' command the Fort Clark Detachment of Scouts had a low rating for desertions, court-martials, and response time for the call to arms.

After Lieutenant Bullis' departure, the command of the scouts rotated through many young army lieutenants until September 1892. Then the Seminole Negro Indians Scouts were transferred to Fort Ringold, Texas. To serve with 3rd Cavalry and to check the stealing of cattle in lower portion of Texas. Most of the scouts families remain living on Fort Clark Military Reservation and the scouts except for furloughs where at Fort Ringold or in field service. March 1899, the six Seminole Negro Indian Scouts were transferred back to Fort Clark. With no hostiles to tract all over the country side, there was no military need for the scouts. The Army is always fortunate in finding garrison duties—mending fences, patrolling perimeters, and more menial jobs–all went to the scouts.

After the Spanish-American War until World War I, Fort Clark had a period of survival—survival to maintain the post from being closed and also justifying the need to maintain the Seminole Negro Indians Scouts. In the period of 1908–1910 the army was under pressure to close Fort Clark but the internal political problems of Mexico and the need to enforce the U.S. Neutrality Laws gave new life blood to the post. The closure pressure brought forth the order to disband the Seminole Negro Indian Scouts Detachment. Each time Fort Clark gained a stay on closure, the order for disbandment of the scouts detachment would be held in abeyance. By 1912, the abeyance of the termination order brought about other conditions. "Sixteen Seminole Negro Indians Scouts are authorized at Fort Clark. As their place are vacated by death or other causes they are not to be filled, and only those now in the service may be reenlisted. The organization will therefore in due course of time cease to exist." At this period the army reported the Indian Settlement on the Fort Clark Reservation consisted of 43 men, 49 women and 150 children, all closely related.

The year 1914 was final decision time for the U.S. Army, all Indians Scout Detachments formed as a result of the Act of 1866 would be terminated and those in the service who desired to enlist in the regular army would be permitted to do so. From the War Department this order filtered to the command level at Fort Clark.

The painful duty of writing the command order for the final disbandment of the Seminole Negro Indian Detachment fell upon Captain Sterling P. Adams, 14th Cavalry. Then the Post Adjutant and Commanding Officer of the Seminole Negro Indian Scout Detachment. Within the parameters authorized, he prepared the "To Whom It May Concern" order to the best military possibility of absorbing the shock of the document and with an attempt to recognize the past faithful service. Since the post was not under eminent orders to close, there was no plot of land the U.S. Army could give the families. Since this was the strongest desire harbored since leaving the U.S. Indian Reservation, the Seminole Negro Indians 53 families were in a state of shock in spite of the tone and consideration offered in their final removal from the reservation.

=====

Captain J. C. DeGress, 9th U.S. Cavalry, Cmdg. Ft. Duncan, letter March 17, 1870.

Headquarters, 5th Military District, Texas, letter March 25, 1870.

Consular Dispatches, Diplomatic Records, Dept. of State, M299 Roll 1.

Papers Relating Return of Kickapoos & Seminoles Indians, M619 Rs. 799–800.

Post Returns, Fort Duncan, March–August 1870.

November 29th, 1877

Lt. John Bullis and his twenty-five Seminole Scouts after returning to the Painted Cave Camp from the engagement with the Mescalero Apaches waited a reply from Lt. Col W. R Shafter at Fort Clark. Colonel Shafter's reply was instructions to go to Pecan Springs on the Lower Road near old Fort Hudson and await the arrival of Capt. S.B.M. Young, 8th Cavalry, who would bring reinforcements and supplies. On November 15th, Capt. Young arrived with Companies A & K, 8th Cavalry and Lt. William Beck with Company G., 10th Cavalry. Capt. Young was anxious to get to the Mescalero Camp, so on the 16th of November, the total command departed Pecan Springs and headed for the Pecos River, Myers Spring, and on west to the Big Bend Country. The command crossed the Rio Grande at Boquilla del Carmen. There they found Apache trails leading to the Sierra del Carmen Mountains. Up to this point the command thought they had rough terrain and rough going but the Carmen mountains gave them a different impression. The trails that led up the mountain were narrow and treacherous, such that the pack mules had to be roped together to prevent their toppling from the steep and narrow trails. Even so, a number of the mules fell and the cavalrymen on foot had to lead their mounts on short bridles as the horses were not as reliable as the mules in this terrain.

The weather was so cold that water in the canteens froze.

The village was in the roughest portion of the mountain and little wonder the Apaches felt secure from the cavalrymen. However, they had misjudged the caliber of Fort Clark's cavalry.

It was little wonder that Alsate's (Arzate's) Apaches were completely surprised when this column of unmounted cavalry first made their appearance in the village area of the mountain. Because of the entrenchment of the Apaches a stalemate in the fighting began to appear.

Capt. Young ordered the troopers and the scouts to encircle the village. After much scrambling for position the troopers and scouts gained the military advantage. After two Indians were killed and three wounded, the remainder abandoned the village and went scrambling up the precipitous incline among the rocks and lengulla.

The troopers destroyed the village after collecting a large quantity of robes, hides, dried meat, saddles, and ropes. They also acquired 30 head of horses and mules from the Indians which had to be led on the return trip down the mountainous terrain in freezing weather.

Capt. Young gave his men a day's rest, before he made the 65 mile trek to the border crossing which he crossed on December 3. He then paralleled the Rio Grande and returned to Fort Clark December 16th.

=====

Capt. S.B.M. Young's Report to AAG, Dist. of Nueces, Ft. Clark, Dec. 18, 1877.

Mackenzie's Second Invasion of Mexico, 1878

On June 1st 1878, an Indian raid killed two herders at Mr. Nicolas Colson's ranch, twelve miles west of Camp Wood. On June 10th, troops started departing Fort Clark for Mackenzie's expedition in Mexico, ostensibly to fight Indians. Some of the force crossed with Mackenzie and the remainder joined across the border. For this Indian fight Mackenzie was leading six troops of cavalry (300-380 troopers), twelve companies of Infantry (600-700 soldiers), a battery of artillery with gatling guns and a platoon of 3-inch guns. The expedition marched to the San Rodriquez River by June 19th. At Remolino, Colonel Valdez (Winkler) of the Mexican Army with some 200 soldiers announced he had orders to resist the expedition's entry into Remolino. Mackenzie ordered his troopers to dismount and he parleyed with General Nuncio. He told the General that he proposed to move forward at 2 P.M. and if the Mexican troops were in his way he would open fire on them. By 1:30 P.M., the Infantry of the expedition had caught up with the cavalry and Mackenzie ordered Lt. Col Shafter to move the infantry nearer to Remolino and deploy them as skirmishers. As the infantry prepared for action, the Mexicans deployed as skirmishers as if to stop their advance. When Lt. Col. Shafter started the advance of the infantry, the Mexicans withdrew for about two miles and then retired from the area.

With no "Mexican standoff," Colonel Mackenzie and his expedition marched to the Rio Grande and crossed at the Las Moras crossing on June 19th. When Col. Mackenzie returned to Fort Clark he sent a coded message to the Department of Texas, "There is no object in humiliating Mexican troops any further, the only thing now that can be done is to capture them and I can not go into a regular campaign to that end without special orders, war ought to be declared on Mexican territory."

Colonel Mackenzie wanted war declared, General Ord, Department of Texas thought the marauders and those abetting them should be punished. Lt. Gen. Phil Sheridan thought Congress should authorize the military occupation of the country between the Rio Grande and the Sierra Madre Mountains. General William Sherman couldn't agree with any of his field men so the "Mexican standoff" now rested with the U.S. Army. This placed Colonel Mackenzie back to trying to catch marauders.

=====

Geo. R. Schneider, "A Border Incident of 1878," *SWHQ*, Oct. 1966, p. 317

Ernest Wallace, *General R. S. Mackenzie on Texas Frontier*, p. 180.

Ernest Wallace, *Ranald Mackenzie's Official Correspondence Relating to Texas 1873-1879*.

Mexico's Reaction to Invasion 1878

R. B. Myers, Brackettville, agreed with Colonel Mackenzie to obtain some intelligence information on the Mexican situation after the June 1878 invasion.

Myers crossed the Rio Grande at Ringold Barracks (Rio Grande City) and arrived in Camargo. From Camagro he went to Monterrey, where he arrived September 29th, and in time to see the first movement of Mexican troops to the Rio Grande for the avowed purpose (as per instructions of President Diaz) to kill the first American soldier who crossed the Rio Grande without a regular passport from a Mexican Custom House. This order was hailed with the greatest joy by every Mexican north of the Sierra Madra.

The troops left Monterrey under the personal charge of General Trevino and in the following order: 26th Infantry, Lt. Col. Trancosa commanding with 592 men; 24th Infantry, Col. M. Gomez, commanding with 720 men; eight pieces of artillery 4-12 pounders and 4-40 pounders with a force of 260 men; 2nd Cavalry (name of commander unknown) with a force of 250 men, total 1,822. Col. Gomez used this expression on the Military Plaza in Monterrey the evening before leaving for the frontier that "they expected to kill "Gringos," rape their women and sell their young as slaves, the same as Cortina in 1859."

He reported that three regiments were still in Monterrey, numbering about 1,230 men, the 22nd Infantry, lest Cavalry and a regiment of mounted riflemen. Col. Noranjo was on the road from the city of Mexico with the 6th Cavalry and 14th Infantry, and also bringing artillery and horses from the 1st Regiment. The whole force was to march to the frontier at New Laredo, Guerro, and Myers. Twelve other regiments (all infantry) were to leave the City of Mexico and Guanajuato on the 25th of the month for Monterrey where they were to await the orders of President Diaz. They would be commanded by either General Roache or General Renioedes. General Trevino said before leaving Monterrey (when asked what he was going to do with the artillery) "that at this particular time he thought large guns would speak more eloquent on border affairs than he could." Colonel Valdez (Winker's brother) left Monterrey with $20,000 to raise 500 volunteers two days before Myers arrived. The headquarters were to be at Zaragoza.

Approximately forty Kickapoos and Mexicans had organized for another raid into Texas. For some unexplained reason this group did not cross the border. Myers completed his report; "General you cannot realize here with what an eager anxiety these yellow-bellies are awaiting war with this country. They say that at first sign of war they will walk into San Antonio with 10,000 men." Trevino says "that each one of his soldiers carries a commission in his knapsack and that all property taken belongs to him who takes it. Hoping that those in power will realize the critical state of affairs in your front."

=====

Ernest Wallace, *Ranald S. Mackenzie's Official Correspondence Relating to Texas, 1873-1879*, pp. 221-223.

Doctor William C. Gorgas Noted Army Doctor Fort Clark, Texas 1880

The military surgeons—both regular and contract—who served with the frontier commands were of varying character, temperament and ambition. A few were escapist, or uniformed "bums," and they were as bad as their counterparts in a command or in the ranks. Many were young graduates seeking the excitement, experience and travel afforded by an army commission or contract. Some Civil War veterans stayed in, hopeful of finding a gold strike or some lucrative venture in the course of their military wanderings. Included, too, were the dedicated career officers who were devoted to the duty they chose. Undoubtedly, Doctor William C. Gorgas was one of the latter as will be noted later.

Doctor George M. Sternberg became the Surgeon General and while in that capacity with rank of Brigadier General, he made an inspection tour of Fort Clark's medical facilities April 11-12, 1895.[1] Not only did he reach the top job in the army for a medical officer but he earned the title of "father of American Bacteriology." His career took him to the frontier west, in Idaho he was promoted to Lieutenant Colonel for gallant service against the Indians. During his career he lost his young wife in a cholera epidemic.

Doctors Walter Reed and William C. Gorgas, both frontier doctors, won fame in the war against yellow fever which took its toll in the army. Doctor William Crawford Gorgas graduated from Bellevue Medical School and became a contract surgeon with the army June 16, 1880, with rank of Assistant Surgeon.[2] His first frontier post was Fort Clark.[3] Two years later he was transferred by the Department of Texas to Fort Brown (Brownsville). Here fate started him on the road to his greatest achievement, the control of yellow fever. While at Fort Brown he visited off-limited areas where the disease was rampant. He was arrested for doing a post-mortem on a yellow-jack victim. Later he was released but ordered to a quarantine sector where his study of the malady was further inspired. Not only was he inspired but he contacted the yellow fever himself and this gave him the answers to the causes of the disease.

Doctor Gorgas continued his study of the yellow jack fever and methods of prevention. When the Spanish-American War developed in 1898 he was recognized as an authority on the yellow-jack and he was sent to Cuba where he gained fame as the sanitation officer who controlled the mosquito. When the U.S. decided to dig the Panama Canal, due to his success in Cuba, Dr. Gorgas was sent to the Canal Zone to help control the yellow-jack fever. His success was considered an aid to building the canal.

Doctor Gorgas worked with Doctor Walter Reed in the war (Spanish- American) with yellow fever. His fame and commitment to duty kept him moving on the promotion ladder, but he didn't neglect his professional education. He obtained a D.S. from the University of Pennsylvania in 1903.[4] In that same year he was promoted to a colonel, a rank that not many obtained in the Medical Department of the Army. By January 16, 1914, Doctor Gorgas was promoted to Brigadier General and made Surgeon General of the Army.[5] He continued on as Surgeon General and March 4, 1915, he was promoted to Major General. He was persistent in his army medical career and held the top army medical position until October 3, 1918, when he retired. He received the "Thanks from Congress for his service" and he was awarded the Distinguished Service Medal.[6] He put forth a medical service career that may have been matched but never outdone.

=====

1. U.S. Army Post Returns, Fort Clark, April 1895.

2. Robert F. Karolevitz, *Doctors of the Old West, A Pictorial History of Medicine on the Frontier*, New York, Bonanza Books, p. 41

3. U.S. Army Post Returns, Fort Clark, June 1880.

4. Official Army Register, January 1903, Washington, GPO, 1903, p. 410.

5. Official Army Register, January 1914, Washington, GPO, 1914, p. 390.

6. Official Army Register, January 1920, Washington, GPO, 1920, p. 67.

John Lapham Bullis Whirlwind and Friend of the Frontier 1881

John Bullis was born on April 17, 1841 at Macedon, New York, the son of Doctor Abram and Lydia (Lapham) Bullis. He attended the public schools of Palymra (Wayne County) New York. On August 8, 1862 (at age of 21 years and 5 months) he answered the call to arms in the Civil War. He enlisted in Company H, 126th New York Volunteers and later was promoted to corporal. While a member of the 126th New York Volunteers, September 12, 1862 (34 days after enlisting), he was involved in the battle of Harpers' Ferry, Virginia, and he was captured by the Confederates but a short time later released. In the spring of 1863, he was in a skirmish near Centerville, Virginia. At the battle of Gettysburg, Virginia, July 2-3, 1863, Bullis was again captured by the Confederates and this time taken as a prisoner of war to the Confederate's capital at Richmond. September 23, 1863, Bullis was involved in a prisoner exchange along with General George Stoneman. Bullis rejoined his outfit and continued to serve with the 126th New York Volunteers until August 17, 1864, when he was discharged.

Bullis was discharged in order to accept a commission on August 18,1864 as a captain in the 118th United States Infantry (Colored). His company was under continuous fire at Dutch Gap Canal, Virginia. At the close of Civil War the 118th United States Infantry was sent to the Texas Border. General Phil Sheridan and 50,000 U.S. Troops were on the border to prevent the remnants of the Confederate Army from joining Maximilian's Army in Mexico. Also, to run the French from Mexico without involving the U.S. in a war with the European forces. Bullis and the 118th U.S. Infantry (Colored) were in General Weitzel's forces which were sent to Brownsville, Texas. January 5, 1865, General Sheridan's Department of The Gulf sent to the General Grangers District of Texas the order to muster out of service a number of the volunteer regiments, one of which was the 118th Infantry (Colored). At that time the 118th was stationed at Clarksville. You needn't try to look it up on a map unless it is 1865 Map of Texas. Clarksville at this time was near the mouth of the Rio Grande in the vicinity of Boca Chica and also across the river from Mexico and the town of Bagdad. French Forces had landed at Bagdad August 1864 and were causing all kinds of problems for the Mexicans and some confusion for the Confederates and Union forces. Of course there are a lot of particulars that weren't discussed in the correspondence between the Generals in command but what developed was that an unspecified number of soldiers of the 118th regiment after taps and prior to reveille on January 5, crossed the Rio Grande, invaded Mexico, and captured the French Forces at Bagdad.

The Commander of the French Forces filed a complaint with Commanding General Wietzel, of the Rio Grande. Immediately that brought a demand from the Commanding General to the Commanding Officer of 118th at Clarksville. The Commanding Officer of the 118th Regiment hurriedly investigated and by reply stated that no officers where involved in such an incident and that all the men were accounted for at bed check and following morning muster. This didn't satisfy General Sheridian because he wasn't satisfied that this couldn't have happened between 11 P.M. and reveille, and he demanded the 118th be retained in the service until a Board of Inquiry completed its findings. In meantime he also issued an order that all arms and artillery taken from the French be returned post haste. By the first of February the field of the enlisted ringleaders was narrowed down and these were arrested and several officers were ordered to be held as witnesses. Bullis' name never surfaced in reports of the investigation but it is hard to believe he failed to have some part or knowledge is such an exciting involvement.

By February 6,1866 the threat of the French involvement in Mexico had disappeared and a large portion of the volunteers of the Union Army were mustered out of service, this also included John Bullis.

After discharge from the army, Bullis moved from Texas to Arkansas. Paul Schaffer, grand nephew of Bullis, reported that his grandmother told that while Bullis lived in Arkansas he was engaged in the business of selling wood to the steamboats plying the Arkansas River.

September 3, 1867, Bullis was commissioned a Second Lieutenant in the 41st U.S. Infantry Regiment (Colored) then commanded by Colonel (Brevit Major General) Ranald Mackenzie and Lieutenant Colonel (Brevit Brigadier General) William R. Shafter. Bullis as a second lieutenant became the third officer in Company D, 41st Infantry, which was under the command of Captain David Sells.

When the 41st Infantry Regiment reported to the Department of Texas (San Antonio), the regiment was assigned to duty in District of Lower Rio Grande,

Fort Brown (Brownsville) and Ringold Barracks (Rio Grande City) Texas. Colonel Mackenzie and the 41st Infantry Regiment were transferred from the District of the Lower Rio Grande on March 30,1868. The Field and Staff plus companies C and F reported to Fort Clark while Company D, Bullis' company, was sent to garrison Fort Inge (Uvalde). Company D was stationed at Fort Inge until Fort Inge was closed as army post (March 29, 1869). During most of this time only

Bullis and Captain Sells were the officers on this post and when Captain Sells was absent, Bullis became the commanding officer. It was during this time that Bullis addressed General Court Martial charges against Captain Sells which terminated his army career.

In March 16, 1869, Colonel R. S. Mackenzie along with the Field, Staff and Companies D & I of the 41st Infantry arrived at Fort McKavett from Fort Clark.

During December 1869, Congress demanded a reduction in the army due to the cost. The most drastic part of the reduction was the consolidations of the four Colored Infantry Regiments, 38-39-40-41. The 38th was chosen to consolidate with the 41st Regiment at Fort McKavett under Colonel Mackenzie. The 38th Regiment had to march from New Mexico to Fort McKavett. When the consolidation of the 38th and 41st was completed it became the 24th U.S. Infantry Regiment (Colored).

Bullis as a Second Lieutenant in the 24th Infantry at Fort McKavett failed to gain any historical recognition. The 24th Infantry was garrisoning the post of the Sub district of Pecos which included the Forts: Clark, McKavett, Concho, and Davis. Bullis and his company probably served at most of them until 1872. In the latter part of 1870, Colonel Mackenzie was given the command of the 4th U.S. Cavalry Regiment. Lieutenant Colonel William R. Shafter became the temporary commanding officer of 24th Infantry Regiment. Both Bullis and Shafter at this time (1870) were both at Fort Davis. In August 1870, Bullis requested a transfer to one of the cavalry regiments serving in Texas from the Commander of the Department of Texas. The timing of this request was such that the Assistant Adjutant General's desk was loaded with information on the transfer of the Seminole Negro Indians from Mexico. The timing of the two most probably helped mark him as the commanding officer in the future. At least his request for transfer to a cavalry regiment was denied.

April 15, 1871, the 24th Infantry gained a new commanding officer, Colonel Abner Doubleday. November 9, 1871, Bullis again captured the attention Department of Texas as General Order Number 17, cited Lieutenant Bullis with four privates of Company M, 9th Cavalry, for attacking Indians and capturing three hundred cattle. Bullis and his men had attacked the 28 Indians and captured the herd. In May 1872, Company D, 24th Infantry and Bullis transferred from Fort Stockton to Fort Duncan.

As early as August 1870, Fort Duncan (Eagle Pass) Texas had a detachment of Seminole Negro Indians Scouts and it was not until August 1872 that Fort Clark also had a detachment of Seminole Negro Indians Scouts. Sometime after Bullis' arrival in May 1872 and May 1873 he was given command of Fort Duncan detachment of scouts. It was usually customary at that time to give the command of the Scouts to the junior of the second lieutenants on the post.

May 17, 1873, Colonel Ranald Mackenzie was at the camp of Captain Wilcox forming his expedition for invasion of Mexico which became better known as the raid of Remolina. At that point Second Lieutenant Bullis arrived from Fort Duncan with his 16 man scout detachment. From Fort Clark came Second Lieutenant Leopold Parker, 4th Cavalry Regimental Adjutant and Commanding Officer of Fort Clark Seminole Scout Detachment. The Fort Clark detachment had 18 Seminole Scouts. Colonel Mackenzie wanted his adjutant available for other duties and he designated Lieutenant Bullis as the Commanding Officer of the Detachment of Seminole Scouts for both posts. After the raid Colonel Mackenzie cited "Lieutenant Bullis for the way the Seminole Scouts charged under the command of that gallant officer." Scout Renty Grayson lassoed Chief Costillitoes and the Seminole Scouts got to escort the 40 Indian women and children captives back to Fort Clark. This evidently set the stage for Bullis' command of the Seminole Scouts until 1881.

After the raid Colonel Mackenzie took military precautions for any retaliatory raids from Mexico by placing his units in outlying camps from Fort Clark. Bullis and his Seminole Scouts were first at San Pedro Springs and later Elm Creek. Following the raid both Lieutenant Colonel Shafter, Fort Duncan, and Colonel Mackenzie, Fort Clark, stayed in close communication as a precaution. In Lieutenant Colonel Shafter's letter of June 27, 1873, he stated: "it is very cheerful to learn from Bullis tonight that old Costillitos has escaped. I shall notify the companies below (Fort Duncan) and try and keep a good look out for him." Costillitos had been held a prisoner at Fort Sam Houston prior to his escape.

When the command felt that the danger from the raid was over, it started a series of field services involving Lieutenant Bullis and the Seminole Scouts. In April 1875, Bullis and the Seminole Scouts: Sergeant John Ward, Trumpeter Isaac Payne and Private Pompey Factor went to the Pecos River where they came across a fresh Indian trail which naturally they followed. At Eagles Nest Crossing (Langtry) of the Rio Grande River, they found the Indians attempting to cross the river with a prized horse herd. The intrepid four decided to take on 20-30 Indians but the Indians were equipped with Winchester repeaters and soon the advance to the rear became a more practical solution than pressing the fire fight. As Bullis and the scouts made a hasty retreat to their horses, they mounted up. That is, all mounted but Bullis. His horse had bolted and he was on foot, fast being surrounded by the Comanches. The three brave scouts came galloping back to rescue their intrepid leader, an act of bravery which earned each the Medal of Honor.

On June 1, 1876, while operating with Lieutenant Colonel Shafter, Bullis with a Mexican guide and three Seminole Scouts entered Mexico, sixty to eighty miles in the unexplored Mexican region but found no Indian villages. July 30, 1876, Bullis with 20 Seminole Scouts and 20 cavalrymen of the 10th Cavalry Regiment, crossed into Mexico over the Del Burro Mountains and near Saragosa they engaged the Indians, killing 12 and capturing 4 women. April 1, 1877, Lieutenant Bullis and the Seminole Scouts engaged Indians on the Rio Grande near the mouth of the Devil's River. September 1877, Lieutenant Bullis and the scouts attacked a Lipan camp 20 miles west of Saragosa and captured 3 women and a boy. After the raid, Bullis and the scouts were pursued by Mexican Colonel Rodiguez and 100 cavalrymen. When Bullis managed to rendezvous with Shafter and his forces on the Rio San Diego River, Colonel Rodriquez decided the American force was too formidable and retreated.

November 10-29, 1877, Bullis and 25 Seminole Scouts joined with Captain S.B.M. Young and three companies of the 10th Cavalry to go to the Big Bend, then crossing into Mexico, and into the Sierra Del Carmen Mountains. The trails were so precipitous that eleven horses or mules were lost and it was so cold that water froze in the soldiers' canteens. In a mountain lair, the soldiers engaged the Mescalerous Apaches and killed two and wounded three. June 12-21, 1878, Bullis and the Seminole Scouts accompanied Colonel Mackenzie expedition on the "war with Mexico." Bullis and his scouts were a part of Captain S.B.M. Young's cavalry force. When the Mexican troops finally undertook military tactics that looked threatening to Shafter's Infantry, Young and Bullis deployed their troops as skirmishers and the Mexicans immediately retired. January 31, 1879, Bullis, thirty nine Seminole Scouts, three Lipan Scouts, Jose' Tafoya (Comanchero), and fifteen cavalrymen trailed Mescalero raiders for thirty-four days but the end of the Indian's trail was at the San Carlos Indian Reservation and the Indian Agent sent Bullis and his men packing back to Fort Clark. In 1880 (January–April) Bullis and forty-six Seminole Scouts accompanied an exploring and mining expedition sent out by the Galveston, Harrisburg, and San Antonio Railroad along with other railway companies. Bullis escorted them to the Chinati Mountains and returned via Pina Colorado and crossed the Military Pecos ford (now the National Park Service boat launching area near mouth of Pecos River).

In 1881, the last of the Indian raids (subdistrict of Nueces), the Indians killed Kate McLauren and two of three children on the Frio River near Leakey, Texas. Bullis and thirty-four Seminole Scouts joined the pursuit party. The civilians who started the pursuit turned back at the Pecos River but Bullis continued the pursuit into Mexico. After six days of trailing the Indians, he located them in their rancheria in the Sierra Burros Mountains. The engagement killed four warriors and captured a squaw and a child.

The above demonstrates the tenacity and the determination of Lieutenant Bullis as an Indian fighter but he had other sides that should be recognized such as a shrewd businessman where real estate and mining interest were concerned. Besides his business acumen, he was likeable, concerned and friendly man with empathy for others, including the Indians he fought and that was later proven by his success as an Indian Agent. Bullis was reported to have owned 60,000 acres of land in northwestern Texas, most of which incorporated a spring where Bullis had camped. He was one of four partners in the Shafter Mine in Presidio County. Bullis was not only the leader of the Seminole Negro Indians Scouts, he was a friend of their families and went to their homes to see the newborn family members. He also conducted the marriage ceremony for some. Bullis was concerned the way the Departments of War and the Interior (Indian Affairs Bureau) failed the Seminoles and he wrote many letters trying to get annuities, food, and travel for them back to the Indian Reservation. When in October 1877, they accused the Seminole Scouts of rustling and killing cattle, Bullis went to James Ballantyne, Kinney County Hide and Animal Inspector, and paid forty dollars of his own money for four cows his scouts supposedly had killed.

On July 23, 1881, the Department of Texas issued General Order 84 which relieved First Lieutenant John L. Bullis, 24th Infantry, Company G, from the command of the Seminole Negro Indian Scouts Detachment at Fort Clark and ordered him to return to his command (Camp Supply, Indian Territory).

In 1882, the newspapers of the southwest Texas: *The Quill* (Castorville), *Hesperian*, (Uvalde), *San Antonio Express*, the *Fort Clark News*, *Bandera Bugle*, and other papers raised a fund to present Lieutenant Bullis with a sword as a testimonial of their gratitude. This sword was made by Bent and Bush of Boston and ornamented by the Goddess of Liberty, American Eagle, and a camp scene in the Chenati Mountains. The inscription reads, "Bullis, the friend of the Frontier." The scabbard has a portrait of Bullis and inscripted: "He protected our home—our homes are open to him, presented to Jno. L. Bullis, by the people of Western Texas." The people of Kinney County not to be outdone also presented to Bullis another sword. The hilt is of seed pearls and the scabbard is a masterpiece. It bears the inscription, "Presented by the people of Kinney County as a token of their undying gratitude." All this publicity for Bullis stirred the Texas Legislature in April 7, 1882, to pass a resolution "to Lieutenant J. L. Bullis of the 24th Infantry, for gallant and efficient services rendered by him and his command in behalf of the people of the frontier of this state in repelling depredations of the Indians and other enemies of the frontier of Texas."

Lieutenant Bullis rejoined Company G, 24th Infantry at Camp Supply in May of 1882. July 4, 1882, he applied to the Secretary of War for appointment as "Major and Paymaster of the U.S. Army upon the occurrence of a vacancy in that corp." This application failed to get any response. December 1885, General Nelson Miles selected Lieutenant Bullis as Inspector of Rifle Practice for the Department of Kansas. By April 1886, Bullis was promoted to Captaincy although he held the brevit rank of Major for gallantry in action. This promotion caused him to be returned to Company G, 24th Infantry and command his company. He remained in command until May 1888 (some 47 years old) when General Miles again selected him for special duty as Indian Agent at San Carlos Agency. November 1891, Bullis once again returned to his regimental duties but in June 1894 he was again appointed as an Indian Agent. This time for the Pueblo and Jicarillo Agency, Santa Fe, New Mexico. In May 1896 (age 55 and 33 years of service), he again returned to his regiment and then applied again for the Major and Paymaster position. This time Bullis had two former Fort Clark "compadres" come to his aid: Brigadier General Zenas Bliss (Inspector General) and Major General Henry C. Corbin (Adjutant General of Army) who helped Bullis obtain the appointment on January 1897.

Upon being commissioned a major and paymaster, Bullis (56) was assigned to the Department of Texas (San Antonio) to travel to the forts of Texas to pay the soldiers. The Spanish-American War made its appearance in 1898 and Bullis was transferred from the Department of Texas. His duty stations changed to: Atlanta, Tampa, Atlanta, Jacksonville, Savannah but by June 1899 he was back in San Antonio. During the Spanish-American War, May 1898, Bullis the paymaster and no longer a field officer, made a request that he be allowed to recruit a regiment of Negroes near Houston and since he and the Negroes would be immune to tropical diseases they could be used to invade Cuba. To give promotion to Bullis' plan four members of Congress sent a message to the President. "Bullis desires a privilege of commanding an army of Negroes immunes in the contemplated invasion of Cuba. Bullis had useful experience in Texas-Mexican Frontier commanding Seminole Scouts. If permitted to organize a regiment of Negroes in the counties near mouth of Brazos River in Texas he would secure men nearly proof against tropical climate and diseases as is possible to have more immune than white men." (signed) Jas. L. Slayden, Rudolph Kelberg, S.W.T. Lanham, Jno. H. Stephens. However, the only invasion Bullis was to make was as paymaster. August 1901 brought another transfer for Bullis, this time he went to Havanna, Cuba, as paymaster and July 1902 he was sent to the Philippines.

September 1903, Bullis made application for his retirement at the required age of 64 and he made the request also that he be retired in the rank of Brigadier General, the rank he felt he would have attained had he remained a field officer instead of changing to the staff corps. Bullis' commander of the Department of Mindanao was none other than Major General Leonard Woods. General Woods reviewed Bullis' application for retirement and put a strong endorsement on it for both the retirement and promotion. The retirement application made its way slowly through the army's bureaucratic hierarchy and by the time it reached the President's desk it was a huge packet with the recommendation of promotion limited to colonelcy which would require an act of congress. "Teddy" Roosevelt (Lieutenant Colonel under Leonard Woods during the war) placed his endorsement to the retirement application, "This is a very good record, can we promote Bullis anyway?" The Secretary of War hastily determined that the appointment to flag rank was at the pleasure of the Commander-in-Chief and no act of Congress was required. So in spite of General S.B.M. Young's endorsement that

Bullis was only a major as a result of his own action. "Bullis had prevented the promotion he might have been entitled to had he remained a field officer as his fellow officers had." The President's endorsement assured the promotion. Bullis was retired April 14, 1905 as a Brigadier General with 41 years of service. His retirement ceremony was at the Army Hospital, San Francisco, California.

Bullis returned to Texas after retirement. Although, he had dreamed earlier in life of making his home at Myers Spring (near Lozier Canyon, Dryden, Texas), his long stay at Fort Sam Houston and the family must of changed his mind to make San Antonio his retirement home. Myers Springs had a special meaning to Bullis. Back in 1881 when Bullis was relieved from the Command of the Seminole Scouts he took an extended furlough and gave his address as Fort Clark but reportedly spent most of the time at Myers Spring. In 1884 the Pecos Land and Cattle Company bought out the Kings Spring Cattle Company and became the owner of some 106 alternate sections of land lying from Dryden to two miles north of King Springs. The Pecos Land and Cattle Company also leased lands from John L. Bullis who also owned the Richland, Geddis, Independence, Cedar, and Myers Springs. Again in 1896 Bullis demonstrated his preference for Myers Springs by taking his furlough there before returning to his regiment from Santa Fe Agency. Evidently, he was considering retirement from the army at this time as this was the period he made the second attempt to become a paymaster. During this stay at Myers Springs, Bullis built a rock reservoir which exist today and bears his name and the date 1896.

When Bullis returned to San Antonio, he built his retirement home almost across the street from the Quadrangle of Fort Sam Houston and near the Staff Post where he had quarters (No. 2, Staff Row) while paymaster for the Department of Texas. Both his home (corner Grayson and Liscum Streets, San Antonio) and his quarters (Staff Row) on Fort Sam Houston are marked with medallions. In 1911, John Bullis suffered a stroke at a sporting event in San Antonio and died May 26, 1911 at the Brooke Army Hospital, Fort Sam Houston, Texas. General Bullis and his second wife are interred at San Antonio National Cemetery. (Not to be confused with Fort Sam Houston National Cemetery.)

To complete biographical sketch of General Bullis the soldier, businessman, and family man, the third aspect needs to be addressed. John Bullis first married Alice Rodriquez, the daughter of Ambrosia and Maria de Jesus Rodriquez. The Rodriquez were descendants of Canary Islanders who emigrated to San Antonio in 1700 in the Duke de Bexar colonization. John Bullis married Alice at an early age (date undetermined), probably before he was discharged from the army at the end of the Civil War. John and Alice Bullis lived in quarters at Fort Clark while he commanded the Seminole Scouts as indicated in the 1880 census.

Approximately 1881 Alice (Rodriquez) Bullis died, probably when Bullis took the extended furlough. In 1885 John Bullis was involved in a civil court case in Davis County (Fort Davis, Texas) with one of his three partners, Lieutenant Colonel William R. Shafter, concerning his ownership in the Shafter Mine. At the trial Mrs. Maria de Jesus Rodriquez's testimony was that Alice had purchased the land but on her death the family felt John Bullis should inherit the land involved.

John Bullis remarried, October 14, 1891 (at 50 years of age) to Josephine Withers (September 8, 1865–December 3, 1934), the daughter of Colonel John Withers. This marriage produced three daughters: Lydia Lapham, Anita Withers and Octavia.

After General Bullis' death the family gave his mementos to the San Antonio Museum Association and they along with the famous swords are under the care and supervision of the Witte Museum of San Antonio.

=====

Returns from United States Military Posts,1800-1916, Microcopy No. 617, National Archives, Washington D.C. Fort Clark, Texas, March 1868–April 1881, Rolls 214, 215, 216.

Fort Inge, Texas, March 1868–. Letters received by Office of Indian Affairs 1824–1881, Microcopy 234, National Archives. Rolls 800, 801, 807.

The Congressional Medal of Honor recipients, Civil War-Spanish-American War-Indian War Campaign, U.S. Army, Microcopy 929, Roll 2.

Papers Relating to Raids into Texas made 1875-1876 by Indians and Mexicans from Mexican Side of border (Investigation in Mexican Border Troubles), Microcopy M666, Rolls 195, 196.

General John Lapham Bullis' Letters, National Archives, Microcopy M1064, Roll 459. The American Historical Society Inc., New York, 1930, American Biography, A New Cyclopedia, Bullis, General John Lapham, pp. 205-209.

Periodicals

Butler, Grace Lowe, "General Bullis, Friend of Frontier," *Frontier Times*, Volume 12, Number 8, May 1935.

Carson, Paul, "'Pecos Bill' Shafter on Texas Frontier, 1870-1875," *Military History of Texas & Southwest*, Volume 15, Number 4.

"'Pecos Bill' Shafter Campaigning in Mexico, 1876-1877, *Military History of Texas Southwest*, Volume 16, Number 4.

Crimmins, Martin L. "Shafter's Explorations in Western Texas, 1875," *West Texas Historical Yearbook*, Volume IX.

Porter, Kenneth W. "The Seminole Negro Scouts, 1870–1881," *Southwestern Historical Quarterly*, Volume LV, Number 3, Jan. 1952.

Schneider, George R. "A Border Incident of 1878 from the Journal of Captain John S. McNaught," *Southwestern Historical Quarterly*, Volume LXX, Number 2, October 1966.

Wallace, Edward S. "General John Lapham Bullis, Thunderbolt of Texas Frontier, I and II," *Southwestern Historical Quarterly* Volume LV, April 1951.

"General Ranald Slidell Mackenzie, Indian Fighting Cavalryman," *Southwestern Historical Quarterly*, Volume LVI, January 1953.

Books

Beaumont E. B. "Over the Border with Mackenzie," *United Service*, Volume 12, 1885.

Carlson, Paul H., *"Pecos Bill": A Military Biography of William R. Shafter*, College Station, Texas A&M Press, 1989.

Cusack, Michael F. & Caleb Pirtle, *The Lonely Sentinel, Fort Clark on Texas's Western Frontier*, Austin, Eakin Press 1985.

Floyd, Dale, E. (Editor), Adjutant General's Office,

Chronological List of Actions, & c., with Indians from January 15, 1837, to January 1891, Fort Collins, Old Army Press, 1979.

Lechie, William H., *The Buffalo Soldiers*, Norman, University of Oklahoma Press, 1967.

Muller, William G., *The Twenty Fourth Infantry, Ft. Collins*, Old Army Press, 1972.

Raht, Carlysle G., *The Romance of Davis Mountains and Big Bend Country*, El Paso, Rathbooks Company.

Scobee, Barry, *Old Fort Davis*, San Antonio, The Naylor Company, 1947.

Sullivan, Jerry M., *The Museum Journal*, XX, 1981, "Fort McKavitt, A Texas Frontier Post," Lubbock, West Texas Museum Association, 1981.

Swift, Roy L. *Three Roads To Chihuahua, The Great Wagon Roads that opened the Southwest 1823-1883*, Austin, Eakin Press, 1988.

Thompson, Richard A., *Crossing The Border with the 4th Cavalry*, Waco, Texian Press, 1986.

Utley, Robert M., *Frontier Regulars, The United States Army and the Indian, 1866-1890*, NewYork, Macmillian Company, 1973.

Wallace, Ernest, *Ranald S. Mackenzie's Official Correspondence Relating to Texas, 1873-1879*, Lubbock, West Texas Museum Association, 1968.

Williams, Clayton W., *Texas Last Frontier, Fort Stockton and the Trans-Pecos, 1861-1895*, College Station, Texas A&M Press, 1982.

Final Action of the Indian Wars October 1881

On October 20, Sergeant Bobby (Robert) Kibbets and nine Seminole Scouts recovered thirteen horses from seven Indians near the Rio Grande. This was the last recorded Indian raid in the Military District of the Nueces.

The Indian Wars came to a early end in this district because General E.O.C. Ord ordered the district to enter Mexico in 1977 when in hot pursuit and punish the Indians. Since the Mexicans began raiding as well as encouraging the Indians, more drastic action was required. Entering into the scene was Colonel Ranald Mackenzie and the Fourth Cavalry. Mackenzie's idea to cure the problem was declare war on Mexico and occupy the country as far as Monterrey and Saltillo from the Rio Grande frontier, while the City of Mexico was being occupied by forces from the coast. While Mackenzie and Sheridan wanted military action against Mexico, Ord and Sherman refused to accept that as the course of action. In the meantime diplomacy went to work on the problem and President Hayes and his cabinet managed to convince President Diaz of Mexico to put aside the post-Civil-War problems and get his country under control. General Trevino made it sound like he was going to war with the "Gringos" but he managed to avoid any confrontation and concentrated on the orders from Diaz to make the Kakapos domestic farmers, control the Lipans, and rid the country of the Mescal Eros. The animosity between the two armies was retarded when Mexican General Geranium Trevino married the daughter of General E.O.C. Ord. On May 18, 1882, a grand ball was given by the commanding officer (Col. D. S. Stanley) at Fort Clark for the bride and bridegroom. In later years the Mexican Army polo teams played matches with the Fifth Cavalry at Fort Clark. The years of animosity were waning to friendship and the Indian was no longer the war tool of the two countries.

Last Indian Raid April 1881

John McLauren had brought Allen Reiss, a sixteen year old, to stay with his wife, Kate, and the young children while he was away for the day. After dinner Kate, Allen, and the children went down to the garden, which was under the bank of the West Prong of the Frio, and out of sight of the house. Kate hearing noises up on the bank, thought that the hogs were in the open house and asked Allen to hike up and run them off. Allen came over the bank and saw that Indians were making the racket. He tried to run back, yelling at Kate to run, but the Indians shot Allen in back of the head. Kate, seeing him fall, caught up her baby and the other children and ran to the garden fence below. The Indians shot her as she climbed over. Severely wounded, Kate lived for two or three hours. The Indians made no effort to attack the children and they laid quietly near Kate until the Indians left.

When it was all quiet up at the house, the oldest McLauren girl, approximately 7 years old, went down the river to find help. She found George Fisher fishing on the river and told him her tale of terror. Fisher lost no time in telling the settlers to gathered at John Leakey's place. Under the leadership of Capt. J.J.H. Patterson, they saddled fresh horses and took the Indians trail at dawn. They also sent a messenger to Fort Clark to notify the commanding officer of the raid.

The settlers trailed the Indians for two days in drenching rain before they were intercepted by Lieutenant Bullis and 34 Seminole Scouts. Since the settlers' horses were becoming jaded, they soon abandoned the pursuit and left it to the soldiers because they were nearing the border. On April 27th, Bullis was on the trail and reached the Rio Grande, ten miles below mouth of the Pecos. On 30th of April, Bullis crossed the Rio Grande and followed the trail which led to the Burro Mountains. Here they spied the Indian camp some two miles distant in a rough and broken country. Bullis concealed his command until midnight, then led 27 of his command to the Indian camp, leaving 7 to safeguard the horses. At daybreak Bullis and his scouts rushed the Indian village. By complete surprise they slaughtered the Lipans and recovered the loot that was taken on the raid. John McLauren and some friends came to Fort Clark later and identified the captured clothing belonging to Kate McLauren.

=====

John Leakey (Nellie Yost), *The West That Was: From Texas to Montana*, pp. 62-64.

Sgt. John B. Charlton
Fourth Cavalry Regiment
Trooper, 1882

As a young lad he had the desire to be a soldier and evidently his father encouraged it by telling him the soldier like qualities he needed to develop. Unfortunately his father died when he was nine years old. As a young lad (15) he ran away from home and joined Company K, Artillery, December 19, 1862, and served until December 19, 1865, almost all of the Civil War. This enlistment and subsequent enlistments were served under his alias, "Robert Fitzmaurice."

The book *Old Sergeant* reports in Charlton's letter that he joined Company K, 1st U.S. Artillery, April 14, 1865. Due to his health and advanced age (75) in his letter he is probably referring to the second enlistment in 1st U.S. Artillery. April 1865, Charlton reenlisted in Light Battery K, 1st U.S. Artillery (Brig. Gen. William M. Graham), and served until April 14, 1870 (22). Charlton then enlisted in April 14, 1870, in Troop F, Fourth U.S. Cavalry then under the command of Captain Wirt Davis (later Brig. Gen.) and still later under Captain Robert C. Carter. He served the Fourth Cavalry in this enlistment until April 1875. He again reenlisted in the fourth Cavalry, April 23, 1875, and he was discharged on Special

Orders, War Department after he made application to President Grant.

On his service in the Light Artillery, he found Captain Graham "to be the hardest taskmaster who ever wore the 'Blue.'" However, when Charlton first enlisted in Light Artillery battery he was counseled by Captain Graham, I have have seen your family tree which dates back to an old royal debauchee in England and I know your people. You should go home and go to school."

Charlton's desire overcame the advice of his commander and he remained in Captain Graham's Company K. During his service he stated Captain Graham "made me" (promoted in rank) and "broke me" (demoted to private) so often that I put my chevrons (non-commissioned officer stripes) on with hooks and eyes. "Once we caught a venerable looking old billy goat and painted 'Old Billy' on his side in big letters and the old rascal went directly up and laid himself down on Captain Graham's porch. Of course Captain Graham sent for the 'dammed boys' and we had to lie fluently and plentifully to 'save our skins.'"

Charlton's service with Fourth Cavalry taken in serious and in a soldierly vein and for this he was noted by his officers as an exceptional soldier. His most recognized soldierly act was when the Kiowas Indian Chiefs Big Tree, Satanta, and Setank were taken prisoners by General of the Army W. T. Sherman on the porch of Colonel Gierson's Quarters at Fort Sill.

General Sherman ordered Colonel Ranald Mackenzie and his Fourth Cavalry to take the three Kiowa prisoners from Fort Sill, Indian Territory, to Fort Richardson, Texas, where they could be tried for the murders of Henry Warren's Government Corn Train. Charlton who was a corporal at that time was ordered in charge of the second wagon to carry prisoners. In the first wagon was Corporal Robinson and Private Cannon, and Setank was loaded aboard for the trip.

On Charlton's wagon was Private Beals along with the other two prisoners, Big Tree and Santanta. After the heavy guarded wagons got underway, Setank began a death song chant but was mostly ignored by the military. After the procession got well on the road to Fort Richardson, Charlton who had been alerted because of death song chant, heard a commotion in the first wagon. Looking out he saw Corporal Robinson turn a back somersault out of his wagon and almost immediately out the other side came Private Cannon, both had left their Spencer Carbines in the wagon.

Setank, with both hands free, had picked up one of their carbines and was trying to work the lever. Charlton immediately raised his carbine and fired at the old Kiowa Chief and he fell over. While Charlton was levering another load into his carbine, Setank had raised himself to a sitting position and was still trying to work the carbine. This time Setank was sitting with his side facing Charlton and Charlton fired the second time sending the bullet clear through the chief's chest. After Setank's body was dumped alongside of the road the procession proceeded on toward Fort Richardson. Due to Colonel Mackenzie's cautions for an attack by the Kiowa tribe on the way to Fort Richardson the two remaining prisoners were staked to ground by hands and feet. The mosquitoes took unmerciful attacks on the Kiowas prisoners and Captain Carter felt sorry for the Indians. He placed sentinels over each prisoner to chase the mosquitoes away with branches. Not to leave the reader in suspense, Big Tree and Santanta reached Fort Richardson, were tried in the Texas Court and convicted, then sent to the Huntsville Prison after sentencing.

Next noted soldierly act by Charlton was performed in September 1872 when Colonel Mackenzie ordered an attack on Qua-ha-da Comanche Indians Camp (Mow-Wi's) Charlton was a junior sergeant that day and he was in charge of the rear column of F Troop. When the troops reached the edge of the camp on the initial charge the order was given "Right Front into line." This caused Charlton and his squad to be on the right of the company. The four in the squad were privates; Ranking, Beals, Kelly, and Dorst. By being on the right of the company, Charlton's squad was in the hottest part of the fight. Charlton's squad as result took the casualties for the attack but Charlton came out of the battle unscathed and he shot "the Indian who shot Kelly and Dorst." The battle resulted in the capture of 130 squaws.

Next on a scouting detail, the detail was attacked by Indians out numbering the troopers two to one. The Lieutenant of detail ran, begging his men to follow him and to "not fire a shot for fear of angering the Indians." Charlton rode beside the officer and said, "Lieutenant, if we stop and make a stand they will run." "No! No! we can do nothing but try to outrun them" the Lieutenant replied. Charlton took command of those who were experienced in such warfare and drove the Indians off. The untried officer came to Charlton afterwards and asked him not to divulge any of this back at the post which Charlton promised and maintained this promise the rest of his enlistment. This story remained such a secret that it was only revealed by Mrs. Charlton after his death.

When Colonel Mackenzie was on a return march from North Fork of Red River Campaign, Indians were harassing the troops all day, the scouts which Charlton was attached to, were kept on the skirmish line all day. That night at roll call a man was reported missing and Charlton and another trooper were detailed to scout out and see if he could be found. This left the two troopers venturing in Indian territory in the dead of night. After sneaking back approximately a mile on road the command had used that day, where the trooper had last been spotted riding in a very feeble manner as if he was wounded. He could barely keep his seat in the saddle.

On this hunt neither of the scouts dared call out to him because of the nearness of the Indians. The scouts spied a gully alongside the road which they used to conceal their movement in trying to reach the wounded trooper. Creeping cautiously along one of these small channels, straining their eyes in the dark for a sight of the wounded man. They had the misfortune to step on a dog and some half dozen puppies. The confusion that followed separated the two troopers but Charlton continued on alone. After crawling for some time on his hands and knees he spotted an Indian camp. By this time Charlton was bruised from stones, a sleeve full of thorns, and an abdominal rupture (an old wound) which was giving him a great deal of pain. By cautiously searching he was able to find the wounded man who had fallen from his horse. Since Charlton dared not carry him for fear of being seen by the

Indians, he felt of the trooper's wounds. Since he was not bleeding Charlton wrapped his head and shoulders in his blouse and rolled him as gently as he and the terrain would permit down to the bottom of the gully. He was able to place the trooper on his back, then carefully avoiding the dogs' den he returned the wounded trooper to the camp for treatment.

While Charlton, Scout McCabe, and two Tonkawas, under the command of Lt. Peter M. Boehm, were scouting some three or four miles from Mackenzie's command, they suddenly came upon four Indians sitting on a grassy plot holding their horses. Upon sight of the troopers the Indians made a spring for their horses. Three succeeded in mounting, but Lt. Boehm shot the horse from under one of them. The demounted Indian engaged in a gun duel but Lt.Boehm won out. The two mounted Indians were making their getaway but were being followed by Scout McCabe and the two Tonkawas. The fourth Indian was left for Sergeant Charlton. Charlton stated that this Indian was the most magnificent specimen of manhood, the bravest, and he was fully six feet, four inches in height. When this fourth Indian saw that he was dismounted and alone, he deliberately starting aiming at Lt. Boehm instead of Charlton. Before the Indian had time to fire at Lt. Boehm, Charlton shot him. Since the shot was not fatal, his attention then was directed at Charlton. Charlton was having trouble controlling his horse as it was sensitive to the firing and every time Charlton tried to fire, the horse either plunged or threw up its head. The Indian was able to keep a string of arrows in the air continually as if he were using a machine gun. One of the arrows pierced Charlton's thigh, midway between the hip and the knee, going through the saddle leather and pinning him to the saddle. After the Indian exhausted his supply of arrows, he began using his rifle. One of the Indian's shots from the rifle struck Charlton's left hand, removing parts of two fingers, mashing them against his quirt and exposing bare bones. One shot from Charlton's carbine shattered the Indian's hips and lower spine, but the Indian laughed, tossed his black hair from his eyes and kept on firing. It finally took a shot through the head by Charlton to end the duel.

The scouts examined his body after the battle ceased and discovered nine bullet holes, any one of which should have killed an ordinary man. Charlton upon returning to the camp had to be removed from the saddle by the doctor after lifting the wounded thigh enough to cut the shaft of the arrow which pinned Charlton to his saddle.

In April 1873, F Troop, along with the rest of the regiment, was ordered to Fort Clark. Charlton stated that it rained on the troop every day until they reached Fort Clark. Since the 9th Cavalry occupied the main post, the Fourth Cavalry was required to camp at Las Moras Springs. After few days Charlton and Troop F were ordered to the "Pintos" (Camp Pinto on Piedra Pinto Creek), which was utilized as a grazing camp. The Troopers kept 15 days' rations in a pack to move at a moment's notice. May 17, when Colonel Mackenzie selected the troops to accompany the raid to Remolino, Mexico, he left Troop F and Charlton at Camp Pinto where they stayed until June 1873. They were then moved to Sabinal Canyon and remained there to scout for Indians until St. Patrick's Day 1874 and then they returned to Fort Clark.

One of the soldiers became insane at Fort Clark and it became necessary to send him for treatment to a government asylum for the insane. This resulted in Charlton drawing another of the detached duties. He left Fort Clark with his charge in handcuffs for Galveston where they boarded a ship for Tampa. Enroute the ship was besieged by a storm and the Captain of the ship ordered Charlton to remove the handcuffs on the insane in case the ship floundered. Due to the situation at the time the insane soldier managed to slip away from Charlton and was discovered sitting astride the yardarm. Two of the ship's sailors managed to bring him down from the yardarm with the greatest of difficulty. The Captain finally permitted the Sergeant to lock the man in his berth for the remainder of the storm. The ship lost its rudder during the storm and drifted for days before it was discovered by a tramp steamer off the coast of South America and was towed back to Florida.

In the late summer 1874 (about August) the Indians in the area of Fort Sill were rioting and General Sheridan was preparing the campaign to end campaigns. General Mackenzie was quartered at Fort Clark and had recovered from his raid at Remolina and a rheumatism attack. Mackenzie sent for Sergeant Charlton and gave him some dispatches to deliver to Fort Sill, Indian Territory (Oklahoma). Charlton was instructed to travel only by night as the country he would be passing through was infested with Indian bands and Mackenzie wanted assurance the dispatches would get through to Fort Sill as soon as possible. (Remember this was a year or two before the military telegraph system was established). Charlton made the trip (580 miles) in six nights by changing horses at each of the five army posts enroute.

On Charlton's return from Fort Sill he was surprised to find Colonel Mackenzie and most of the Fourth Cavalry at Fort Concho. Mackenzie ordered Charlton to a scouting party under the command of Lt. William A. Thompson and consisting of six white men, thirteen Seminole Negro-Indians Scouts, twelve Tonkawa Indian scouts, and two Apache scouts. Their job was to scout out in advance of Mackenzie's expedition that was going to clear the staked plains of Indian menace (commonly referred to as the Red River War of 1874). Mackenzie's expedition left Fort Concho almost immediately for Blanco Canyon (Yellow House Canyon). The supply trains accompanied by four companies of Infantry from Fort Concho followed. After several days' marching the destination was reached and a supply camp (Camp Supply) was established. That night rain fell in torrents and a norther blew in, all of which added to the discomfort of soldiers and animals. The next morning, September 27, 1874, with fifteen days' rations for each man, the troops were on the march again, this time the destination was Tule Canyon, about another day's march. When the command reached the level of the plains the scouts were ordered out ahead of the command and to deviate their path somewhat from that of the main command so the flanks would also be guarded. The scouts rode all morning without seeing any signs of Indians, but about noon with a break in the plains the scouts stopped to survey the landscape. Some distance away Charlton spied what appeared about 100 buffalo and called the Lieutenant's attention to it.

He raised his field glasses and exclaimed, "They are Indians, Sergeant, and they are going to attack us. Get our men ready for action." The Old Sergeant dismounted the men, assigned six to take charge of the horses and had the remainder form a line around the horses. Lieutenant Thompson continued to watch the approaching Indians with his field glasses and determined his force was outnumbered by at least four to one. "Hold steady, men, and reserve your fire until they are within easy reach!" When the Indians reached a point about sixty yards distant they made a right turn and started circling the scouts. In the meanwhile the Lieutenant had decided that being that outnumbered they would have to fall back gradually, holding the Indians off with hopes they could gain contact with the main force. Step by step they fell back fighting cautiously to create the most damage on the enemy. Almost sundown they had reached the trail of the command. Realizing the size of the trail and the command approaching, the Indians bid the scouts goodnight.

After receiving the reports of the skirmish, Colonel Mackenzie ordered one third of the command on guard that night for he strongly suspected they would attack before sunup. His experience proved him correct, for at moon up, the Indians were back in full force. At the first concentrated fire from the troopers the Indians withdrew, no doubt surprised at the readiness and number of troopers involved. This certainly clued the old Indian fighter Mackenzie that somewhere in the region was a large encampment of Indians. After the troops had breakfast, Colonel Mackenzie sent for Sergeant Charlton and ordered him to take two Indian Scouts and follow the trail left by the night raiding Indians. Charlton choose two Tonkawas, Johnson and Job, and departed following the well marked trail. The country seemed level as far as the eye could see and numerous other trails joined the one the scouts were following. Unexpectedly, there was before the three scouts the colossal Palo Duro Canyon.

They dismounted immediately and Job was assigned to hold the horses while Charlton and Johnson crept to the precipice for a scout of the whole canyon. The walls of the canyon were a sheer drop of fifteen hundred feet and the distance from wall to wall was about a half mile, with a small stream of water running through between the walls. In the open were hundreds of horses grazing, and from the immense height they appeared no larger then chickens. Teepees thickly dotted the banks of the stream as far down the canyon as was visible (later it was determined to be three miles long). Johnson viewing over the precipice said: "Heap Injuns!." Charlton reportedly replied:" you bet your life, old scout, and some canyon too." Realizing they had a twenty-five mile ride to get back to the command and report to Mackenzie, they hastily but cautiously departed.

As soon as Mackenzie was briefed, he ordered a Troop of the Cavalry to remain with the Infantry to protect the supplies at Camp Supply. With less than six hundred men, Mackenzie headed for the twenty-five mile march to meet the foe of twice as much or more. At sunrise the next morning the command had reached the Palo Duro Canyon. He quickly surveyed the narrow, steep approach to the canyon, then walked over to Lieutenant Thompson's scouts and said: "Mr. Thompson, take your men down and open the fight." "Very well sir," and Lieutenant Thompson led off with the scouts in single file to descend the fifteen hundred feet into a land teeming with Indians.

About two thirds down the precipitous buffalo trail, an Indian sentinel spied the attackers and let out a war whoop. That whoop brought a shot from the scouts and although it silenced that sentinel, its echo throughout the canyon immediately caused the whole canyon to come to life. (Custer aficionados should compare this action with Custer's "Last Stand" to learn why Mackenzie was the better combat general.) Kiowas, Comanches, and Arapahos attacked the scouts from every quarter, first by dozens, later by hundreds, as warriors hastily gathered at the lower part of the camp attempting to block the path of the attacking scouts and then the troopers. Many of the defending Indians concealed themselves behind rocks or cedars for protection as they were able to observe the continuous line of troopers descending the trail. The scouts had to take the blunt of the battle but were quickly reinforced by the troopers descending behind them.

By the time the warriors were battling the total command, they began to give ground, fighting desperately to cover the exit of the squaws and pack animals. The Indians retreat followed the banks of the stream to the pass some five miles where the squaws left the canyon. The warriors more slowly retreated to the same destination but it was sunset before they made the pass. The troopers broke off the pursuit so they could burn the Indian teepees and Indians' personal belongings, herd the Indian ponies and tend to their own wounded. The trooper causalities were two dead and a number of wounded. Charlton who went up the far reaches of canyon, said he passed over dead Indians everywhere.

After the village was burned, the herded Indian ponies (some 2,200) were rounded up and driven out of the canyon with a battle-weary command following on a return to Tule Canyon and their base camp. They departed the canyon about dark and continued on to Tule Canyon, arriving in the early morning. Charlton confessed after such a strenuous night-day-night combination that several times he slept in the saddle but he would feel General Mackenzie's hand on his shoulder shaking me, "Wake up, Sergeant, wake up your men and look after the horses." When the command reached Tule Canyon, Mackenzie ordered the captured horses shot.

Mackenzie knew he couldn't burden the command in Indian country with that many horses and he was for sure not going to let those Indians to become mounted again. Putting the Indians on foot was attributed to making them sue for peace and later going to the reservation.

After the completion of the Red River Campaign, the Fourth Cavalry returned to Fort Clark. February 1875, the Fourth Cavalry swapped with the Ninth Cavalry for the garrison of Fort Clark and departed to Fort Sill. Now the Fourth Cavalry was to police and protect the Indian Territory. When April rolled around Charlton's first enlistment in the cavalry was complete and he gave consideration to returning to civilian life. The purchase of civilian clothes and its fit plus being self-conscious in them after wearing the uniform convinced him to take on a new suit of "blues" instead, so he reenlisted. At Fort Sill Charlton was the Sergeant of the Scouts and thereby adding to his collection of military anecdotes and rare experiences.

The most noted of his military duties after his reenlistment was to get Mow-wi, the Qua-ha-da Comanche chief, to come in to Fort Sill and surrender. In April 1875, Colonel Mackenzie sent for Charlton and told him he wanted him to go on a very dangerous mission. Mackenzie emphasized that it was "not an order." Henry Strong, a civilian scout was also induced to volunteer and to be the interpreter with Mackenzie's message to the chief. "If Mow-wi and his band will come to Fort Sill and surrender, giving up his arms and ammunition, he would be made comfortable and be taken care of by the Government. Mow-wi would be free so long as he gave no trouble, but if he would not come that he (Colonel Mackenzie) would follow him until his band was exterminated."

On April 24th, Charlton, Henry Strong, and two friendly Comanches departed on a three day trip to Mow-wi's camp. On reaching the camp, the Indians removed the guns and horses and placed the scouts in a teepee which was heavily guarded. Three days of captivity were endured before Mow-wi decided to accept Colonel Mackenzie's terms.

Charlton stated that "once General Mackenzie passed me, on his way to take a swim in a little stream." You may come in too, if you wish, Sergeant," he said. His scars were plainly visible and by looking at him when he wasn't looking, Charlton learned much of what he had suffered and would suffer until his dying day. Charlton stated his own wounds were similar to Mackenzie's but did not trouble him as much until later years. (Mackenzie was wounded four times and Charlton three times.) Charlton's wounds and waning interest in the military life caused him to accept Lt. Fred Grant's assistance in obtaining a discharge by President U.S. Grant. Now his lust for the military life may have waned but he was only 28 years old. He had remaining still a very adventurous and wanderlust spirit which he displayed at least until 1890 if not until the time of his death in 1922.

In the civilian life he first went to Cheyenne, Wyoming, and started freighting for the Army Quartermaster's of

Cheyenne and ended up in a three-day Indian fight with Utes at Mill Creek. Next he took a job of caring for the horses of a trick rider in a circus and traveled to Alaska with the circus. His next venture was to Australia which ended up in returning to United States. The wanderlust still persisting he joined up with a gold prospector and went to South America for gold and then goat ranching but this failed and he returned to U.S. In the late 1880s he was in Mexico grading for the Mexican Railroad but due to his quick temper reaction to notable Mexicans, he had to flee for his life. Now at 33 years old where would you think he would head next? Wrong, it was Brackettville, Texas. In 1884, Charlton settled in Bracketville and operated "Jacks Bar or Jacks Place" and Livery Stables. In 1892, he married Miss Letitia Walling of Brackettville.

In 1894, Charlton sold his interests in Brackettville and bought a ranch on the Nueces River near Uvalde. He sold this ranch in 1904 but continued to live in Uvalde until he died of congenital heart trouble in 1922.

He was buried with military honors in the Fort Clark's "New Post Cemetery." The Old Post Cemetery had a grave of another soldier of Fourth Cavalry, Peter Corrigan, Corrigan's epitaph is also applicable to Charlton's military career.

> "Oh, pray for the soldier, you kind hearted stranger,
> He has roamed o'er the prairies for many a year,
> He has kept the Comanches from off your ranches,
> And chased them far over the Texas Frontier"

Brackettville-Fort Clark's Contribution in the Spanish-American War

On April 22, 1989, when John L. Bullis' swords were on display at the Old Guardhouse Museum, Fort Clark Springs, Mrs. J. Lee Ballantyne, an aficionado of the swords, came accompanied by several members of the Fritter family to view the swords.

During a conversations with the museum curator it was revealed that Stafford Fritter had a trunk which belonged to his father, James Edward Fritter, which of all things possessed his Spanish-American Army uniform and other artifacts of his service during this historical period. Due to the interest it created, Stafford donated the uniform and unidentified medal which is most probably the marksmanship medal of that period. Since a Soldier's Memorial Certificate was also in this trunk of valuable artifacts, a copy of it was made and also donated to the Old Guardhouse Museum by Mr. Fritter. This Memorial Certificate lists all the personnel in Company L, 23rd U.S. Army Infantry Regiment. Of primary interest in the list is the most prominent names of the older Brackettville families: James Edward Fritter, Walter S. Ballantyne, and Arthur J. Veltman. Of the 118 names on this list, there may well be others from Brackettville and surrounding territory as Company L of the 23rd Infantry was recruited to bring the regiment to a wartime strength while the 23rd Infantry was garrisoned at Fort Clark.

On June 21, 1894, the 23rd Infantry Regiment arrived at Fort Clark primarily from Fort Sam Houston (San Antonio). Arriving at Fort Clark was the Field, Staff, Band, and Companies C, E, G, H, I, K. Companies B and D arrived from Fort Bliss (El Paso). Colonel J. J. Coppinger commanded the regiment and as senior ranking officer, automatically commanded the post of Fort Clark. April 1895, Colonel Coppinger was promoted to the rank of Brigadier General and transferred to another command. Replacing him as Commanding Officer of the Regiment and Post was Colonel Samuel Ovenshine. Colonel Ovenshine remained the commanding officer of Fort Clark until May 16, 1898, when the 23rd Infantry Regiment departed Fort Clark for New Orleans and wartime duty overseas in the Philippines. Prior to the departure of the regiment, the 23rd Infantry was recruited to wartime compliment by the addition of two more companies and Colonel Ovenshine was given a wartime promotion to Brigadier General, United States Volunteers.

Evidently, with the impending departure of the 23rd Infantry Regiment there must also to have been a severe shortage of officers, as Chaplain J. A. Potter was the senior officer and became the commanding officer of the post, something that seldom was repeated in the history of the army. The population of Fort Clark as a garrison dropped from 490 to 134 or less.

June 10, 1898, the 3rd Texas Volunteer Infantry reported to Fort Clark and the 3rd's commanding officer, Colonel Rawleigh P. Smyth, relieved Chaplain Potter as the commanding officer of Fort Clark. The 3rd Texas Volunteer Infantry remained at Fort Clark until February 22, 1899, when they were mustered out of Federal Service and replaced by 10th Cavalry Regiment. The 10th Cavalry Regiment had just returned from Cuba where they had fought the Spanish-American War and rescued Lt. Col. Theodore Roosevelt (Col. Leonard Wood and Rough Riders from the Spanish Insurgents.)

=====

Fort Clark's Post Return, May 1898.
Fort Clark's Post Return, June 1898.
Fort Clark's Post Return, Feb. 1899.

Hazards of the Occupation

In Fort Clark's Interment Journal in the period of 1852–1879 there are some 10 deaths of enlisted men whose deaths were noted as "Gun Shot" since these were not noted as "killed by Indians" and with no further research we are left to assume it must have been self-inflicted or caused by other soldiers. So how did the officers fare in non-combat situations of "Gun Shots"? There are two situations which are very prominent because of the officers involved and the situations which prompted the shooting.

The earliest case reported in the Fort Clark Post Returns involves Lieutenant Charles L. Hudson. Lieutenant Hudson was with Colonel Mackenzie's Remolina Raid, May 23, 1873. Colonel Mackenzie's official report on Lieutenant Hudson stated, "I mention Lieutenant Hudson this time and should have done as before for gallantry on the North Fork of the Brazos. He is a very gallant officer but inclined to be a little rash." Lieutenant Hudson's actions had been well noted as he was designated by a Brevit as Captain. December 9, 1873, he was in command of a group of the 4th Cavalry which engaged a large Comanche War Party and defeated them. Many of the Indians wounded and killed were young braves, sons of famous Comanche and Kiowa chiefs whose grief triggered a general uprising of the Kiowa and Commanche tribes.

The Army's Department of Texas, San Antonio, Texas, December 26th, 1873, issued General Order Number 4 which congratulated Lt. Hudson, 4th Cavalry, as result of his scout of December 9, 1873. After Lieutenant (Brevit Captain) Charles Hudson returned from San Antonio where he had been congratulated by the Department Commander, General C. C. Augur, he was enjoying the glory of his successful engagement.

This glory period was of a very short duration for on January 4, 1874, Lieutenant Hudson was laying on his bunk in Officer's Quarters at Fort Clark when his roommate grabbed up Hudson's rifle. The roommate admirably handled the Winchester Rifle (non-regulation), and asked, "Is this the gun you had in the Indian fight?" and not knowing that it was loaded pulled the trigger. He accidentally killed Lt. Hudson instantly. Brevit Captain Hudson was interred San Antonio National Cemetery, January 10, 1874.

Four years and 26 days later another officer, Lieutenant Charles J. Crane, was wounded accidentally in his room by "horse-play" from fellow Lieutenants. Later as a Colonel, Crane reports the accident. Lieutenant Jacob R. Pierce, 24th Infantry, returned from attending reveille and brought with him to our joint room over Captain John B. Nixon's quarters two other officers, Lieutenants Frank Mills, 24th Infantry, and Fred Phelps, 8th Cavalry. I was still in bed, lying on my iron bunk. The three youngsters came in rather boisterously. The weather was cool that January morning, and they had been out in it and felt good." Phelps caught hold of my bedding at the foot of the bed and said to the others, "Here's how we done it at the Point," and pulling hard and suddenly he jerked me out of bed on the floor in the middle of the floor, where I landed on my seat, with hands and feet in the air. There had been a loud noise resembling a muffled explosion, or perhaps the falling of the old time wooden bed slats on the floor. From my position on the floor I seemed to rise without effort about six feet away, slapping my back and feeling very much dumbfounded, like the others. They asked, "What's the matter?" Still slapping my back I answered, "I believe that pistol went off," and looking around I continued, "Yes it did. See that smoke." Hurriedly all three of them inquired at the same time, "Are you hurt?" "I don't know," I said, and I began to examine myself to find out if I had been shot, and where. After quite a search I found the exit hole and then the others discovered where the ball had entered. That injury could not be duplicated without death in a hundred intentional efforts. The caliber .45 bullet from my old time Colt revolver had passed between two flanges of my back bone, entering at the small of the back on the right side and coming out just to the front of my right hip bone, then it went up through top of the house which had no ceiling.

In eight days I was out of the house walking around with a crutch. Meanwhile about half of the 4th Cavalry had arrived, under their Colonel R. S. Mackenzie, whom I will never forget, and do not wish to ... He promptly came to me while I was still in a bed and many others did the same.

=====

Fort Clark Interment Journal, NA Micopy 2014, roll 1.

Col. R. S. Mackenzie Action Report, May 17, 1873, to AAG, Dept. of Texas, Headquarters, San Antonio, Texas.

Nye, W. S., *Carbine and the Lance, The Story of Old Fort Sill*, Norman, Univ. of Oklahoma Press, 1937, pp. 182-184.

Bliss, Zenas R., *Reminiscences*, Volume V, p. 159.

Fort Clark Post Returns, January 1873 and January 1878.

Charles Judson Crane, *The Experiences of a Colonel of the Infantry*, The Knickerbocker Press, New York, 1923, pp. 65-67.

U.S. Army Turns to Bicycles for Mobility and Fort Clark's Bicycle Corp

In 1891 bicycles were being used for nearly all roads at favorable seasons of the year between the Atlantic and Pacific. I consider it quite important to demonstrate their utility by practical use in the military service.[1] Thus was General Nelson A. Miles, as commander of Department of Missouri, appeal for permission from Secretary of War to continue experimentation. General Miles, an impetuous army figure or as many of his contemporaries considered, a promotion climber, started experimentation with bicycles at Fort Sheridan, Illinois. Early on (January 1892) General Miles was notified by Adjutant General Office that he was violating Army Regulations since only the Secretary of War could approve testing of military equipment.[2]

General Miles first experimentation was on November 25, 1891, and this date is important not as a history lesson but that it was before the advent of the automobiles, freeways, or paved roads. Colonel R.E.A. Crofton, commanding 15th Infantry at Fort Sheridan, was ordered to organize a detachment of one officer (Lt. W. T. May) and nine noncommissioned officers to conduct experiments using bicycles which would be furnished by the Pope Bicycle Company at no expense to the government.[3]

Since this experiment was stopped by the Adjutant General of the Army, General Miles went directly to the Secretary of War with the urgency to continue the Pope Bicycle Company's promise to furnish them at no expense to the government.

February 1892, General Miles received authorization from the acting Secretary of War to continue his experimentation with a Bicycle Corp.

As of May 31, 1892, General Miles, a speaker in Chicago honoring Charles L. Burdett, League of American Wheelmen, spoke on military cycling and noted that on May 30, 1892, soldiers from the 15th Infantry had conducted a practice march on bicycles from Pullman to Chicago.

Not much has been recorded about the experimentation up to 1895 when General Miles was promoted to Major General and ordered to command the U.S. Army. In his first annual report to the Secretary of War, in 1896, he recommended that one full regiment be equipped with bicycles ... it was his intention "to use to some extent troops stationed at different posts to make practice marches and reconnaissances, and thereby obtain a through knowledge of their own country, especially the topographical features, conditions of roads, sources of supplies and all information's of military importance."[4]

With the above information on the U.S. Army's experimentation in a Bicycle Corp it isn't hard to understand how Fort Clark, the lonely sentinel on the Texas frontier, was drawn into the experimentation. The Post Returns documented the first Fort Clark venture in October 1895. The 23rd Infantry which was garrisoned at Fort Clark from June 1894 until April 28, 1898 (deployed to Philippines). This particular practice march gained fame for reasons other than the bicycle experimentation. Frederick Remington's painting "A Practice March in Texas" depicts this march. Two companies of the 23rd Infantry under command of Captain Lea Febiger, marched from Fort Clark to the East Nueces River in Texas.[5]

Captain Lea Febiger's orders for the march, via

Commanding Officer of 23rd Infantry and Post, Colonel Coppinger, from the Department of Texas contained the provision for the bicycle experiment. "The command not having transportation of any kind on the march, should it become necessary to communicate with the post for any purpose whatever, may do so by bicycles, the use of which on the march by enlisted men owning them is hereby authorized."[6]

Six lucky soldiers, because they owned bicycles, were to make the march but not in the old Infantry fashion. "Four privates and one musician, with Corporal Jim Reeves in charge, constituted the bicycle corps. They carried their haversacks and blanket rolls on the handle bars, and rifles strapped to the frame. They constituted daily, on the march, as the advance guard, and were ready for use as messengers and couriers. Two of bicycles being second handed, very old and worn, gave out on the march; the other four came successfully through, though not of the most expensive pattern." This was the report of the first Fort Clark experimentation with bicycles.

The march in October 1895 was not only a practice march but a warm up for the one that was ordered to commence December 18, 1895, and lasted until January 21, 1896. This march again involved the 23rd infantry, Companies G and H. Company G was in command of Captain R. J. Eckridge and Company H commander was Captain E. B. Bollon. The basic purpose of march was to re-station the two companies: Company G at Fort Ringold and Company H at Fort Brown. The 400 mile march from Fort Clark to Fort Brown took some 23 days. This march did include the bicycle experiment but the post returns were a little sketchy.

The bicycle detachment was commanded by Lt. H. G. Cole. This detachment acted as an advance unit and it was able to explore the roads a day ahead of march and make any necessary repairs. The two companies left Fort Clark December 18, 1895, marched to Eagle Pass (Fort Duncan) in three days, to Fort McIntosh (Laredo) in eight days, and to Fort Ringold (Rio Grande City) in another seven days. Company G took station there and Company H slogged on for another 106 miles to Ft.Brown, covering this last lap in five days.[7] One anecdotal event happen on this march, soldier Harry Orgelman of Company H got lost the third day out of Eagle Pass. It was a dull, still day with heavy fog, so he had little to guide him. He wandered helplessly for 48 hours with nothing to eat but finally he wandered to the Rio Grande River and joined in with some trappers.[8]

The next experiment with the bicycle at Fort Clark came in February 1896. This time instead of accompanying a marching contingent, it was a bicycle detachment that made the march without the hindrance of marching infantry. 1st Lieutenant W. H. Sage and 2nd Lieutenant H. L. Lauback 9 of 23rd Infantry with one sergeant from Company C, 23rd Infantry and one Private, Company B, 23rd Infantry made a reconnaissance of the road from Fort Clark via Eagle Pass to Del Rio and return to Fort Clark. These bicycles (private property) left Fort Clark at 9:30 A.M. on February 20, 1896, and returned at 11:15 A.M., February 24, 1896. In support of this operation, 1st Sergeant Frank E. Miller, Company B, 23rd Infantry was ordered in charge of one teamster and one four mule team and wagon. This wagon was loaded with rations and other necessities for this detachment. On February 21, 1896, Sergeant Miller proceeded as instructed to the mouth of Sycamore Creek, Texas, where on arrival he was to wait until the bicycle detachment arrived and to report to Lieutenant Sage. The Sergeant was to continue under the orders of Lieutenant Sage until relieved of the detachment at Fort Clark. The total distance traveled by this bicycle detachment was 137 miles.[1]

The above is last official report found on U.S. Army's experimentation on bicycles at the national level or Fort Clark's. Perhaps it was a good thing this developed in 1890s because the Indian Wars in military district of the Nueces was terminated in 1881. The Indians thought it humorous when the U.S. Army placed the Infantry on mules to combat the mobility of the Indians. Can you imagine what the Indians would have thought of infantrymen on bicycles?

1. File No. 23672, AGO, RG-94, NA.

2. Charles M. Dollar, *Putting The Army On Wheels: The Story of the Twenty-Fifth Infantry Bicycle Corps.* Prologue, Journal of National Archives, Spring 1985, Vol. 17, No. 1, pp. 7-8.

3. File No. 23672, AGO, RG-94, NA.

4. Report of Secretary of War 1896, Volume 1, p. 69.

5. *Harper's Weekly*, January 4, 1896.

6. Fort Clark Post Return, October 1895.

7. Fort Clark Post Returns, December 1895 and January 1896.

8. William U. Feeman, "The Snails of the Army Marched," *San Antonio Express Magazine*, March 16, 1952.

9. 2nd Lt. Howard L. Lauback reported to Fort Clark June 1893. He was the subject of a Ghost Story in the Officer's Quarters #1; Commanded Camp Del Rio in 1919; Brig Gen. in WWI and again 1931.

10. Fort Clark Post Returns, February 1896.

A Ghost Story from Fort Clark 1894

The author Kenneth Wiggins Porter wrote this story as originally told him by Mrs. Hollbrook, widow of General Lucius R. Holbrook, in 1955. Mrs. Holbrook stated this story was told her by General Howard L. Laubach. Howard Laubach reported to Fort Clark in June 1894 as a recent graduate of Military Academy at West Point. As a very junior 2nd Lieutenant, Laubach was assigned Company B, 23rd Infantry under the command of Colonel J. J Coppinger who also commanded the post at Fort Clark at that time.

Lt. Laubach was intending on marriage in the very near future. At the time of reporting to the regiment he made an inquiry to the Commanding Officer on the availability of Married Officer Quarters. The Commanding Officer stated the only quarters available was a little square one-story building at east end of the officer's row. He also emphasized the reason that one was vacant was due to general belief by members of the post that it was haunted.

As a background for this belief the commanding officer stated that a colonel who formerly commanded the post had lived in that house. He had a colored cook who was always accompanied by a big black cat. The colonel drank heavily and when in his cups sometimes beat the cook. Eventually, after one such beating, the cook died. After that, people in the living room of the little house would hear footsteps on the ceiling which would come down the wall and halfway across the room, and then stop. People then began to see visions of the cook and her cat.

Finally, no one could be found on the fort who was willing to live there. A colored servant who was lodged there temporarily overnight without being told of the house's reputation was sitting on the porch next morning. He had heard the cook's footsteps on the ceiling and made a fast decision to leave the house to the cook and her cat.

Lt. Laubach who was about to be married and was concerned over the effect such visitation might have on his future wife. The commanding officer was concerned also and he repeated all the stories he had previously been told, with some new ones added, in support of his belief that the bride would not wish to live there. However, being a young, brave, lieutenant and to lose the only opportunity for married officers quarters would require indefinite postponement of the marriage plus living in the Bachelor Officer's Quarters. So for the want of any other place to live, he moved into the little house.

Laubach had two dogs, one was rather valuable, the other less so. For some time neither he nor the dogs heard or saw anything out of the ordinary. Then one night at 11 o'clock, as the Lieutenant was getting ready to inspect the guard as Officer of the Day, he heard footsteps across the ceiling which moved down the wall and came toward him in the middle of the floor. The dogs were so terror stricken that they dashed through the screen window and screen porch. The most valuable dog lost his senses and had to be tied up and eventually destroyed. The other could never be coaxed into the house again.

Later Lt. Laubach married and brought his bride to live in Quarters No. 1. To his relief, she never heard anything at all alarming. Whether her presence "laid the ghost to rest" for good or not the general did not know; at any rate, after leaving Fort Clark he never heard anything further about the "haunted house" he had once occupied. (The present long vacancy of that still standing quarters makes one wonder whether the cook and her cat have ever returned.)

======

Mody Boatwright, Wilson M. Hudson, & Allen Maxwell (editors), "And Horns on Toads," *Texas Folklore Society Publication*, No. XXIX, 1959.

Other Units That Served at Fort Clark, 1852-1945

1st Artillery Regiment, U.S. Army: Jan. 1856–Oct. 1856: Aug. 1859–Jul. 1860

2nd Artillery Regiment, U.S. Army: May 1878–Oct. 1880

Lipan Indian Scouts Dec. 1878–Jan. 1880

Tonkawa Indian Scouts: Dec. 1881–July 1882

Coastal Artillery, 12th Co., U.S. Army: Mar. 1901–June 1902

Coastal Artillery, 125th Co.,U.S. Army: Oct. 1901–June 1902

Machine Gun Platoon, U.S. Army: Sept. 1912–April 1915

Machine Gun Troop, U.S. Army: May 1915–June 1916

Signal Corps, U.S. Army (element of) Oct. 1904–Sept 1916

Hospital Corps, U.S. Army (element of) Oct. 1904–Sept. 1916

Seminole Negro Indian Scouts: Aug. 1872–Sept. 1892: Mar. 1899–Sept. 1914

99th Field Artillery: February 1943–February 1944

First Cavalry Brigade Commanders

Fremont, Jonathan C. 1903-1904
Parker, James C. 1914-1915
Booth, Edwin E. 1924-1925
Etringe, LeRoy 1927-1928
Hawkins, Hamilton C. 1929-1930
Lear, Ben 1936-1937
Joyce, Kenton 1937-1938
Wainwright, Jonathan 1939-1940
Chase, William C. 1940-1941
Millikin, John 1941-1942

First Cavalry Division

First Cavalry Brigade		Second Cavalry Brigade	
5th Cavalry Regiment	12th Cavalry Regiment	7th Cavalry Regiment	8th Cavalry Regiment

General Hugh S. Johnson

Hugh Johnson first military assignment after graduation from the Military Academy, West Point, was at Fort Clark. As the first duty post it made an indelible impression on his memory. In his writings in later life he more or less glamorized Fort Clark.

"Full of anticipation, I went to join my regiment at Fort Clark, Texas, twelve miles from the railroad and twenty-five miles east of Del Rio on the Rio Grande. It was an antebellum post, put there to guard the marches from the Comanches. I lived in one of the oldest adobe houses—built eighty years ago. Indeed there were only a few modern quarters there—no conveniences—the slenderest communication with the outside world. But as I look back, it was a young man's paradise and I had more fun in the years I was stationed there and at San Antonio than in any of my life. Built on a slight rise from a mesquite-covered limestone plain of illimitable extent, it guarded one of the finest and largest never-failing well-springs in the country—Las Moras River flowing through some underground limestone channel into the open."

"The mesquite was full of quail. The Pinto was full of fish. Ducks came in season to near-by lakes. You didn't have to go far for bear, deer, or javelina. There was no prohibition and the First Cavalry Mess and Club was one of the best-provided in the Army. You could buy a polo pony for five dollars and among all the fifteen regiments of cavalry, there was none like the First.

"As I have said, the (officer's) club was above reproach and there was all outdoors and over eight hundred horses to absorb anybody's youthful ebullience. Across the creek (Las Moras) was a typical frontier town rejoicing in soldier saloons with such names as 'Bucket of Blood' and 'Blue Goose' and everything that goes with them—everything. In January, 1904, I went back to New York and got married to my classmate's (Henry S. Kilbourne, Jr.) sister.

"My wife had (previously) lived four years at Fort Clark, where her father (A Civil War veteran-sic, post Civil War) had been stationed when she was a little girl."[2] Her father was Dr. Henry S. Kimbrough, Sr., Surgeon.[3]

"As a cavalry regiment the First left something to be desired just then. It had just come back from guerila warfare in the Philippines where each troop had been isolated in control of some barrio—the Captain usually acting in civil government, the troops as gendarmes. As the officer's brides and wives began flocking in, the First Cavalry was settling down. It had a good old colonel (Col. Martin B. Hughes)[4] and several veteran majors and captains of the plains and Indian fighting days. They knew what discipline ought to be and they finally got it to the nth degree. In those months of hard work and hard play the First Cavalry became what I of course shall always regard as the best regiment in the Army. General Malin Craig, Chief of Staff of the First Army in Argonne, had a distinguished record in the World War I and throughout his whole service. He was my captain during most of the many years of my lieutenancy. General Joseph Gaston at Fort Clark was the major commanding my squadron. General H. J. Breese [Brees], then was a brilliant captain and a buddy of mine as was General G.V.H. Moseley, also then a captain. General E. J. McClernand, whose father was the General McClernand of Vicksburg and the Civil War. He was my colonel for many years (at Ft. Clark-Lt. Col.). General De Rosey Cabel, who averted a dangerous situation at Nogales during the war, was a captain and lived next door to me at Fort Clark, Texas. He was a much older officer and always

195

took a fatherly interest in me. He was a peppery little man with bristling moustache and shoe-brush hair and once when I was relieving as Officer of the Day he took me to one the cells in the guardhouse where a man was raving in delirium tremens."

"That, young man," said he, "is what whisky will do." I looked at him in askance and perhaps a trifle astonished. He liked his toddy as well as the next. He bristled all over. "I mean bad whisky!" he amended. "Bad whisky—Bad whisky—very bad whisky."[5]

Although Hugh Johnson doesn't mention it in his book written in 1935, a young Lieutenant joined the First Cavalry in 1906 who later became a famous army general, his name, Jonathan M. Wainwright. Also Johnson is pointing out the officers who gained the recognition and fame from his unit, the First Cavalry at Fort Clark. Fort Clark never has received much recognition for the number of officers who moved to the top ranks. Many had their careers laced and interlaced with duty at Fort Clark.

Hugh S. Johnson attended West Point in the class of 1903. He was a classmate with Douglas MacArthur. June 1906 he graduated as Second Lieutenant. He was assigned to the First Cavalry Regiment which in 1903 was garrisoned at Fort Clark, Texas. His record states he was assigned to Fort Clark from 1903 to April 1906 prior to his transfer from Fort Clark, San Francisco had its great earthquake and fire. He was rushed to San Francisco as Quartermaster of Refugees in the Relief Camp at Camp Presidio, May 5–June 5, 1906. June 6 he was changed over as Quartermaster with the San Francisco Relief Corporation. He maintained this position until September 5, 1906. After the San Francisco Relief assignment he returned to Fort Clark until November 26, 1907. The First Cavalry Regiment then returned to the Philippines, this time to Camp Stotsenburg.

To prevent this biographical sketch from being too long, the military career will entail only a few of the highlights of an interesting career. His civilian career which followed has many interesting highlights. There is one aspect he is most noted for by the people who lived during that time.

While enroute to the Philippines, Johnson was ordered by the Treasury Department to oversee the delivery of five million dollars in nickels and dimes. Upon return to United States the First Cavalry Regiment was assigned to the Presidio of San Francisco. Johnson's squadron in the summer was detailed to guard National Parks—Yosemite and Sequoia. The biggest task was fighting forest fires. Later he was involved with General Pershing in chasing Pancho Villa.

"The most engaging personality of my Mexican service was my tent-mate, "Georgie" Patton. He came from a distinguished Virginia family. His father used to own Catalina Island. He went to V.M.I. before he came to West Point and what cadets call "tin-soldier antecedents" do not help a plebe at all. But when the yearlings asked Georgie what he was going to be, he said, 'First, Adjutant of the Cadet Corps and then Chief of Staff of the Army, sir."

"He had an antique idea that to be a good cavalryman, an officer should be expert in swordsmanship, pistol shooting, swimming, walking, and horsemanship, and he proceeded to make himself so. He used to sit in his tent by the hour practicing "trigger-pull" with either hand on a pistol fitted with a spring and a rod which would dart out at a swinging pith ball at which he aimed."

"We used to call Georgie a Sears-Roebuck cowboy, because he wore a pistol cartridge belt low about his hips with two pearl (ivory) handled forty-five revolvers in holsters, one on each groin—he never used an automatic pistol."[6]

Johnson was transferred from Pershing's staff as a Judge Advocate to be the Assistant to the Law Officer of the Bureau of Insular Affairs. He was in charge of civil litigations arising from U.S. Island possessions. Since this was 1916 and relations between the United States and Germany were growing steadily more strained. General Crowder at the War Department required several officers to study the history of the various attempts at conscription in this country and in England. Especially during the Civil War on both the Confederate and the Federal sides. The President came to the War Department and wanted a bill drawn to organize a large army. Johnson was assigned to write the sections dealing with raising the army. The draft was successful and Johnson was one of the authors. This WWI Conscription Bill incidentally laid the foundation for draft that was utilized in WWII.

In 1918, President Woodrow Wilson appointed Hugh Johnson as the War Department representative on the War Industries Board with rank of Brigadier General. Johnson was thirty-five years old, 15 years in officer's status. Prior year, a first lieutenant (acting captain's rank), suddenly he was elevated to a Brigadier General.

In spite of the plush job assignments and success in his undertakings, he was a soldier. He wanted to get to the front and fight. Through his previous connections with General Pershing, now commanding American Expedition Forces, he was transferred to command the 15th army brigade. However, the war ended before he and his unit were able to serve. This with other factors convinced General Johnson to resign from the army in 1919. He then became the Assistant General Manager to Moline Plow Company and worked in an industry until 1932. Next he found himself involved in the Franklin Roosevelt's election campaign.

With the election won, Franklin Roosevelt's New Deal was to bring recovery to the United States. A product of the New Deal was National Recovery Administration (NRA) which was greatest social and economic experiment of its time or perhaps our age. To head the NRA as administrator the President named General Hugh S. Johnson. At this job he gained national recognition. Many people at the time questioned why an army general was the administrator. The administration of NRA incorporated so many battles only a soldier could have handled it.

=====

1. Hugh S. Johnson, *The Blue Eagle From Egg To Earth*, Doubleday, Doran & Company, Inc., Garden City, 1935, p. 30.

2. *Ibid*, pp. 31, 32.

3. Henry S. Kilbroune accepted appointment as Assistant Surgeon June 26, 1875. Promoted Captain, Assistant Surgeon, 1880. Assigned to Fort Clark, May 8, 1893, as Captain and assigned as Assistant Post Surgeon. October 26–November 10, 1893, as-

signed duty at Fort Bliss, Texas. Returned to Ft. Clark as Assistant Post Surgeon. March 1894 promoted to Major and made Post Surgeon of Ft. Clark. Sept. 10 to Oct. 6, 1894, on practice march with 3rd Cavalry. Oct. 6, 1894 to April 2, 1896, Post Surgeon, Ft. Clark. April 2-16, 1896, on practice march with 23rd Infantry. May 6, 1897, transferred to Madison Barracks, N.Y. Retired August 1904. (U.S. Post Returns, NA, MC 617, Roll 217, Registers of the Army of U.S., January 1894, 1905.)

4. Colonel Martin B. Hughes, Cadet Military Academy, July 1, 1865, 2 Lt. 9th Cav. 1869, (At Ft. Clark April 1872–March 1873), 1st Lt. May 1873 9th Cav. 1st Lt.-Maj., Lt. Col. 10th Cav. 1901, Col. 1st Cav. 1903, Retired 1906 disability in line of duty. Geo.W. Cullem's Biographical Register of Officers and Graduates U.S. Military Academy, Seeman & Peters, Saginaw, Supplement, Volume 5, 1920. 2309.

5. Hugh S. Johnson, *The Blue Eagle From Egg to Earth*, p. 33.

6. *Ibid*, pp. 67 & 68.

General of the Army George C. Marshall

In the 92 years of active service in U.S. Army the post Fort Clark, Texas, had many of the important military men pass through its gates. Probably from his record of accomplishments General George C. Marshall tops all of them. From Fort Clark's position it is great to claim the likeness of General Marshall but from his standpoint he probably wouldn't be as ready to claim Fort Clark. General Marshall is quoted about his duty at Fort Clark as, "the hardest service I ever had in the Army."[1]

George Marshall was born December 31, 1880, to George C. Marshall and Laura (Bradford) Marshall. He graduated from Virginia Military Institute in Lexington Virginia, in 1901. On February 11, 1902, soon after he received his commission in the army, Marshall married Elizabeth Carter Coles of Lexington, Virginia. His first duty with the army was with the 30th Infantry in the Philippine Islands, 1902-1903. His next duty was at Fort Reno, Oklahoma, 1903-1906, and it was during this period in his career that he was assigned the detached duty at Fort Clark. He drew several assignments of duty but by 1913 he had been selected as aide-de-camp to Major General Hunter Liggett. His ability in that post pegged him for another aide-de-camp assignment with Major General J. Franklin Bell, 1916-1917. World War I was now in progress, he was assigned assistant chief of staff, G-3 with American Expeditionary Force in France. This duty led him to be aide-de-camp to General Pershing in France and later in Washington, 1919-1924.

Although, Marshall later commanded several army posts he seemed to be assigned more frequently to the staff positions. In 1939 Marshall became the acting Chief of Staff then later that year he was named the Chief of Staff, the position he held until the end of World War II. While General of the Army, Marshall was named Special Representative of the President with rank of Ambassador to China. January 1947 Marshall was selected by President Truman to be Secretary of State. It was in this position that he devised the Marshall Plan to aid in revitalizing of war torn Europe. This endeavor he will probably be remembered most for in history. In 1949 he became the President of the American Red Cross but by 1950 President Truman had reappointed him in his cabinet, Secretary of Defense. September 1951 he retired from public life. In 1953 he received the Nobel Peace Prize for his initiation of the European Recovery Act and he died on October 16, 1959.[2]

Let's stop this great officer's career at the period of 1905, when he was a Lieutenant, in order to review the time "that was the hardest service he ever had in the Army." From Fort Reno Lt. Marshall was transferred on detached Service to the First Cavalry Regiment Headquarters, Fort Clark, Texas. The specific duty Lt. Marshall was to perform on this detached service was to map 2,000 square miles of territory and to survey an area between Comstock and Langtry, Texas. This was an area of desert and scrub with deep ravines and no water at all except for a small section near the Devils River. The Southern Pacific Railroad had found it difficult in 1881-1882 to build a railroad through this area. Due to the terrain the SPRR had to return in 1890 to change the route and its crossing for the Pecos River.

In order to perform this duty Lt. Marshall was given a team consisting of a 1st Cavalry sergeant, a driver, a packer, his assistant, and a cook, two horses, an escort wagon, a four-line mule team, and a pack train of twenty mules. He was told that the only place where he would get food and supplies in the area for men and animals was at Langtry. Langtry in 1905 was probably best noted as a watering stop for the train and Judge Roy Bean's "law west of the Pecos." Although Fort Clark had in the past had an outlying camp at Langtry it was closed April 31, 1891, and the Pecos High Bridge which became an outlying outpost of Fort Clark, much later, after the 1910 Mexican unrest started. So the population of the area Marshall was to map consisted mainly of railroad workmen, some hearty ranch men, and bars with their followers, a rough area as to people and terrain.

To conduct the extensive detached service from Fort Clark, Lt. Marshall placed a requisition with the Quartermaster requesting rations and forage be shipped to the train stops along the railroad between Comstock and Sanderson (probably Dryden). This way he and his team could come to the stops and replenish their supplies as needed. The requisition was still being passed from post to post between Texas and Oklahoma when Marshall and his men were in the middle of the Southwest desert and it was never executed. Luckily the Lt. took the precaution of getting vouchers for buying supplies and forage enroute.

This mapping expedition departed Fort Clark in July 1905 and had all the making of a vintage western film. His mule driver was Nat Cox of Brackettville, who was a veteran of the Indian Wars that had stood as a child at his father's, Nathan Cox, knee and watched him shoot at a Comanche raiding party trying to storm their cabin. Marshall's sergeant was a cavalryman with 20 years of service, overly proud of his luxurious drooping mustache and his capacity for bad liquor.

The midsummer heat was fierce by the time the team started out from Comstock. "The thermometer would go up to a hundred and thirty" Marshall recalled. The team followed the railroad to begin with as Marshall had to walk the track and count the sections of rail. That would give him an exact measurement which he needed as a base line. He got his distances otherwise from the odometer on the wheel of the wagon or from the time scale on the walking of his horse.

Forage was not too difficult to come by, but food was

another matter. The onions and potatoes that the group took with them were exhausted by the end of the first week. Thereafter, they had to subsist on canned bacon and other meats, and Marshall did badly on it. Lacking fresh vegetables, his digestion suffered, and he was soon in great pain from heartburn. He stated "I could barely drink without gasping. As I recall, I went in there weighing about a hundred sixty-five to one seventy, and I came out weighting a hundred thirty-two pounds."

But the lack of water was the greatest trial. The lieutenant made sure his animals were watered first and then carefully rationed the rest of the water among his men, but toward the end Marshall denied himself any liquids at all. Nat Cox, claiming he was used to desert conditions, volunteered to abstain with him in order to sustain the rest. Marshall and the old one (Cox was sixty) marched or rode the last fifty miles without any water and all but collapsed when they reached Langtry but were quickly revived by the hospitality of the citizenry.

Langtry, the old frontier town west of the Pecos, which had been named by its gun-toting Judge Roy Bean after a famous English beauty, Lillie Langtry, was a pretty wild town in 1905 and was prepared to give its visitors a hearty welcome, particularly if they had money. It so happened that there was mail awaiting the expedition in Langtry, and it included pay for the men. The sergeant, an old hand at paydays, promptly loaded up with liquor from the local store, found Langtry's principal bar and brothel, and moved in, threatening to shoot anyone who tried to interrupt him. He declared he was going to sit back and enjoy both drink and girls until such time as they, and his money, were used up. But if the girls were willing, the citizenry were not. They objected to having their main source of entertainment and relaxation requisitioned by the U.S. Army and demonstrated before the entrance to the saloon. Threatening to burn it down if the sergeant kept the padlocks on its doors. A panicky little town committee roused Marshall from his well-merited slumbers to demand that he resolve the situation before all hell broke loose. He was taken down the street to the place where the riotous townsfolk were demonstrating and he was interested to note that many of the protesters seemed to be wives and other respectable looking womenfolk. Marshall having listened to their complaint, went up to the door of the saloon, loudly demanded admittance, and he was allowed in by one the girls. The Lieutenant found his sergeant sleeping upstairs like a baby, a blissful smile on his face, with one handlebar of his rich mustachios missing (he and the girls had been playfully shaving each other) and no one was willing to wake him up since he still had his revolver belted around his longjohns. With his eyes averted from the girls, who were by no means bashful in welcoming this handsome young newcomer, the lieutenant took the sergeant in his arms, dunked him in a bathtub full of cold water, and then told the half-sobered and shaken veteran to share the place with the irate citizens. He readily agreed to do so, and Marshall went below to inform the crowd. But when the men swarmed inside, Marshall was not among them. He went back to his quarters and gave no sign whatsoever that he had been tempted to stay.

It was three months later that the small unit of men and mules eventually limped back into Fort Clark, Texas, where Marshall and his sergeant reported to the Officer of the Day. Marshall looked by that time more like an Indian scout than an officer of the United States Army. His face and arms had been burned black by the sun. His old campaign hat, which a mule had bitten the top out of, looked like a headgear for a scarecrow, and his uniform was in tatters. The Officer of the Day was so embarrassed by Marshall's appearance that he wouldn't look at him. He didn't think Marshall could be an officer and talked entirely to the old sergeant, despite of the fact that the noncom's facial adornment had not yet grown back in place.

But Marshall had a warmer reception when he reported with his findings to the chief army engineer, Southwest Division, who found his map the best one received and the only complete one. In the office of the commanding general in San Antonio he was welcomed back by the military secretary, Captain George Van Horn Moseley. Marshall was near exhaustion, he stated that he had a pretty hard time, as a result of the climate and a harsh terrain, but Moseley's sympathetic reception more than made up for it. It was through Moseley's recommendation that the commanding general issued an immediate order granting Lieutenant George C. Marshall four months' leave.

Marshall took the train at once for Virginia and a reunion with his beloved Lily. It was three and half years since their marriage and she was still the bride he barely knew.

Thirty-three years later the former captain who had been the Officer of the Day at Fort Clark when the then Lieutenant Marshall reported in was now General Malin Craig the newly appointed Chief of Staff of the Army. General Craig at this juncture in Marshall's military career was an added influence although General Craig may not have remembered the previous meeting but it was for sure Marshall hadn't forgot it.

Marshall had been recently promoted to Brigadier General at the time. General Craig had succeeded General Douglas MacArthur as Chief of Staff of the Army. This fact put a wholly different complexion on the face of Marshall's future. Craig was a Pershing man and, in marked contrast with his predecessor, was very much inclined to look with favor on any officer who had been with Black Jack at Chaumont. He strongly admired his old Commmander in Chief, would do anything to please him and was well aware that Marshall was one of his protégée's. On that basis alone he was determined to see that the new Brigadier General got preferment and so much the better that his record made it plain that he surely deserved.

=====

1. Leonard Mosley, *Marshall, Hero of Our Times*, New York, Hearst Books, 1982, pp. 29-33.

2. Clarence E. Wunderlin, Jr. (ed.), *A Chronology, George Catlett Marshall*, Lexington, George C. Marshall Foundation, 1986, pp. 2-4.

Fort Clark's Chinese 1919

In 1979 Colonel Paul Mattee, U.S. Army retired, from Melbourne, Florida, responded to Don Swanson's inquiry about duty at Fort Clark with an audio tape. He entitled his tape "Honeymoon on the Mexico Border" as he explained that he had "gone over the head" of his commanding officer at Fort Myers to get furlough at end of World War I to get married. While on furlough he received orders reassigning him or as he put it, "shanghaied" to Fort Clark. Now he was not to specific on the date, 1919 or 1920, but he was assigned the duty as Fort Clark Post Exchange Officer.

The important aspect of this is that in accepting the responsibility for the duty he was required to sign all custody cards for the equipment held by the former Post Exchange Officer. Among these cards were two, each for a Chinaman as property of the Post Exchange. Poor Colonel Mattee spend 30 years in the army never understanding why he had accepted custody of two men the same as other equipment.

Well, I have an odd story for you and the worse part is it is true and historic. When General John J. Pershing and the Punitive Expedition invaded Chihuahua, March 1916, in pursuit of Pancho Villa they learned there were Chinese in Mexico besides the Mexicans. Originally, there were some 30,000 Chinese in Mexico, mostly imported like in United

States, to build the Mexican National Railroad. Seems like they were less accepted in Mexico than in the U.S.

As an example, in 1911 in Torre'on 303 were massacred. Pershing and his army found they had a strong following and it was only Chinese who were anxious to do anything for the "yankee" dollar. Soon the Provost Marshal found himself controlling the Chinese population and their business at the main camp in Colonia Dublan area and on the fringes of the little stations along the trail to Columbus, New Mexico. The Provost Marshal not only controlled the kind and location of the business but he also fixed the prices. Stores, restaurants, and laundries broke the miseries for the soldiers of the Mexican boredom, dust, and army chow.

When the Punitive Expedition came to an end in 1917, the Chinese posed a special problem. The entry of the Chinese into the U.S. was forbidden by Immigration Laws, but common decency and humanity demanded that they not be left to the mercies of the Mexicans.

General Funston (General in charge of Army) ordered General Pershing to bring his 527 followers to U.S. regardless of the exclusion law while he endeavored to get the Immigration Service to set aside the law. Permission was finally granted by the Immigration Service provided they became wards of the Army and not become public charges.

In June 1917 the army moved most of the Chinese to Fort Sam Houston in San Antonio and others were assigned to various other forts in Texas. Ft. Clark had at least two: Bock Lin and Chu Lee. Bock Lin worked in the Post Exchange Restaurant. Chu Lee did tailoring dry cleaning in Post Exchange. In 1927 Fort Clark published a booklet on *History of Fort Clark and Fifth Cavalry* by Chaplain Bateman. Two of the supporting advertisements were inviting the soldiers to visit Bock Lin's PX Restaurant and Lee's tailor shop. Chu Lee worked at the PX Laundry.

All the Chinese remained wards of the army until 1921, when a special act of Congress, passed at the urging of General Pershing, granted the right of residence to 365 Chinamen who had been wards or as Colonel Matte thought, equipment in the army.

Many of Chinese descendants in San Antonio are traceable to this incident and what became of those two from Fort Clark is unknown.

=====

Handy, Mary Olivia, *History of Fort Sam Houston*, San Antonio, The Naylor Co., 1951, p. 86.

Rhoads, Edward J. M., "Chinese in Texas," *Southwest Historical Quarterly*, Vol. LXXXI, July 1977, pp. 1-2.

Cubbison, Maj. Gen., *Foreign Relations*, 1917, pp. 1088-1092.

Clendenen, Clarence, *Blood on the Border, The U.S. Army & The Mexican Irregulars*, London, The Macmillan Co., 1969, pp. 331-339.

I.G. Inspection 1928

Inspector General, Colonel H. C. Whitehead, reported his inspection of Fort Clark, January 14, 1928. "Fort Clark had been practically abandoned prior to 1912 when certain Mexican difficulties caused its reoccupation. The permanent stone buildings of this post were built during a period extending from 1842 to 1888. The material is native limestone procured from quarries on the reservation (?) and evidently put together by soldier labor or unskilled native mechanics(?). The masonry is of very poor quality, the stone has softened and is crumbling, the mortar and plaster has lost its life. A soft dust and sand is constantly falling. Due to this deterioration the foundations, which are simply laid on the rock formations are insecure. The walls are from 2 to 3 feet thick.

They show the effect of uneven settling. Cracks have been filled in and in most instances an examination shows them to be bulging. This particularly evident in the two story barracks buildings (3) which are full of old cracks. The walls are tied together with heavy iron rods running clear through the buildings. All timber work is combination of hand hewn and modern 6 by 12 patchwork. Some buildings have been provided with ceilings in relatively modern days. In general, the repair work must be done so to speak "long hand." No repair to any buildings can be done any other way than by patch work. The woodwork is full of dry rot so that nails cannot be driven with security into any of old beams. Hence the appearance of patchiness, and instability of floors and roof timbers. It will be necessary to entirely rebuild all the barracks to make them serviceable.

In early 1930s the three (3) two story barracks were torn down although the two wings (mess hall and supply section) of each were retained. The barracks were rebuilt and limestone veneered with rock quarried on the Nueces River near Uvalde. A trooper reported that the rock was hauled in one of the hard rubber tire trucks (Packard or Reo) from that quarry to Fort Clark and the primary masonry work was completed by a sergeant who later committed suicide. In 1933 the hospital (built in 1856) was torn down. It had been replaced by the hospital built in 1873-1874 (Adult Center). The old Hospital had been used in latter years for the 5th Cavalry Band. The two story barracks (Seminole Hall) was also built during this period.

Animal Sense Prevails Trooper's Story 1936

There was a period in 1936 when the Fifth Cavalry was furnishing horse troopers to supplement the Del Rio Custom Headquarters. The four troopers were primarily utilized to make mounted patrols on the U.S. side of the Rio Grande to apprehend smugglers.

On days when the trooper weren't patrolling, they would be at the check station supposedly to assist the duty custom inspectors. However, the troopers felt they were there more to observe the inspectors so they could be impressed with their duties.

One of the troopers who was a better observer and more eager in trying to apprehend smugglers watched with great interest all that transpired at the check station.

He became aware that each morning there came an elderly Mexican man leading a donkey with a homemade pack saddle on it. When the trooper asked the inspector about the old Mexican he was told that he was Pedro. He comes each morning, seven days a week, and goes to Del Rio to pick up whatever junk he can find and brings it back to Acuna. He is very poor and probably the most harmless of the Mexicans who pass through this station.

Now the trooper from his observations wasn't as assured of the harmlessness of old Pedro. The next time this trooper was on duty at the check station he was on the alert for old Pedro's entrance into the U.S.

As Pedro meandered down the road to the station the trooper was watching the donkey all the way. As Pedro approached the Inspector at the station he received the usual, "Buena's Dias" and the usual wave to pass on by. The trooper said to the inspector, "Stop that man." After years of this routine, the inspector felt his authority and ability was being questioned, and he demanded to know why he should. The trooper wasn't sure why but he was assured the donkey had some abnormal reactions. So he replied, "I am suspicious of that donkey and want to inspect him." The inspector accommodated him and stopped Pedro. The trooper purposely went to the donkey's head. Starting like he was giving the animal and its equipment a thorough inspection. However, his interest was really centered on the tail of the animal and when he reached to rear of the animal, the trooper jerked the tail as high as he could. Automatically a leather pouch was extracted from the donkey's anus. The pouch was found to contain three fairly large diamonds. Now old Pedro's true character was revealed and his complete innocence was reversed. The haughty inspector was embarrassed by a horse trooper who knew animals better than the inspector.

Pedro had been making the daily excursions for several years and might still be going strong had he trained his donkey not to be twitching his tail when there were no flies around.

=====

Trooper's Tale revealed at 1988 Trooper's Reunion, Ft. Clark.

General Quinones 1938

General of the Brigade, Jesus Jaime Quinones was stationed in Piedras Negras, Coahuila, Mexico, in 1938. He was a frequent visitor to Fort Clark earlier and later after it became Fort Clark Springs.

General Quinones had long been appreciative of fine horses and during the 1920s, early 1930s, he became the Captain of the Mexican Army's Polo Team. He was one of the finest players in all of Mexico and the American Southwest. There are families around Marfa who still remember the General for decades before when he came from Ojinaga with a fine string of polo ponies and put on a spectacular performance on the polo field at Fort D. A. Russel (formerly Camp Marfa).

There are also those of Kinney County who remember when the General's polo team came from Piedras Negras to compete at Fort Clark with 5th Cavalry Regiment's team. General Quinones was a friend of Brigadier Generals Ben Lear, Kenton Joyce, and Jonathan M. Wainwright, who each in succession commanded the Post of Fort Clark and 1st Cavalry Brigade. He also was a friend of Colonels (later Generals) Richardson and Patton who were commanders of the Fifth Cavalry Regiment when it was stationed at Fort Clark.

In 1938 during an after-match gathering at the Officers Club at Fort Clark, General Quinones was asked by General

Joyce to relate an incident many years previous that he had told Joyce regarding a Lieutenant in the Pershing's Punitive Expedition.

Quinones' story went back to June 16, 1916 after the then Captain Quinones had switched to the Mexico (Carranista) Army. At that time there existed a crisis between the United States and Pancho Villa. Captain Quinones was then in his early twenties, and was stationed with a small garrison (about 100 soldiers) some miles east of the state capitol of Chihuahua at San Antonio Arenales. San Antonio Arenales was hardly more than a railroad station in 1916 and the station itself was merely a converted railroad box car.

One night Colonel Carlos Carranza, nephew of the First Chief Venustiano Carranza, brought the word to Captain Quinones by order of his uncle, the Americans were not to advance any further south than the railroad. The Captain deployed his men and kept a constant vigil for the Americans along the railroad.

During this hot day of June 16, 1916 an American Cavalry column of over 100 men, Negro troopers with white officers, all uniformed and well equipped with weapons, ammunition and supplies came riding in the vicinity of San Antonio Arnales with the following of a huge dust cloud. Captain Quinones accompanied by two of his men, rode out from his company to meet the approaching American column. The American commander, a lieutenant, advanced from his company to meet the Mexican officer with an interpreter.

"Who are you?" the young American lieutenant bluntly asked. "Captain of the Mexican Army," he was told. "And what do you want?" the Lieutenant demanded through his interpreter. Captain Quinones told the Lieutenant that orders were issued to prevent the Americans from advancing any further south. The American officer replied that they were merely heading to a nearby ranch where they hoped to buy food and horses. He was told by Captain Quinones a second time not to cross the railroad line, and to emphasize the point, the captain added, they had to kill all of the soldiers in the Mexican garrison before they could indeed proceed south.

The Lieutenant listened to the translation and eyed the

three Mexicans. The Lieutenant had a square cut face and pale eyes under the brim of his campaign hat. He had the appearance of an intelligent man and he mused for a moment over this frank reply. The American Expeditionary Force had orders to avoid gunfire, the Lieutenant seemed satisfied to comply with the order, and they parted company with a wave of the hand and an "hasta luego." The American column turned north and returned in the direction from which they came.

After General Quinones finished the story at the Officer's Club, a Colonel arose and exclaimed "that is just how it happened" and he told the surprised storyteller that he was that young Lieutenant who Quinones had confronted. The Colonel was none other than George S. Patton, Jr., the two men reminisced about the tense meeting the summer of 1916. Nor did Patton explain he had previously raised the ire of General Pershing by killing bandits and at that time was treading cautiously to prevent any other mistakes.

Shortly after this meeting at Fort Clark Colonel Patton received orders to command Fort Meyers, Virginia, and to relieve Brigadier General Jonathan Wainwright who had orders to Fort Clark to command the post and 1st Cavalry Brigade. Colonel Patton wrote on December 2, 1938, to General of Brigade, Jesus Jaime Quinones, Piedras Negras, Coahuila, Mexico.

"I regret from the bottom of my heart that circumstances are such that I cannot call on you in person but can only express gratitude by the written word. I must also take this occasion to bid you farewell. It is a source of profound sorrow to me to leave here and so deprive myself of seeing more of you. With renewed expression of thanks and esteem,

I am, my dear General your devoted admirer."
George S. Patton, Jr.
Colonel, U.S. Army

=====

James Hyndman, "James Secrets: Memoirs of a Revolutionary Soldier," *Southwestern Historical Quarterly*, Volume XI, 1973, No. 1, 57-60.

Martin Blumenson, The Patton Papers, p. 931.

Recollections of an Airman Stationed on a Horse Soldier's Installation, 1939

My first, and only, contact with General Jonathan Wainwright happened in Dryden, Texas in the summer of 1938 (1939?). I had recently been transferred from Fort Sill, Oklahoma to the Army Airfield just west of the town of Dryden to assume duty as a Weather Observer. One day in mid-summer while I was preparing a weather report with my back to the front door of our building I heard a voice ask if he could have a cold soft drink from our ice box. My response was that he could if he had a nickel. When the same voice said: "Let me have a nickel Stinky" I turned to see who had been insulted with such a name. Standing before me was one of the tallest and thinnest persons I had ever seen with a shorter companion. They were both in military uniforms and when I caught sight of the star of brigadier general on the tall one's collar, I immediately froze to attention. General Wainwright told me to relax that they had just stopped to quench their thirst. I learned later the other officer was his Aide by the name of Pugh (Capt. Johnny Pugh—later Maj. Gen.) ... thus deriving the moniker of "Stinky." Little did I know that in less than one year later I would be performing duty on the same installation with these two men.

On reporting to the Dryden Airfield I was accompanied by my wife who at that time was about four months into her confinement for the birth of our first child. Since Dryden proper was very small there was no housing available in the town, so we purchased a "home-made trailer about 8'x12' which was parked across the runway from the other installations. After the delivery of our first child (a daughter) at the Fort Sam Houston Station hospital (now Brooke Army Medical Center) we returned to Dryden determined to make the best of the inadequate housing we had. When our baby was about six weeks old, my Commanding Officer from Barksdale Field, Louisiana transferred me to Fort Clark, Texas.

Our first reaction in reporting to Fort Clark was that we had entered paradise since we had graduated from a small trailer to a fully furnished two bedroom house. We arrived to take charge of the Weather Station and Airport in March 1939 (1940?). The Airfield as you know was situated a few miles south of the Main Post and because of this isolation two sets of quarters were provided for the two men assigned to report weather conditions, keep the landing field in order and refuel any visiting aircraft. The other set of quarters was occupied by PFC. Oren B. Jolley and his wife, Katherine, who had formerly worked as the secretary to the Kinney County Judge.

My working partner and myself would alternate days preparing weather reports on conditions of Fort Clark from 8 A.M. through 5 P.M. five days each week (Saturday and Sunday excluded). I well remember that during the coming winter when I sent out a report of snow at Fort Clark, the Weather Bureau called back for confirmation. Periodically we would take turns in taking the tractor drawn mower and cut the high weeds from the landing strip during the summer. Our most demanding task came about when a flight of small aircraft would fly in from Kelly or Randolph for refueling. At that time the trainers (PT-13's) could only fly about 150 miles without refueling. Since there were no starting devices on these planes as we know them today, we had to hand crank the so called "energizer" near the engine until it gained enough speed for the pilot to start his aircraft. After a few of these crankings, our arms would become leaden and our backs would begin to ache ... I can still feel the pain in my mind.

At the time we were stationed at Fort Clark, General Wainwright was the Commanding Officer of the 12th (1st) Cavalry Brigade. Major Richard W. Carter signed my discharge as the Post Commander and he was also the Acting Finance Officer. Since the two of us at the Airfield were enlisted men, the officer-in-charge to see we performed our assigned duties was Captain Leif Neprud (CAC) and the Post Quartermaster. Our weather reports were sent out through the Signal Office, the NCOIC was Staff Sergeant Parker. I do not recall many persons by name from that period of time except that there was a First Sergeant Bailey in C Troop.

Our working relationship with the Cavalry Troops on the Post was amicable enough although there may have been a twinge of jealousy on the part of the younger Troopers since I was wearing the stripes of a Corporal and had only four years active duty. Plus the fact we were allowed to be married and had fine quarters furnished by the government. There was one event that I recall where friction developed from the actions of a visiting aviator. As we sat outside the Weather Office adjacent to the hanger some of the officers from the Post rode by on their way to play polo. The visiting aviator took exception that none of them would return his salute, so when he got ready to leave he taxied his airplane down to the polo field at the end of the runway and ran his engine full force, blowing up a dense dust storm until the polo game had to be suspended for several minutes.

Duty for us at the airfield was pretty routine. Several times during the year the 5th Cavalry Troops would come out on horse back to use the airfield for training purposes. This was the only cleared place on the Post large enough to conduct their maneuvers. I remember that on a few occasions the entire Regiment would come out and do a Parade using the entire Airfield. We were greatly impressed by the colorful men on horse back wheeling and charging and the band playing. During some of the training time on the Airfield some of the Drill Sergeants would forget the proximity of the two ladies in the nearby quarters and would favor their orders with some "basic Anglo-Saxon" expletives.

Being a separate unit from the Main Post, we were not required to perform the menial task of C.O. (K.P.?) or guard duty, etc. I did however have to take my turn as Sergeant of the Guard and stay at the Old Guard House while the Regiment was on maneuvers at Balmorhea, Texas. The secluded areas surrounding the Airfield became a favorite spot at night for "visiting" automobiles during the time the troops were away ... probably just stargazing! A lot of our free time was just walking along the beautiful banks of the creek flowing from Los Moras Springs. We enjoyed the cool water and the nut harvest from the pecan trees during the fall. We did attend the movie theater on the Post, but were cautioned not to let our small daughter cry during the showing of the film.

I found that the quarters we occupied at the Airfield are both gone. The large gasoline storage tank that was located on the north side of the hanger is missing as well as the hanger doors. However, the old Weather Station just south of the hanger is still standing but long out of operation. In my mind I can still see the old weather instruments and the adjacent instrument shelter that we used more than 50 years ago. If I "dream" hard enough, I might even hear the hoof beats of the 5th Cavalry Troopers on horse back.

=====

Major Ralph C. Skinner, 840 Vindicator Drive, #306, Colorado Springs, Co.

Officer Quarters Assignment Fort Clark, Texas

10 November 1941
112TH CAVALRY GARRISONED*

Capt. Ira J. Berk	Quarters 13
1st Lt. George A. Burgess	" 16
1st Lt. John G. Carter	" 1-F
Capt. Forrest M. Cowman	" 39-6
Capt. Jack Dews	" 1-C
Lt. Col. John Dunlap (112th Executive Officer)	" 23
Capt. David Fisher	" 9
Maj. Austin Getz (Post Veterinarian)	" 12
Capt. Clyde E. Grant	" 1-D
Capt. William M. Hill	" 39-21
Capt. Manley E. Hood	" 14
Capt. Sam L. Hunnicut	" 8
Maj. Robert Hurt	" 39
B. Gen. H. H. Johnson (C.O. 112th)	" 24
Capt. Rupert H. Johnson	" 27
Capt. Harold H. Jones	" 39-1
1st Lt. Jack King	" 7

2nd Lt. Tom King	"	1-
Lt. Col. Waldo B. Lasater	"	17
1st Lt. Max T. Leyendecker	"	18
2nd Sam L. Martin	"	39-15
Capt. George S. Metcalfe	"	22
1st Lt. John L. Minter	"	25
Capt. D. M. McMains	"	11
1st Lt. F. B. Robinson	"	39-16
Maj. J. W. Savage	"	20
1st Lt. W. R. Shaw	"	3
2nd Lt. Edward Shroeder	"	39-4
Maj. Henry M. Shue	"	15
Maj. B. L. Smith (Chaplain)	"	39
1st J. D. Stallings	"	1-E
1st Robert W. Swinney	"	19
1st Lt. Quentin Tipton	"	2
1st Lt. Hugh B. Thaxton	"	39-13
Lt. Col. John P. Wheeler (Post Commander)	"	29
Maj. Charles R. Williams	"	1-A
2nd Lt. Edward Wright, Jr.	"	39-14

*Officers assigned quarters on main post

Maj. Gen. William C. Chase
1942

After World War II commenced, Colonel Chase was assigned to Maj. Gen. Holland (Howling Mad) Smith, U.S. Marines, Amphibious Force, Atlantic Fleet. The Amphibious Force was in training at Quantico, Virginia, for a expedition to Martinique, French West Indies, to capture a small French Fleet with a large amount of gold which had escaped from France when the Nazis had captured France.

While training at Quantico with the marines, Colonel Chase learned that Colonel O'Brien of 113th Cavalry at Camp Bowie was on the selection list for Brigadier General. Colonel Chase called General Walter Krueger, San Antonio, to inquire about the replacement for Brig. Gen. O'Brien. Gen. Krueger said, "Chase, get on the first plane and come, you have the regiment." Colonel Chase went to General Smith and told him that he had been assigned to command a regiment at Fort Clark, Texas and requested his permission. General Smith said, "Go ahead, good luck to you. Every colonel should command a regiment."

"The 113th Cavalry was a topnotch National Guard regiment from Iowa, and when I assumed command in February 1942, it was stationed at Fort Clark, Brackettville, Texas. It was a horse-mechanized regiment—one squadron mounted on horses and one squadron equipped with armored scout cars, light tanks, and motorcycles. This was a little bit of everything and somewhat of a compromise between the old horses) and the new (tanks). To complicate the whole business there were 40 large horse trailers to carry the horses on long marches. It was a weird looking outfit on the road. The regiment was in fine shape with high morale, with very high class enlisted and commissioned personnel.

The mission of this outfit on the border was to guard the Southern Pacific Railroad from Uvalde to Spofford, Texas, both inclusive. The most important part of this was the high bridge (R.R.) over the Pecos River where all trains stopped while the 113th men shook them down to get rid of bums and hobos who were aboard. An amazing number of the worst looking thugs imaginable were taken from each freight train. I doubt if there was one genuine Nazi saboteur among them, but at any rate, it assured us of an uninterrupted southern railroad route from east to west. The 113th remained at Fort Clark only a month or so and then marched via Del Rio and San Angelo to Camp Bowie in Brownwood where it had been stationed previously."

"In late March 1943, I received orders from the Pentagon detailing me to the 1st Cavalry Division as a brigade commander, as I had won my first star. I was following my old friend Gen. J. M. (Skinny) Wainwright in my first command as a general officer but Skinny by this time had been a prisoner of war for a year or so after having to go through the humiliation of surrender to the Japs on Corregidor in May 1942. I reported to Fort Bliss, Texas, where I found the First (Cavalry) Division had been alerted for duty under General MacArthur in the Southwest Pacific."

In June 1943 the First Division went to Australia. Just before Christmas 1944 the Division had its final parade Brisbane prior to the northern advance on New Guinea. The First Division went through the Admiralty Island Campaign, the Leyte Campaign, the Luzon Campaign, and on to Tokyo. Chase was promoted to Lt. Gen. in the Philippines and took command of 38th Infantry Division. General Chase after WW II served in Germany and later in Formosa prior to retiring in 1955.

=====

For more information see *Front Line General, The Commands of William C. Chase, An Autobiography*, Houston, Pacesetter Press, 1975.

1917-1919 4th Division, France , World War I
1920-1921 16th Cavalry Regiment, lower Rio Grande Valley
1921-1925 Michigan State College teaching R.O.T.C.
1926-1928 Cavalry School, Infantry School, Command & General Staff School
1927-1929 14th Cavalry Regiment, Fort Sheridan, Illinois
1931-1934 26th Cavalry Regiment (Philippine Scouts), Ft. Strotsenberg, Philippine Islands.
1934-1935 Army War College, Washington, D.C.
1935-1938 Instructor, Tactics, Cavalry School, Ft. Riley, Kansas.
1938-1940 Instructor, Tactics, Command & General School, Ft. Leavenworth, Kansas

Pecos River Viaduct
(Old Pecos River RR High Bridge)

Perhaps you have read the story previously written concerning the German spy plane. This story's main theme is the same subject and area that story was centered on. The old Southern Pacific Railroad Bridge was an outstanding historical subject. The old troopers who spent a good deal of time guarding it were more likely to consider their story as a more important story than other stories that have been written about it.

The bridge was built in the 1890s and the urgency of wartime transportation in WWII caused it to be replaced. To keep its history we will repeat some of the facts concerning it that was described in the previous story.

Approximately ten years after the Southern Pacific Railroad expended so much money, time, and effort to cross the Pecos River (1883) by building tunnels on both sides of the river such that they could utilized a short span bridge, later they were faced with abandonment of that project. The Southern Pacific Railroad claimed the cost, the grade and danger from falling rocks made them seek a different method of crossing the Pecos River. After a unique engineering feat for that day and time they later constructed what became known as the "Pecos River Viaduct."

The Pecos Viaduct was the highest railroad bridge ever

built in this country in the 1890s. There was nothing to rival its length of 2,180 feet at a height of 325 feet above low water anywhere in the U.S. (1893).

Almost from the day it was built it became an important military strategic spot and it fell to Fort Clarks' command to protect this bridge. To the military and the soldiers it became the "Pecos River High Bridge." As early as the Mexican civil wars it fell Fort Clark's lot (1910, 1912, 1914, 1917) to ensure the safety of this high precarious steel span.

It became more important when the Punitive Expedition was in progress, after all think what it would have been like if Pancho Villa had immobilized the transcontinental rail shipments. It seems as through out Mexico's earlier history there was a series of revolutions and then there was the concern about Mexico aligning with Germany in World War I. These events caused a Mexican border patrol to be established, always resulting in the guarding of the illustrious Pecos High Bridge. Mexico internal unrest continued on after WWI and these periods (1920, 1923-1924, and 1927) made the Pecos High Bridge an outpost of Fort Clark.

Then along came World War II and like its predecessor World War I, Mexico favored the axis powers (Germany) over the allies at least until June 2, 1942, when Mexico decided to side with the allies, and declared war. Perhaps there is a history lesson here for the United States but it meant a great deal more for Fort Clark as they prolonged its active duty beyond the Indian Wars period.

Without all these concerns for military protection and enforcement of the neutrality laws, Fort Clark would have been closed in 1912 instead of 1945. Not only did Fort Clark remain open but Congress throughout this period was encouraged to sweeten the appropriations. Each time as the public was concerned for protection and the Southern Pacific Railroad's awareness arose for the security of the Pecos High Bridge. Fort Clark took great care of the bridge like a mother hen with her nest egg.

I think all the early troopers who were stationed at the Pecos High Bridge remember it in awe and also had a least one good tale to tell about his experiences there. One of the best written accounts was written by Colonel Alonzo Gray in the *Brief Memoirs of Colonel Alonzo Gray*, chapter 12. "In August 1916, I was promoted to Colonel and left in command of Fort McIntosh (Laredo). In October 1917, I was assigned to the 6th Cavalry Regiment and joined it at Marfa, Texas. The regiment was under orders to march to San Antonio and prepare for service in France (WWI). The regiment—1600 men and 1600 horses—left Marfa on October 18, 1917, and arrived at San Antonio, Texas, on November 10th, having marched a distance of 440 miles. The march was very interesting and with many problems to be solved, the greatest of which was crossing the Pecos Canyon.

"We camped at Shumla, four miles west of the canyon, on the Southern Pacific Railway. After looking over the situation, the decision was to run the wagons across the railroad bridge, the draft animals should all go to the Bullis's Ford, 6 miles below. On reaching the west end of the bridge, the draft animals were unhitched and each troop dismounted twenty men, who reported to the Regimental Quartermaster. All trains stopped before crossing the bridge. The plan was timed so as to run the wagons by hand across, between trains. The bridge was 1,000 feet long and 340 feet above the river. The ties were six inches apart and planking about three feet wide, ran lengthwise between the rails. A freight train appeared just as the last wagon was leaving the bridge.

During the previous night, a severe windstorm arose, blowing down tents and filling the air with dust. Breakfast was mostly "slum" highly seasoned with sand. I had lost my glasses and sent my orderly back to look for them. He found them but, instead of catching up with the horse column, he led his horse across the railroad bridge, behind the last wagon and the dismounted men. The command having completed its crossing, proceeded to its camp, four miles further east" (probably painted cave stop on the railroad).

Undoubtedly, the Pecos River Railroad Bridge was a marvelous feat of engineering in its day. However, it is almost as marvelous today to obtain the correct measurements of the span. You will note than in the above dimensions they each vary and to add more confusion to the length and height of the span we will add this quote from a newspaper article at the commencement of construction." The masonry work of the bridge over the Pecos river, being built by the Southern Pacific is now underway. L. R. Marston of Cleburg is in charge of operations for the contractors, Richer, Lee and Company. The bridge will be the third highest in the world. It will be 334 feet high and 1,900 feet long, with twenty-four piers of masonry. This bridge is being built for the railroad company across the Pecos River, 300(?) miles west from San Antonio. The banks of the river are solid rock and 200 feet perpendicular. Everything has to be lowered down by derricks. The employees have to climb down on ropes to get to their work. At present there are 110 men at work, and all who apply for work are given a trial. The masonry work of this bridge will probably be completed by the first of August next (1891). Prior to this we were led to believe all the variations in the dimensions were natural "trooper tales."

=====

1. Dan Bus, "Original Pecos High Bridge Scraped Clouds," Del Rio Guide, October 1983.

2. Kenneth Baxter Ragsdale, Wings Over the Mexican Border, p. 3

3. Southwestern Historical Quarterly, January 1992, Vol. XCV, No. 3 pp. 388-389.

4. Colonel Alonzo Gray, "Brief Memoirs of Colonel Alonzo Gray" Crossed Sabers Cavalry Journal, Ft. Riley, U.S. Cavalry Association, p. 8.

5. Brackettville, Brackett News, May 23, 1891.

6. Alonzo Gray wrote about his military career which was published as "Recollections of Col. Alonzo Gray." This has been quoted by other authors. In January of 1898, then Lieutenant Alonzo Gray's troop (Company H, 5th Cav.) was ordered from Ft. Ringold (Rio Grande City) to Fort Clark. His family traveled in a buckboard, while he marched (mounted) with the troop. His bed springs were lashed to the tailgate of a wagon and at night laid on the ground inside a conical walled tent. The trip, 300 miles of it was made with such comfort and such pleasant weather that it became an outing rather than a march. The troop arrived at Ft. Clark and were escorted into the post by the 23rd Infantry Band playing, "There'll be

a hot time in the old town tonight." Lt. Gray noted there was little to say about Ft. Clark, at that time, because of the blowing up of the Maine (battleship) which was the start of the Spanish-American War. The 23rd Infantry left first for the Philippines with a number of Brackettville men as volunteer soldiers. On May 14, 1898, Companies H & I of 5th Cavalry departed for New Orleans and Philippines. Chaplain Potter became the ranking officer (one of very few) and thereby inherited the command of the fort.

    Macly P. Burg, "Service on The Vanishing Frontier 1887-1898" Military History of Texas and Southwest, p. 20.

Prisoner Chasing Duty

The Guardhouse was designed to house two types of prisoners; the garrison prisoner and those convicted by Courts-Martial. The large prison cell was designed for the garrison prisoners which included those who abused alcohol and those who committed a military crime and were awaiting trial. On the other wing were five cells for those convicted by a courts-martial (military trial) provided their sentence was for one year or less. Those whose sentence was for more than one year were sent to Lansing Penitentiary at Fort Leavenworth. The cell time was primarily to isolate them from other soldiers and not necessarily to punish for the crimes they were guilty of. No one in those days identified confinement with punishment. Punishment was in addition to and usually consisted of work details that were primarily reserved for the prisoners.

Prisoner-chasers ensured that the prisoner was able to get to the work detail and complied with the work assignment. Prisoner-chasers usually were appointed by the Sergeant and since it was not one of the most relished duty details, it too might be used by the sergeant to gain the attention of some lower ranked soldier. If the soldier appointed the prisoner chaser who was not enamored with the job, how was it the military could count on him performing the assignment as necessary? Basically if the prisoner failed to perform the duty as was considered appropriate both the chaser and prisoner would return to that "choice" duty until it was completed. It might seem like the prisoner chaser under such circumstance might not invest the alertness to prevent the prisoner from escaping. There was a military insurance clause that stated if a prisoner chaser lost his prisoner through escape then he automatically had to complete the prisoner's remaining sentence. Security of prisoners was usually better and more rigid than the supervision of the detail he had to perform.

Jessie Aylor (not his real name) returned to Fort Clark for a visit after some 45 years absence. Jessie was a trooper in the 112th Cavalry who joined Fort Clark for active duty under the Emergency War Powers Act. Jessie came to the Old Guardhouse Museum and his memory was activated to his prisoner-chaser duty in 1941. He stated he had been promoted to Private First Class which was a step or two from "Draftee." He recalled that the sergeant would appoint him quite frequently to the Prisoner-Chasing Duty. On the day assigned such duty Jessie had to report to the Sergeant of the Guardhouse where the details for the Prisoner Chaser were assigned. This included the area of the work detail, work to be performed, and the prisoner assigned to his charge.

The particular assignment Jessie recalled was that three prisoner chasers were to take their assigned prisoners to work on the golf course fairway and the green on hole 9. In those days the golf course was 9 holes which ran along the front fence parallel to highway 90. The 9th Green was in the corner of the reservation formed by Highway 90, Farm To Market Road 135 and Las Moras Creek.

On Jessie's assignment of prisoner he was unlucky, so he stated, to draw George McWatty who happened to be a member of his own troop. Jessie disliked the assigned prisoner because he was a frequent visitor to the guardhouse. In other words George seemed to be more wrong than right so his duty tours between the guardhouse were very short. Being so familiar with the prisoner was certainly a disadvantage to the prison chaser. After all if you were too harsh you could get repaid later in the troop quarters.

The Prison Chasers marched their prisoner details out to the assigned area at Green No. 9. When the hoeing detail got underway each chaser stayed close to his prisoner. As the other prisoners and chasers moved down the fairway George and Jessie stayed on the green removing the weeds near the perimeter. Since the others were out of earshot of George, he began pestering Jessie to let him get some whiskey. At first Jessie's no was very positive but George was persistent and kept nagging Jessie.

Jessie was confident George couldn't get the whiskey anyway but as his resistance melted he allowed George to realize he had him psyched. How would you manage to get the whiskey and keep from getting caught at the Guardhouse? Now old George showed his veteran stripes. "First, I don't have to leave the job as Hilltop Liquors is just across the highway. If you will look the other way the proprietor would deliver a half pint to the fence." Oh, he wouldn't have to pay for it as he had a charge account with the Hilltop. George would work his way later over to the fence and pick up the bottle and hide it in his fatigue jacket. Experience had taught George that he would be searched by the Officer-of-the-Day when he returned from the work detail but he bragged he had done this number of times without being caught.

Jessie's curiosity was overcoming his resistance so he told George, "You get me in trouble and I will shoot you for trying to escape." That was all the permission George needed as he let out on shrill whistle. A short time later the proprietor from Hilltop came out and crossed the highway. At the corner of the fence, he glanced around to see if he was being observed by others, and quickly set his package down by the fence. Then nonchalantly walked up the fence a piece and crossed the highway. Later George worked his way in the direction of his prize and hung his jacket on the fence. George was even more industrious about hoeing now than he had been before.

When time for the work detail was up, George was notified and requested to go pick up his jacket. His prize and jacket were retrieved without anyone else knowing the better. On the march back to the Guardhouse, Jessie's conscience began to work on him but at this stage of the game he had to have confidence that George wasn't going to let anything happen that would further jeopardize his position. Jessie stated by the time he reached the Guardhouse he was a nervous wreck but George was so cool it was instilling confidence in him.

At the Guardhouse, the detail was marched around to the back to deposit their tools in the tool shed which was attached on the back wall opposite the latrine. In the tool shed was a window without glass but with bars on it. So while George was depositing his hoe he also placed his half pint on the window ledge.

The detail was then marched to the front of the Guardhouse where the Officer-of-the-Day searched the prisoners. As soon as the Sergeant accepted the prisoners, Jessie was relieved of the duty as Prisoner Chaser. Jessie not only was bothered about being such a fool then but 45 years later he referred to it as an awful stupid stunt.

Trooper's Tale, September 1987.

3rd Medical Battalion Veterinary Troop 1944

Dr. R. Leland West, Veterinarian, was stationed at Fort Clark, October 1943–February 1944 and attached to Second Cavalry Division, 3rd Medical Battalion, Veterinary Troop. The training program for the 2nd Cavalry Division at Fort Clark was largely oriented to mounted marches by the regiments (27th and 9th Cavs., 77th Field Artillery), with 3rd Medical Battalion providing medical support for sick and injured troopers and animals (horses & mules). The Veterinary Troop of 3rd Medical was equipped with semi-trucks to transport incapacitated animals, and the veterinary technicians (troopers) who were trained in the use of lead-lines for the movement of walking wounded cases.

Dr. West recalled a particular occasion when a detachment under his command was having some difficulty in loading a lame horse into the truck. The Division Commanding Officer (Maj. Gen. Henry H. Johnson) and a carload of his aides came by inspecting the march, stopped, and "helped" the veterinarian detachment load the fractious patient. By some miracle the horse was loaded in only two or three times the length of time that it would have taken Dr. West's well trained troopers to accomplish the task without all the "command" aid.

=====

Correspondence from Dr. R. Leland West, Colorado Springs, Colorado, Ill. August 1990.

Officer's Quarters Assignment Fort Clark

January 1944

Maj. W. W. Agnew	Quarters	#13
Lt. F. B. Avery	"	#10
Capt. W. L. Bolin	"	#27
Lt. Col. Loren Benton		BOQ 1
(Post Commanding Officer)		
1st Lt. Myron L. Carr		BOQ 1
Capt. Charles B. Coker		BOQ 1
2nd Lt. P. H. Curran	Quarters	#28
2nd Lt. F.A. Drafseke	"	# 28
Maj. C. A. Furr		BOQ 1-G
Maj. G.W. Hudson	Quarters	#27
Capt. Joseph D. McKenzie	"	2
1st Lt. J. S. Mense	"	#27
Capt. DeForrest Morton	"	#16
Maj. Alvin P. Noyes		BOQ 1-C
Lt. Col. Alfred Oliver		#18
Lt. Col. John R. Porterfield	"	# 9
Capt. M. M. Roland	"	#27
Maj. W. H Seale	"	# 8

Capt. J. H. Sutherland	"	#12
1st Lt. Joseph H. Szalecki	"	#23
Col. C. M. Thirlkeld		BOQ1-H
Capt. Fred F. Thompson		BOQ 1
2nd Lt. W. A. Ward		#27
Maj. W. I. Salisbury	"	#17

*Capt. Winfred E. Chapin Ranch House (20)

Army Telephone Directory, Fort Clark, Texas
January 1944
(Quarters 3-4-5-14-15-21-22 not listed in directory)

Last of the Cavalry Mounts 1944

After the 2nd Cavalry Division failed their combat readiness test (Feb. 1944), they were ordered to be dismounted and to turn in their mounts. Troops C and D of 253rd Quartermaster Remount Squadron were charged with receiving the mounts and transporting them to the remount posts of Fort Reno and Fort Robinson. The mounts of the Division were assigned to 9th Cavalry Regiment, 27th Cavalry Regiment and 77th Field Artillery at Fort Clark and 10th Cavalry Regiment, 28th Cavalry Regiment, (Headquarters 4th Cav. Brigade, & Weapons Troop) at Camp Lockett, Puente, Calif. The Division had approximately 5,000 mounts with approximately 3,000 being at Ft. Clark.

Captain Delano L. Proctor, Jr., Veterinary Corp, and 5 enlisted veterinarian technicians were assigned from D Troop of 253rd Remount Squadron to move the first contingent of horses from Fort Clark. They loaded the box cars with 30 horses per car and the first movement consisted of 27 cars (810 horses). The cars were loaded on the Fort Clark spur track and the 27 cars were connected to the engine and caboose at Spofford Junction to make the train for Fort Reno. Capt. Proctor stated that at Fort Worth he and his crew of veterinarian technicians had to offload, feed and rest the horses and then reload the 810 horses to continue the trip. All this was accomplished in a cold rain.

Capt. Proctor recalled that on the trip from Fort Clark to Fort Worth the train crew had hooked up a extra box car to accommodate the veterinarian crew. This car was unheated and had no facilities. "We heated coffee by pouring gasoline in a can of sand to make an improvised stove." In Fort Worth after reloading the horses, the crew wandered into the caboose car attached for train crew and found plush seats, roaring fire and coffee brewing on the stove. Being dead tired after their arduous task of loading the horses, they curled up on the seats and were soon fast asleep, before the engine was hooked up to train for final leg of the journey.

Captain Proctor said shortly after the hookup he was violently shaken out of a sound sleep by the train conductor demanding to know what he thought he was doing in the train crew's quarters. Captain Proctor recalled that none of the past few days had been very pleasant and his exhaustion failed to contribute to the best mental attitude. His reaction to the violent and abusive reception was to draw his .45 automatic which was carried loaded to relieve any horse accidentally injured. In this case he was tempted to relieve one not so diplomatic train conductor. After banging his side arm on the table in front of a startled conductor, he informed the trainman the army was in charge of this shipment and the cargo in the government's name and be damned if he was going to take any guff from a civilian train crewman. He left no doubt in the conductor's mind that he was in charge and he would give the orders. Later he learned the train crew had felt sorry for the GIs and had swapped the box car they had previously for an old passenger coach but it was without water or heat for the remainder of the trip for the veterinary crew.

According to Captain Proctor when the train crew was relieved at the junction point north of Ft. Worth, the brakeman who was under the orders of the conductor, "Windmill Jackson," said he was glad some one had been able to take that character down a peg or two. "Windmill" was known as the meanest train conductor in the southwest.

Captain Proctor said he made only the first movement of

horses from Ft. Clark but he was sure the remaining animals were transferred to Ft. Reno or Ft. Robinson. He recalls sending a shipment of some 200 horses to a regimental command (124th Cav.) on the Mexican border. They had been specially selected as the regimental commander wanted only brown horses. (124th Cavalry Regiment, with Col. John H. "Cactus Jack" Irving, commanding, was stationed at Fort D. A. Russell (Marfa). In April 1944, they were the last mounted cavalry regiment in the army to be dismounted and the mounts transferred to Fort Riley.) Captain Proctor said that he thought most of the horses from the Second Cavalry Division (Ft. Clark and Camp Lockett) served the remainder of WWII in the China-Burma Theatre.

=====

Interview July 20, 1990, with Doctor Delano L. Proctor, Jr., 567 Muir Station, Lexington, Ky, 40516. He was, at that time, still a practicing DVM, and he had served as Veterinary Officer, Feb. 1943–June 1946, serving the later portion in Burma.

American Statesman
June 30, 1946

Brackettville, June 29.–(AP)–An old army veteran who helped bring civilization to a wild western frontier and then stayed through four wars and almost a century of military duty to keep it there, is about to be discharged from service. The "Discharge" will read: "Fort Clark, established June 15, 1852; declared surplus 1945; disposed of 1946." Under the heading "Honorable Military Service" will be "Numerous Indian Raids," "Civil War 1861-1865," "War with Spain 1898-1899," "Mexican Bandit Raids and Cattle Rustler Fights," "World War I 1917-1918," and "World War II 1940-1945." Even for an old soldier that is quite a record.

Last year the little regimental post, just a few miles from the Mexican border, was declared surplus by the Army. It was turned over to the War Assets Administration for disposal. First the WAA asked for bids for outright sale of the post and its facilities. The highest was a $411,250 bid from the Texas Railway Equipment Company, Houston.

Recently two bills were introduced in the house to authorize the transfer of the abandoned post to the "Fort Clark Military Institute." The institute is incorporated under Texas Laws as a non-profit educational enterprise. Among the directors are ex-vice President John N. Garner and Amon G. Carter, *Ft. Worth Star-Telegram* publisher.

San Antonio Light
June 29, 1946

Garth Jones, an old army veteran who helped bring civilization to a wild western frontier and then stayed through four wars and almost a century of military duty is about to be discharged from service. The "discharge" will read; "Fort Clark, Brackettville, Texas, established June 15, 1852, declared surplus, 1945; disposed of, 1946." Under the heading "honorable military service" will be "Numerous Indian raids."

But the War Department says it is time for retirement. Last year the little regimental post, just a few miles from the Mexican border, was declared surplus by the army. It was turned over to the War Assets Administration for disposal.

First the WAA asked for bids for outright sale of the post and its facilities. Several were received. The highest was a $411,250 bid from the Texas Railway Equipment Company, Houston.

Recently there has been a new development. Two bills have been introduced in the house to authorize the transfer of the abandoned post to the "Fort Clark Military Institute." The Institute is incorporated under Texas Law as a nonprofit educational enterprise. Among the directors are ex-Vice President John Nance Garner and Amon G. Carter, Fort Worth publisher.

The Army's Training Is Lasting

One winter weekend in 1988, a couple came to the Old Guardhouse Museum and the man commenced to sign the registration book. Due to the nature of this story, the couple will remain unidentified. The man had already introduced himself as an ex-trooper who had served in the Fifth Cavalry in 1937. The recall mechanization failed as it so often does during examinations or when you became emotional in later years. So the husband said to his wife "What's our address?" That question ignited a bomb and he received a lecture for forgetting his address.

As is natural for old troopers he started reciting his former days in the Cavalry. Since he had been in the Machine Gun Troop, he had been assigned two horses, one as his mount and the other horse was the pack horse for the machine gun and equipment. A good trooper is always fond of his horse or horses and this ex-trooper was no exception. The thought of his horses stirred his memory to new highs and also revived his recall mechanism. Why he even remembered the army serial number that was tattooed under the mane of each horse. To the other listeners this added authority to the trooper's tale but his wife had a complete different view. "How is it that you can remember your horse's serial numbers when you don't know where you live?" The moral of this story is "The Army's training is lasting."

Fort Clark Guest Ranch Old Guardhouse Museum 1949-1964

During the period Brown and Root (Texas Railway Company) operated Fort Clark as a guest ranch, the Old Guardhouse was called a Museum. Since the old Guard-ouse floor plan was not conducive to many other operations but the basic design made it intriguing, it was almost a natural to become a museum unless one wanted to use it for what it was originally designed to do—confine people.

Brown and Root's Museum was to say the least somewhat strange. First of all, reports have it that little if anything was done to change the building from a guardhouse to a museum (deteriorating and accessible to birds). The selection of the artifacts to be displayed neither reinforced the history of the post nor had any direct association with the operation of the fort during the 92 years of the U.S. Army operations. Old timers who remember seeing the museum during this period described it as being a army guardhouse filled with aircraft parts.

Let see if a little background of the time will bring the operations into better focus. "After the war (WWII), Brown and Root had a salvage operation at Walnut Ridge, Arkansas, where they scrapped out salvage aircraft fuselages for the aluminum under the name of Aircraft Conversion Company. The overall operation was so large, that at one time after World War II they owned more combat aircraft than the U.S. Government. This would have made them the first or second largest air force in the world."

"Minot (Tully?) Pratt, general manager of the company, took a fancy to the nose art panels, and had workman remove the 'the interesting' nose art with a fire axe. It seems that his idea was to build a fence around his property out of nose art. This never came to pass so the panels were stored in the barn for a short time and later moved to west Texas (Fort Clark) when Pratt started a cattle company there. In the mid-1960s the panels were given to the Confederate Air Force, Harlingen, Texas. Regardless of the whys and wherefores, we are all in debt to this man for saving a piece of history."

Pratt's cattle operation in west Texas was located at Brackettville where he purchased a portion of Fort Clark WWII property and started a cattle ranch. His ties with Brown and Root kept him closely connected to the Fort Clark Guest Ranch operation. The old Guardhouse probably lent itself to a good storage place for the nose art while affording some interest to the dude ranchers.

=====

Gary M. Valant, *Vintage Aircraft Nose Art, Ready For Duty*, Osceola, Motorbooks International Publishers & Wholesalers Inc., 1987, p. 11.

About the Author

Donald A. Swanson

I retired as a Naval Aviator in 1963 in Corpus Christi, Texas. I went to work for the State of Texas Comptroller and retired once again in 1977.

While my wife and I were traveling around Texas we discovered Fort Clark Springs in Brackettville, Texas. Fort Clark Springs was a U.S .Cavalry Post from 1852 to 1945.

My wife, Frances and I bought a membership and a house built in 1874 and moved to Fort Clark Springs in 1981. I was on the Board of Directors from 1982 to 1985. I then volunteered to assume the duties of Director/Curator of the Guard House Museum on Fort Clark Springs. Due to my wife's illness I resigned as Director/Curator of the Guard House Museum in 1994.

As curator of the Museum I found that visitors were seeking historical background that a Naval Officer would not know so I researched US Army/Cavalry Records. It seems books and records are scarce or out of print with costly price tags.

I established a repository of books, documents, photographs, and maps relating to Fort Clark in order to ensure the historical record of the officers and men who served here from 1852 to 1946 is preserved for future generations.

In my research I discovered many interesting stories, hence the *Chronicles of Fort Clark, Texas.*

www.ingramcontent.com/pod-product-compliance
Lightning Source LLC
Chambersburg PA
CBHW071428150426
43191CB00008B/1082